EIGHTEENTH-CENTURY WRITERS IN THEIR WORLD

Eighteenth-Century Writers in their World

A Mighty Maze

Andrew Varney

First published in Great Britain 1999 by
MACMILLAN PRESS LTD
Houndmills, Basingstoke, Hampshire RG21 6XS and London
Companies and representatives throughout the world

A catalogue record for this book is available from the British Library.

ISBN 0–333–67972–5 hardcover
ISBN 0–333–67973–3 paperback

First published in the United States of America 1999 by
ST. MARTIN'S PRESS, INC.,
Scholarly and Reference Division,
175 Fifth Avenue, New York, N.Y. 10010

ISBN 0–312–22531–8

Library of Congress Cataloging-in-Publication Data
Varney, Andrew.
Eighteenth-century writers in their world : a mighty maze / Andrew
Varney.
p. cm.
Includes bibliographical references and index.
ISBN 0–312–22531–8 (cloth)
1. English literature—18th century—History and criticism.
2. Literature and society—Great Britain—History—18th century.
3. Literature and history—Great Britain—History—18th century.
I. Title.
IN PROCESS PR448.S64 V
820.9′005—dc21   99–22174
                                                    CIP

© Andrew Varney 1999

This book is printed on paper suitable for recycling and made from fully managed and
sustained forest sources.

10   9   8   7   6   5   4   3   2   1
08   07   06   05   04   03   02   01   00   99

Printed in Hong Kong

Contents

Acknowledgements   vi

Preface   vii

1   Other Worlds – Narratives of Travel:
    Robinson Crusoe and *Gulliver's Travels*   1

2   Wit and Virtue: *The Way of the World* and *Clarissa*   33

3   Money and Government:
    Roxana and *The Beggar's Opera*   62

4   Men and Women – Love and Marriage:
    The Rape of the Lock, Roderick Random and
    Tom Jones   87

5   Writing by Women: the Female Poets and Mrs Manley   117
        Appendix: Mrs Manley's Preface   140

6   The Harmony of Things:
    An Essay on Man and *Moral Essays*   145

7   Science and Nature:
    The Spectator, Gulliver's Travels and *The Seasons*   171

8   Country and City, the Choice of Life: Dr Johnson   197

Notes   221

Suggestions for Further Reading   231

Index   234

Acknowledgements

I hope this book shows some marks of how enjoyable it was to write. It was a rather diffuse project and in the course of completing it I have incurred debts promiscuously. I am profoundly grateful to all those whose names occur in the annotation, and to those whose names no doubt ought to appear there. I am always tremendously impressed by the way in which eighteenth-century writing elicits some of its own characteristics in those who study it, so that eighteenth-century scholarship takes on something of the flexibility, wit, mordancy, zest and humanity of its subject. I cannot aspire to match the diligence, knowledge or perceptiveness of those to whom I owe so much, but want to record anyway how exhilarating being in their debt can be.

I do, of course, owe more particular debts too, not least to Margaret Bartley at Macmillan for her enthusiastic support and tolerance as an editor. I am also extremely grateful to my friends and colleagues Mark Loveridge, a source of intriguing and original ideas over many years, and Ian Bell, who as Head of Department has given me continuous encouragement, and who as eighteenth-century scholar has been a source of valuable practical information and advice. I wish that I had designed into this book a chapter on friends and families: the eighteenth century in England was bracketed between periods which placed supreme importance on individual experience, but in the period itself the sense you get of the national life is of life and experience held in common, in some measure shared in a spirit of intimate acquaintance, amusement and tolerance. Had I written such a chapter it would have registered not only my sense of the period, but also my gratitude for the extraordinary kindness and supportiveness of my own friends and family while I have been writing this book.

Preface

All works of literary recovery are to some degree a negotiation between the picayune and the grandiose, or between obsession and understanding. One chapter here spends rather a long time talking about pineapples; another outlines the impact of Newtonian science on the human imagination. This veering between Lilliputian detail and Brobdingnagian gesture reflects a conviction that the cultural world of early eighteenth-century Britain exhibited a kind of promiscuous interest in everything. The literary world was the real world, the world of common experience. Defoe made bricks and bred civet cats; Pope invested the money he received from translating Homer in the South Sea Company; Swift dined regularly with the prime minister and wrote political pamphlets; Thomson studied science; Addison bought a country estate so that he could become a member of parliament; Lady Mary Wortley Montagu was married to a diplomat, lived in Turkey and brought inoculation for smallpox to Britain. None of these facts receives particular attention here but the book is an attempt to record an awareness that writers of the period were citizens and that one way to approach their work is to understand something of the tidal flows which they were navigating.

Cultural recuperation is, however, barren without the cultural products – narratives, plays, poems – in which people represent themselves, construct a picture of their world and articulate their anxieties. Each chapter here attempts to describe a feature of the culture of early eighteenth-century Britain and to read some major works of the period in its context, but there were no rigid demarcations between topics and writers; culture is a conversation, not a discourse, and so there is inevitable repetition and overlapping. Some topics, the legal status (or non-status) of women for instance, and some passages of texts, such as Gulliver's observations on the relative scale of things, recur here in different discursive contexts. Culture is about recognition and repetition as well as about novelty and discovery, and it is accordingly proper to find an expression like Pope's 'Order in Variety' from *Windsor-Forest* at home in a discussion of landscape and of eighteenth-century political economy.

One conspicuous recurrence is reference to Thomson's *The Seasons*.

This is not because a case is being made for his verse, which swerves between the sublime and the daft, but because his lifespan, 1700–48, coincides almost exactly with the cultural period this book covers, and because his poem is so compendious and so hospitable to many of the ideas and responses that filled the emotional and intellectual atmosphere of his times that he becomes in almost all fields a useful point of reference. His comparative ordinariness makes him useful in a way that a figure of scintillatingly idiosyncratic genius such as Swift cannot be. But an account of his times cannot be just an account of him; it has to take in the inventive vitality and distinctive energy of Defoe, Swift, Pope, Smollett and the others. Thomson's role here is a bit like that of Prufrock: '... not Prince Hamlet, nor ... meant to be; ... an attendant lord, one that will do / To swell a progress, start a scene or two ... Full of high sentence, but a bit obtuse; / At times, indeed, almost ridiculous – / Almost, at times, the Fool.' But it is none the less important in a culture with so many voices as the first half of the eighteenth century.

This book quotes those voices extensively, more perhaps than many academic works choose to do. This is partly because some of the material is unfamiliar – not many general readers, not all undergraduates or even all academics have Mandeville or Mrs Manley at their fingertips – but more importantly because the period was a polyphony of articulations, a play of tones, witty, variable, intense, allusive, and they need to be seen and heard if the age is to come alive again at all. And some are irresistible and need no excuse. I have also quoted quite a lot from modern commentators, to all of whom I am profoundly in debt. The eighteenth century is not particularly buoyant in undergraduate literary studies at present, but cultural and scholarly investigation of the period is extremely vital and productive and, most importantly, pan-disciplinary. The eighteenth century is part of the discourse of our times; it is not locked away in the past. I have in the main not quoted much from studies of literary discourse or cultural theory, although certain assimilations and assumptions will be obvious. The voices I want to record are those of and about the culture of the first half of the eighteenth century.

Some of these voices are those of women, and there is now an increasing interest in and awareness of their significance. Apart from such writing as survives by women, the lives of women play a much bigger role in writing of this than of any earlier period: *The Rape of the Lock, Moll Flanders, Clarissa* – such major canonical works, though written by men, are about women and the conditions in which they had to negotiate their lives. The familial, literary, cultural and political power bases were of course dominated by men, but there is more and more recognition in the period that men shared the world with women and that women mattered. I have tried to register this here, but without falsifying the account.

Many of the works I discuss are familiar canonical texts of the first half of the eighteenth century – *The Rape of the Lock*, *Robinson Crusoe*, *Gulliver's Travels* and so forth. The aim is not to endorse the canon but to work with what is familiar, and of course with what undergraduate readers and other readers are commonly confronted with. Too often the texts are encountered as mighty islands in an unknown sea. One function of this book is to help chart that sea so that the texts begin to acquire meaning in terms of the cultural geography of their times and so to become more fully rewarding. This in its turn should facilitate access to the many-lesser known works which modern scholars are increasingly bringing into view and whose exploration is a source of enormous interest and entertainment.

Each chapter here can be read separately, but none offers a full account of its topic or of the texts for which that topic supplies a context. No full recovery of the period – of any period – or of the texts that animate it is possible, but the intention here is to offer an accumulation of contexts and texts that will help to fill some of the white paper on the map of the literate culture of the first half of the eighteenth century.

1   *Marriage à la Mode*, Part 1: *The Marriage Settlement* by William Hogarth (1697–1764); © National Gallery, London.

2 *An Emblematical Print on the South Sea Scheme* by William Hogarth (1697–1764); reproduced by kind permission of British Museum Press from *Hogarth and his Times* by David Bindman (1997).

1
Other Worlds – Narratives of Travel: *Robinson Crusoe* and *Gulliver's Travels*

In Chapter 22 of *Northanger Abbey* one of the minor clues given about General Tilney's character as a somewhat despotic and unnatural head of a family is that he prides himself on a huge kitchen garden with walls 'countless in number, endless in length' and comprising 'a village of hot-houses' and 'a pinery', which had produced one hundred pineapples in the last year. The point about pineapples is that since their introduction to Britain in the seventeenth century they had always exerted a curious fascination over the English imagination, witnessed not least in their frequent use as architectural ornaments in seventeenth- and eighteenth-century architecture. They were an exotic luxury; they were outlandish in appearance; and not being native to Britain they could be raised domestically only in expensive artificial conditions. But they were nevertheless enticing and delectable and appealed to the sophisticated and privileged palate that could alone afford them. A measure of at least unnaturalness is hinted at in General Tilney's cultivation of them. A passage in Thomson's *The Seasons* catalogues the exotic fruit of the world, 'the lemon and the piercing lime', 'the deep orange', 'the spreading tamarind' with 'its fever-cooling fruit', 'the massy locust', 'the Indian fig', and so forth, most of which Thomson, whose travels were restricted to France and Italy, had never seen growing. The catalogue reaches its climax in his celebration of the pineapple:

> . . . thou best Anana, thou the Pride
> Of vegetable Life, beyond whate'er
> The Poets imag'd in the golden Age:
> Quick, let me strip thee of thy tufty Coat,
> Spread thy ambrosial Stores, and feast with *Jove*![1]

1

These lines are, unsurprisingly, not the last word on eighteenth-century British culture's encounters with worlds beyond its own, but they none the less inscribe more of their elements than might appear. Thomson begins with the apostrophic address, 'thou . . .', which is a rhetorical mode normally directed to what is superior or wonderful. The use is partly jocose here, but not to the extent that its extravagance is conclusively contested. Next, the word *anana*, which is not part of the English lexicon. Nothing in British experience corresponds to the anana and so the word is properly untranslatable. Of course, there is the term pineapple, but this is just a borrowing. In medieval usage a pineapple was the fruit of the pine-tree, a pine-cone, and ananas were so called because that is what they roughly resembled. Otherwise , the term is misleading: the anana is not an apple and it does not grow on a pine-tree, or any tree. It is a term of convenience: an analogy might be the pronunciation of Swift's word for the horses in *Gulliver's Travels* Book Four, houyhnhnms. There is a kind of agreement among scholarly readers that it may be pronounced something like 'whinnims', but this is not the answer to the question 'how should *houyhnhnm* be pronounced?' as the word has only an orthographic and not phonic existence.

Unexampled as it is in British culture, to leave the anana as an unparalleled, inexplicable phenomenon would be discomforting to the systematising and assimilative temper of eighteenth-century epistemology, and so one function of the ensuing lines is to familiarise the unfamiliar, to bring the anana home. The phrase 'the Pride of vegetable Life' draws it into the scientific discourse of a culture increasingly obsessed with the Linnean enterprise of botanical classification.[2] To call it the Pride of vegetable Life no more indicates what it is like than the Brobdingnagian scholars' identification of the diminutive Gulliver as '*relplum scalcath*, which is interpreted literally, *lusus naturae*' [trick of nature],[3] but at least it sounds like science, or knowledge. In the next phrase, however, the remarkable quality of the anana is restored in its transcendence: it is 'beyond' what is known, or even what was ever imagined in the literature of the classical world, which is the constant yardstick of cultural attainment for many eighteenth-century writers. In works dealing with the experience of unfamiliar territories in this period the concept of the other as 'beyond' is of profound significance. Despite all the geographical and navigational specification in *Robinson Crusoe* it is clear that the island is off the map: Crusoe notes his ship's position at the beginning of the tempest which will lead to his eventual shipwreck, and then, in one of those resonant expressions that he so often uses that reach far deeper into his experience than at first appears, he records that 'a violent tournado or hurricane took us quite out of our knowledge',[4] beyond what was known.

The next impulse in the lines is to reclaim or repossess the unfamiliar other: 'Quick, let me strip thee of thy tufty Coat.' (I want to hold in suspension the preposterousness of detailed interpretation of lines like this, and will just for the present note that absurdity or preposterousness is part of the discourse of eighteenth-century travel narrative.) The urgency of the line is almost violent. The reclaiming or repossession that is the rhetorical function of this line could also be seen as registering the imperial impulse to claim and to possess, to colonise and to despoil the exotic other. The bathetic and unpoetic, 'low' phrase 'tufty Coat' takes from the anana its primitive exoticism, demythologises it, and so in a way legitimises the greedy rapine of 'let me strip thee'. This graceless urgency is rehabilitated into cultural acceptability in the concluding phase of the passage, as the last line glamorises the physicality of 'spread' with the classically allusive 'thy ambrosial Stores'. If he consumes this food of the gods the subject will 'feast with *Jove*' and so participate in the transcendent and unexampled otherness of which the pineapple is the ontological record.

Apart from whatever cultural significations are inscribed here it might be reasonable to respond, 'what a way to write about pineapples!' But this can equally excite the question, 'Well, how *do* you write about pineapples?' Is there a decorum or a convention determining the style and mode of discourse of the pineapple? There are plenty of acknowledged ways of writing and thinking about the other proud examples of vegetable life in the British cultural register – about roses, for example, or about, especially in the early eighteenth century, tulips – but how does one render the exotic and unfamiliar? In the anana lines there is a radical instability as Thomson swings between at least four ways of distinguishing pineapples: as exotic wonder, as object of science, as mythological glory, and as imperial object. The instability is nevertheless not quite out of control. The authorial intelligence supervises and seduces the reading experience; by its arch allusions to high culture ('golden Age', 'ambrosial', '*Jove*'), its scientific positiveness ('vegetable Life') and its comic sense of deflation ('tufty Coat') it establishes a manner of superiority to its topic. And yet the pineapple survives its own consumption, as it were: as the anana it has been registered as an object of contemplation, as a still exotic and unaccountable phenomenon of our experience in a way it had never been before. The world with the anana is different and richer than the world without it.

In being written about it has acquired an ontological status, been culturally accommodated into a world of discourse and, yet, is still 'beyond' familiarity. Inscribed as it now is, however, it remains a little absurd and in that absurdity unthreatening. If it really were a consciousness-transforming 'magic' fruit, or if it contained hallucinogenic pharmaceutical compounds, it might be rather alarming. If Thomson really thought he was feasting with Jove as he ate a pineapple, or, to go as far as the lines actually assert, he were in point of fact feasting with Jove, then the lines would have a power nothing could defuse, and Catherine Morland would have serious cause for concern about General Tilney. As it is, they afford little more than a *frisson* of cultural amusement. But there are real pineapples, and what if there were a real Robinson Crusoe who had lived twenty-eight years on a Caribbean island, as there was a real Alexander Selkirk, four years alone on Juan Fernandez; and what if there were real houyhnhnms?

The tension which gives Thomson's lines what animation they have is generated between the contesting principles of familiarity and otherness, or of recognition and perplexity, and this tension is inscribed in early eighteenth-century writing on alien cultures, irrespective of whether they are real or imaginary – not that that is a particularly telling distinction, as they only exist as they are recorded. It is a tension which may be crystallised in two contrasting cosmologies. The first is that which Watt quotes, and takes as a key to his understanding of eighteenth-century fiction, as it was formulated by Berkeley in 1713: 'it is an universally received maxim, that everything *which exists is particular*'.[5] The countervailing principle can be taken as it is expressed in Whalley's *An Essay on the Manner of Writing History* (1746): 'human Nature hath, in all Ages and Nations, a great Conformity to itself'.[6]

In terms of the very many narratives of the early part of the eighteenth century which record real or invented histories of – or voyages to – remote places, this opposition manifests itself in on the one hand discovering outlandish wonders in such places, and on the other in finding that they are in fact very like home. One of very many possible instances is a narrative of 1712 that offers itself as *The History of the Proceedings of the Mandarins and Proatins of the Britomartian Empire at their Last General Diet*. The terms Mandarins and, less recognisably, Proatins indicate that this is a narrative with a Far Eastern provenance, and so exotic and strange. The word Britomartian, however, hints that this may be domestic history in disguise, as of course it is, being a history of Harley's Tory administration that began in 1710. Even so, accounts of remote places are only offered because they are remarkable and challenge credulity. The satirical implication generated by the publication is thus that the history of the 'Britomartian' Mandarins (Lords) and Proatins (House of Commons) is almost as strange as fiction. In a much more familiar instance, the Preface to *Robinson Crusoe* (1719) exploits the unfamiliar/familiar antinomy in asserting first that 'The wonders of this man's life exceed all that . . . is to be found extant; the life of one man being scarce capable of a greater variety', and then in suggesting that 'this example' can be usefully applied 'to the instruction of others', unremarkable readers with unwonderful lives.

It has become part of the modern intellectual tradition to see this kind of opposition in terms of dialectic. The intricate conceptual structure which informs, for instance, Michael McKeon's *Origins of the English Novel, 1600–1740* (1987) could not exist without it. And it is true that more than ever before British culture in the early eighteenth century figured itself in a series of binary constructions: it imaged itself as divided into a variety of absolutely opposed groups. In party politics, which is often thought of as a creation of the early decades of the eighteenth century, there were Whigs and Tories; the national religion was divided into High Church (conservative, possibly leaning towards France and popery, maybe Jacobite) and Low Church (progressive, leaning towards dissent, pro-trade, constitutionalist); in broader cultural terms the Ancients took the achievements of classical culture and its tradition as their benchmark, while the Moderns believed in progress, science, and the vernacular culture. In modern terms, society could be divided between the traditional, aristocratic and ethically based values of 'civic humanism' and the proponents of society as a non-moral, dynamic system driven by industry and trade, the 'political economists'. But these oppositions were not scientific descriptions of society; in use they almost always had a rhetorical charge and so were almost by admission misrepresentations. The division of Lilliputian politicians into Slamecksan and Tramecksan is not so much an exact mirror of English political life in Swift's time as a way of representing that life. There were other, non-binary, constructions of the culture current in the period: it might be represented as the primal chaos, in which all the elements of creation were jumbled together before they were ordered by divine fiat, or as a Concordia Discors, in which all the diverse parts of society retained their distinctiveness but together composed a harmonious system.

It may therefore be misleading to approach the body of travel narratives of the early eighteenth century with too much interpretive expectation. If it appears a bit unruly, or perplexed by contradiction and inconsistency, if it invites several different kinds of understanding and interpretation at once, then this appearance may have its own significance.

The fascination with travel was a complex cultural phenomenon with many aspects that issue in the literary characteristics of all narratives of travel in the period, and especially in works of such imaginative fullness as *Robinson Crusoe* and *Gulliver's Travels*.

Firstly, in very broad terms, the seventeenth century could be seen as having been fundamentally introspective, a period preoccupied with scrutiny and testing of the national body politic, religious and constitutional, a preoccupation which had issued in the trauma of civil war with the horrors of regicide for the royalists and of restoration for the parliamentarians. Furthermore, for the individual the agenda of personal religion was determined by forms of protestantism and puritanism, which although their dominance was ultimately questionable, none the less contested many more or less established values and attitudes, and did so by exacting a rigorous and unending self-scrutiny. One could argue that it was not until after the 1689 Settlement that Britain began to recover the stability and self-assurance that allowed it once again the security to turn from scrutiny of the self to the large outer world and to become interested again in exploring and exploiting it.

Secondly, the late seventeenth century saw a burgeoning of global commerce. Many things fed this, not least in Britain the development of more and more sophisticated instruments for the direction and manipulation of capital that facilitated the funding of expensive commercial and speculative expeditions. The establishment of the Bank of England, granted its charter in 1695, had as its first purpose providing means of raising money for William III's military campaigns abroad, but it was also a symptom of the existence of a reservoir of capitalistic expertise that could, from London, fund enterprises that reached out to the distant corners of the earth.

Thirdly, Britain was beginning to exercise itself as an imperial power, so that travel was not just a matter of individual expeditions going out to see what they could bring back in the way of goods, trophies, profit, curiosities or knowledge, but of a nation exporting and establishing its authority and culture. In the words of one commentator on British maritime experience in the first half of the eighteenth century, 'English trade routes constituted the arteries of the imperial body between 1650 and 1750.'[7]

Furthermore, with the gradual loosening up of theological speculation from the period of the Restoration onwards it became, broadly, more and more respectable and acceptable to evince and foster a lively interest in this world and all it contained, rather than focusing on the life hereafter. Preoccupation with this world was no longer a blasphemous neglect of the central nature of divinity: it was another mode of worship and respect. The godhead could be honoured in the study of the bounteous magnanimity of his creativity: it could become an alternative way of learning and knowing about him.

This went hand in hand with the growth of British empirical science in the same period, extending itself outwards and downwards from Charles II's Royal Society, founded in 1662, generating enthusiasm and sophisticating methodologies all the time. 'Science' was a term with broader connotations than its now rather confined significations: it meant knowledge and the ways to it, and so a scientific understanding of the world need in no way preclude piety and religious respect: it might even foster it, almost in the spirit of Whitman's ecstatic recognition:

... the running blackberry would adorn the parlors of heaven
And the narrowest hinge in my hand puts to scorn all machinery
...
And a mouse is a miracle enough to stagger sextillions of infidels.
(*Leaves of Grass* (1855) 'Song of Myself' 31)

Scientific enterprise and the astronomical and mathematical developments which accompanied it, together with more scrupulous and accurate techniques in the production of maps and charts and the construction of instruments, promoted improvement in the science and skills of navigation (even in the absence of a practicable way of calculating longitude) and this in its turn facilitated all kinds of exploratory, commercial and imperial activity.

Lastly, extensions in popular literacy, in desire for improving knowledge, in the eagerness to read about amazing phenomena and 'wonders', together with a rapidly expanding printing and publishing industry, nurtured the translation of travel into text.[8] So keen was the market that in some cases the appetite for the book prompted the journey, and certainly inclined the narrators of voyages to supplement narratives wanting in excitement with lively invented detail, or indeed to invent voyages which had not taken place at all.

These factors do not amount to a complete account of the cultural moment that generated the frequency and prominence of travel accounts in early eighteenth-century writing, and they are all discussed more extensively elsewhere in this study, but they do suggest how what might be seen just as a literary fashion or cult of the strange and exotic was a manifestation of a broad transformation in cultural consciousness. Equally, none of these factors existed uncontested, and travel literature of the period incorporates a reaction against as well as assimilation of them, so that the literary corpus becomes a site of contesting systems of vitality and resistance.

The impulse to acknowledge the wider world was not of course a peculiarly British phenomenon. Chambers notes how as early as the middle of the seventeenth century, 'among the eagerly awaited cultural events each year in the French court was the publication of the *Jesuit Relations*: accounts of the French missions in North America, among which certainly were surveys of the culture and beliefs of the first-nation peoples'.[9] The interest was obviously two-fold: on the one hand in the missionaries' success in exporting Catholic religious culture to the 'savage' world, and on the other in anthropological curiosity. From *Robinson Crusoe* and *Gulliver's Travels* alone it is notable how British voyagers in visiting worlds new to them are travelling a world already at least partially frequented by other Europeans – Dutch, Spanish and Portuguese in particular. British travel had a context not only in the mind-expanding cultural phenomena of the pre-Enlightenment era, but also in the tissue of international relationships, rivalry, alliance, jealousy, envy, contempt and admiration, that was the working business of late seventeenth- and early eighteenth-century Europe.

Voyages to remote places frequently had multiple functions. Traders looking for opportunities would necessarily explore. Mercantile and intellectual quests went hand in hand. Voyaging can virtually be seen as an enactment of ambivalence. It is interesting that the term 'privateer' first enters the English record in 1664, and continues through into the eighteenth and nineteenth centuries. A privateer was a privately owned vessel, whose primary function would be commercial, but authorised by letters of marque from a government to carry armaments and to deploy them against hostile shipping, and by extension to prey upon enemy merchantmen. And of course privateering became an enterprise in itself, not readily distinguishable from piracy. In the term privateer were thus encoded meanings that were official and unofficial, peaceful and belligerent, private and public, legitimate and criminal. This ambivalence also characterised more respectable voyages. Merchant voyagers often carried with them charts and instruments to be tested, or passengers whose interest was both scientific and commercial. Relations were established with correspondents in remote places who could bring forth not only goods and products but information of both commercial and intellectual value. McKeon cites Thomas Sprat, historian and early fellow of the Royal Society, on the way in which scientific enquirers were making merchant voyages in knowledge. As he writes Sprat's language effortlessly fuses the discourses of commerce and learning:

> They have begun to settle a *correspondence* through all *Countreys*; and have taken such order, that in short time, there will scarce a Ship come up the *Thames*, that does not make some return of *Experiments*, as well as of *Merchandize* ... [Merchants] have contributed their labours; they have help'd their *correspondence*: they have employ'd their *Factors* abroad, to answer their *Inquiries*; they have laid out in all Countries for observations.[10]

This ambivalence or multivalency inherent in the enterprise of the voyage is one reason why the form of the voyage account became so fruitful for imaginative writers, who discovered in the form a vehicle ideally suited to the representation of a subtle, multifold and often ambiguous response to the phenomena of strange or of familiar cultures.

Voyages can only exist for anyone other than the voyager once they are recorded. The astounding stories of the wanderings of Odysseus only become known when King Alcinous, after having received the destitute Odysseus into Phaeacia and treated him with great courtesy and hospitality, asks his guest,

> ... for a true account of your wanderings; To what parts of the inhabited world did they take you? What lovely cities did you see? Did you meet hostile tribes and lawless savages, or did you fall in with some friendly and god-fearing folk?
>
> (*The Odyssey*, trans. Rieu, Book eight)

The next four books of *The Odyssey*, which contain the narratives of his encounters with the Cyclops, Circe, Scylla and Charybdis, and so on, constitute Odysseus' in every sense telling Alcinous what he wants to hear. There is thus a natural link with voyage and narration: it is central, though, that the character of the narration is determined not only by the nature of the voyage but by the desires of the audience, and this was as true in the early eighteenth century as it was in the period of Hellenic expansion to which *The Odyssey* belongs. Alcinous carefully specifies the kind of thing that he wants to hear about. He notably does not ask about storms, or scenery, or geography, or navigation, or mutinies. He wants to hear about the social and cultural characteristics of the places Odysseus visited. It is interesting how these preoccupations are echoed in what Francis Bacon in the early seventeenth century advises travellers to take note of: 'The Things to be seene and observed' are institutions, civic organisations, structures, artefacts:

> The Courts of Princes . . . The Courts of Justice . . . The Churches and Monasteries . . . The Wals and Fortifications of Cities and Townes . . . Colleges . . . Navies . . . Gardens of State and Pleasure . . . Ex(c)hanges: Burses: Ware-houses . . . Trayning of Soldiers . . . Comedies . . . Treasuries of Jewels, and Robes; Cabinets, and Rarities . . . [11]

It is the record of these things that will be worth having. One might almost figure Swift having this open before him, studiously turning it into sardonic travesty, as he composed the narratives of Gulliver's travels. And again, it was in a manner of speaking Defoe's problem to generate a travel narrative that would gratify the desires of an audience when absolutely none of these things were available in his figuration of Crusoe's uninhabited island.

The voyage does not of course transform itself directly into text. The recording of the voyage was a cultural exercise. The navigational log is not the only account that can be made of a voyage. Discussing the exploitation of voyages for scientific purposes, McKeon notes how seamen were urged both to keep a detailed day-to-day journal of their observations and experience, and to prepare out of this at regular intervals a narrative digest.[12] Clearly the second is an ordering of the first, giving to the experience a shape inherent neither in it nor in the instant journal. Famously, in *Robinson Crusoe* Crusoe first gives a retrospective account of his arrival and early days in the island, he then reproduces a journal which he says he kept as long as his ink lasted, and then resumes retrospective narration. But as the journal part proceeds it is increasingly penetrated with the hindsight, selection and summary that characterise retrospection, to the extent that the point at which the journal mode yields to the retrospective mode is in effect imperceptible. The text which is generated from the voyage is something other than the voyage itself, and may be governed by different cultural criteria, as well as by the technical impositions of narration. This is one of the reasons why in the extensive record of eighteenth-century voyage narrative the distinction between accounts of voyages which actually took place and of voyages which were wholly or partly imagined (a distinction which it is in any case often extremely difficult to make when there is only a single record to go by) is far less fundamental than might at first thought appear.

Robinson Crusoe

If Robinson Crusoe is in respect of his character, attitudes and provenance a representative figure, a son of 'the middle state, or what might be called the upper station of low life' (p. 28; all references are to edition given in note 4) in mid-century York, why has he got so extraordinary a name? What other Crusoes has one ever heard of? Has one ever met a Crusoe? Are there Crusoes in the phone book? Does eighteenth-century writing feature Crusoes originating independently of Defoe's hero? Overwhelmingly the answer to these questions will be 'no'. Crusoe himself offers a derivation in the first paragraph of his narrative: his mother's family name was Robinson; his father was 'a foreigner of Bremen', and so 'I was called Robinson Kreutznaer' (27) and the family name became corrupted to Crusoe. That his father was a mercantile North European protestant may be a nice prolepsis of the themes of economic individualism and spiritual pilgrimage which inform the narrative. Possibly 'Kreutz' and 'Crus' invite the ear to 'cross' and so anticipate the Christian theme, or even the cross Crusoe has to bear in life. Defoe was interested in names: the naming of Moll Flanders is a complicated issue in her story. The central character of *Roxana or The Fortunate Mistress* is referred to by three names on the title page of her novel, none of which is properly her own, or none of which is more her own than any other. The author himself during his writing career effected several variations on the name he received from his parents James and Alice Foe, until his initial became incorporated in his surname as the quasi-aristocratic 'de' prefix. So the naming of Crusoe would seem to be an important signifier. There is nothing to suggest it is not, but at the same time it is slightly deflating to discover among Defoe's classmates at Charles Morton's academy at Newington Green one Timothy Cruso.[13] Is Robinson simply named after the boy at the next desk? Even so limited an issue as this seems to position the narrative in the flux of suggestion between the familiar and the arcane, the banal and the exceptional, that characterises so much in the record of encounters with other spheres of existence in the eighteenth century.

Robinson Crusoe is one of the three most famous literary works of the first three decades of the eighteenth century, the others being *The Rape of the Lock* and *Gulliver's Travels*. Each of these recounts a story or stories of translation from a place identifiable as home to somewhere very different. The journeys made by the central characters effect various changes in their personalities or circumstances, and the fact of being the subject of translations is, to put it simply, what makes each of them famous, or is represented as the most significant episode of their lives. The narratives are not romances, in the sense that the essence of the story lies in the plot or episode rather than in significant human experience. Paul Hunter makes the point, talking of the evolution of the novel form in the eighteenth century:

> romances had traipsed all over the world without having any significant effect on how people thought, acted or felt, and with little difference in whom one met, but the novel is a product of serious cultural thinking about comparative societies and the multiple natures in human nature.[14]

Beyond these similarities there is, however, another. All three narratives are, in some of their aspects, either mock-heroic or anti-heroic. In other words, they find their identities in difference, difference from other narratives that exist or could exist. They are thus self-defined intertextually. I have already mentioned the problem confronting Defoe in fabricating a narrative when his central character could bring back no account of the sorts of things Bacon said the traveller should see and observe because they did not exist on Crusoe's island. That *The Life and Strange Surprizing Adventures of Robinson Crusoe, of York, Mariner* exists in a kind of rivalry with other texts of a related kind is made clear by the first two paragraphs of the Preface:

> If ever the story of any private man's adventures in the world were worth making publick, and were acceptable when published, the editor of this account thinks this will be so.
>   The wonders of this man's life exceed all that [he thinks] is to be found extant; the life of one man being scarce capable of a greater variety.

What is commended here is not simply Crusoe's life as he lived it, but more importantly his 'Life' in the sense of a biography. It is a narrative to challenge and outdo all others extant.

In claiming for this narrative a position in relation to other publications the Preface to *Robinson Crusoe* is not making a simple claim; Defoe or whoever wrote the Preface is exercising himself in a minor literary form, much as one might say that the acknowledgements page of a modern academic monograph, with its fulsomeness, its inclusion of illustrious names and its elegant modesty is doing the same. One can compare with Defoe's Preface the Preface supplied by the translator of Petis de la Croix's *Turkish Tales* (1708) in which he deliberately creates blue water between his and other kinds of work:

> They are not . . . the bare Invention of some *Frenchman*, designing to recommend his Fictions to the World under the Umbrage of a Foreign Title . . . they are not to be consider'd as a confus'd Heap of extraordinary Events jumbled together without any Design or Judgment, but the deliberate Work of one whose principal Aim was to render Virtue amiable, and Vice odious.[15]

A voyage account published in the same year distinguishes itself from 'a great number of false Voyages, and some of them ill enough related' and, interestingly, in reference to the matter of the narrative, anticipates the point that I have noted as one of Defoe's authorial problems in *Robinson Crusoe*. He claims publication to be justifiable even though,

> I found neither Cities, nor Temples, nor Palaces, nor Cabinets of Rarities, nor Antique Monuments, nor Academies, nor Libraries, nor People, on whose Religion, Language, Government, Manners and Customs, I might make observations.[16]

The voices of the author of *Robinson Crusoe* and of those other two authors might well have been raised indignantly against a voyage narrative of 1705 called *The Consolidator: or, Memoirs of Sundry Transactions from the World in the Moon*, in which a traveller after one or two false attempts manages to get to the moon by jumping off a large spring, only to find in the moon a world very like Western Europe. Its author was Daniel Defoe.

Robinson Crusoe, Gulliver's Travels and *The Rape of the Lock* define themselves against precursor, rival or alternative, narratives, and one aspect of this self-definition is in being mock- or anti-heroic. Crusoe's is a story of extravagant and outlandish adventure; it is in part the story of a transition from destitution to affluence; it traces a return from anonymous exile to home and status; in countless local episodes it recounts confrontation with difficulties and dangers, and success in overcoming them. Thus it has the outline, trajectory and features of romantic adventure. Offered with the racy and unreflective self-confidence of, say, Nash in the Elizabethan period or with the cultural arrogance of class and empire of John Buchan in the twentieth century, it would be such a thing. But Defoe's eighteenth-century narrative is not like this. It is of course open to heroic reading, as for instance David Blewett's history of the illustrations to *Robinson Crusoe* makes clear: at various times graphic representations of Crusoe show him as noble solitary, triumphant or benevolent imperialist, Christ-like saviour of Friday, Lord of Nature, or *Boy's Own Paper* hero.[17] This, however, is re-presentation: in the discourse of his own self-presentation Crusoe is not, except in such episodes as his seeing off the Pyreneean wolves with a train of gunpowder, like this. His self-presentation is determined by who he is in his time and place.

An instance of how Crusoe's conduct and manner is not distinguished by noble or romantic heroics may be found in the visit which Crusoe pays after many years of his isolated life to the ship that he finds wrecked on a reef miles to the east of his island. His first response when he becomes aware of the wreck is to experience 'a strange longing or hankering of desires' (193) for companionship. In his loneliness his longing that even one man might have been saved amounts to a passion that expresses itself in frustrated physical energy:

> I believe I repeated the words, 'O that it had been but one!' a thousand times; and the desires were so moved by it, that when I spoke the words, my hands would clinch together, and the fingers press the palms of my hands, that if I had had any soft thing in my hand, it would have crush'd it involuntarily; and my teeth in my head wou'd strike together, and set against one another so strong, that for some time I could not part them again.   (193)

In the literature of romantic love this kind of behaviour marks the disappointed or rejected lover, but in that case the elevation of the passion warrants the violence of the response. Crusoe is desperately lonely, but otherwise there is no spiritual correlative of his violent impulse.

After a few days Crusoe has the affliction, as he puts it, of seeing 'the corps of a drowned boy' washed up on the island. He goes through the boy's pockets, finding only 'two pieces of eight, and a tobacco-pipe; the last was to me of ten times more value than the first' (193). He then equips himself for a voyage out to the wreck in his canoe. He finds only one living being on it, a dog 'almost dead from hunger and thirst'. He relieves 'the poor creature' with food and water and then searches the ship for whatever he can get, including a dozen and a half of some dead sailors' white handkerchiefs, which were 'very welcome, being exceedingly refreshing to wipe my face in a hot day' (197). He also finds 'two pair of shoes . . ., which I took off the feet of the two drowned men who I saw in the wreck'. They are not very good though, and Crusoe grumbles, 'they were not like our English shoes, either for ease or service; being rather what we call pumps, than shoes' (197). He also gets some money out of the ship, but regrets that the state of the wreck was such that he could not get more:

> . . . however, I lugged this money home to my cave, and laid it up . . . but it was a great pity . . . that the other part of the ship had not come to my share; for I am satisfy'd I might have loaded my canoe several times over with money, which, if I ever escaped to England, would have lain safe enough, till I might have come again, and fetched it.
>
> (198)

Psychologically all this is excellent. Crusoe's desperate disappointment at finding himself still alone issues in a kind of angry resentment against these sailors for dying on him. He can feel for the dog, but seems wilfully affectless about the men. He scavenges the ship for whatever might be of use to him, and quarrels with it for not being good enough. If he is going to have solitude forced upon him he is going to have his own back in selfishness. This apart, what is striking about the episode is the absence of any other ways of talking or acting in this situation. There is no sense of reverence or compassion about the dead; there is no attempt to commit the corpses to eternity with a burial or prayers; there is no expressed resistance to taking the clothes and property of the dead, even the shoes from their feet; there is no sense of moral compunction about looting other people's clothes from the ship; there is no piety, no gratitude for even small mercies. Crusoe now seems exiled not just from home, but from all the home culture valorises – religion, humanity, decency, even simply property. In romantic or heroic narrative the essence of the hero's conduct abroad is that he carries with him, and lives true to, the core values of his cultural provenance. Here Crusoe behaves and talks like a lost soul. In all the desolations Crusoe faces this is one of the bleakest moments.

The establishment of difference which Defoe claimed for this narrative as a way of giving it distinctiveness and worth in a cloud of competing narratives is not just a matter of commercial or authorial opportunism: the difference is concretised as the essence of Crusoe's life and *Life*. In a luminous phrase deployed just pages before this episode Crusoe describes his unaccompanied island existence as 'my unaccountable life' (185). To tease out fully the implications of this formulation would take one into almost every thematic and discursive corner of *Robinson Crusoe*, but two are particularly salient. Firstly, what this publication purports to offer is an 'account' of Crusoe's story. If it is unaccountable the enterprise is impossible: the full story cannot be told. We cannot have the life, only the *Life*. We have, to use the words of the Preface, 'the story' of this 'private man's adventures in the world', one which the editor says he believes to be 'a just history of fact'. 'Stories' and 'histories' are verbal constructs, perhaps abstracted from some body of actuality but none the less fabrications. Crusoe's experience, his intuition tells him, is properly 'unaccountable'. It is, like the anana, 'beyond whate'er' might be told by the poets. It is an untranslatable wonder that lies, like the island on which it took place, 'quite out of our knowledge'. The second sense in which Crusoe's life is unaccountable is more literal. It is impossible to draw up an account of it: this meaning becomes clear in the light of Crusoe's earlier exercise in accounting when, not long after his arrival in the island, 'I drew up the state of my affairs in writing . . . like debtor and creditor' (83). His parallel columns under the heads of 'Evil' and 'Good' were the written statement of his 'accompt' (84). Crusoe had used the precise denotative discourse of the counting house as a mechanism or a metaphor for articulating the various good and bad aspects of his predicament. He had at that stage found a way of making his life 'accountable'. In his later perception, however, his experience of the civilised world has no resources that will supply him with the descriptive, discursive or calculating language that will render his life accountable.

This is, of course, an extension of those memorable moments in the narrative when Crusoe flags up the present meaninglessness of money to him. The point that gives these moments their particular significance is not just that money has no present value for him, but that it has in fact no value. Money, gold or paper, only has significance as it is given it in the play of discourses of value and transaction. Gold is only an agreed token of exchange-value, and paper money, bills of exchange, are only the tokens of a token. When in the most famous of these moments, when Crusoe finds 'about thirty six pounds value in money, some European coin, some Brasil, some pieces of eight, some gold, some silver' (75) in the wreck, he apostrophises it with the words 'O drug!' Clearly he is not thinking of money as a drug in its beneficial medical sense as a therapeutic pharmaceutical (although in some eighteenth-century writing on political economy this would be a perfectly feasible reading, as when Pope is able to talk of how the Man of Ross uses his money to bring 'Health to the sick' – *Moral Essays*, 2.258), but as a malign compound that stupefies or enslaves the mind. Crusoe's address to the money he has found goes on like this:

> what art thou good for? Thou art not worth to me, no, not the taking off the ground; one of those knives is worth all this heap; I have no manner of use for thee, e'en remain where thou art, and go to the bottom as a creature whose life is not worth saving.
>
> (75)

This clearly indicates that Crusoe's predicament has removed him from the world where money has significance, where agreed discourses and systems of exchange have given money 'worth'. Crusoe is now in a world where money is not 'worth' anything at all, and as money only exists as a token of worth it can be said no longer to exist for Crusoe. An alarming concommitant of Crusoe's translation from the culture of agreed significance, and perhaps a measure of the extent of that translation, is indicated in the words with which he dismisses money from his new life: 'go to the bottom as a creature whose life is not worth saving'. There is a chilling heartlessness about this. Which creatures is it whose lives are not worth saving? Who is Crusoe to decide? The callousness of this seems all the more extreme in one who, not strikingly deserving himself, has in his very immediate history just been singled out for deliverance, alone saved from being sent to the bottom from among a whole ship's crew. With his alienation from the world of money and accounts Crusoe seems to have lost touch with the reticulation of values, social, ethical, religious and humane, on which human nature has been constructed as it is recognised.

This is not, however, the end of the story, as it is not the end of this little episode. Crusoe is redeemed by a small act of inconsistency, an act of moral banality, utterly familiar and recognisable. Immediately after his withering excoriation of money for its worthlessness he reports, 'However, upon second thoughts, I took it away.' The heroic rhetoric of his repudiation of the drug by which we are all enslaved is simply set aside; in a moment of weakness, or of prudence, more impulsive than calculated, he takes the money with him. As, in all likelihood, anyone who was, in Conrad's phrase, 'one of us' would.

As has been suggested by the presentation of these two incidents, by the time Crusoe is much deeper into his island life and visits the second wreck he is far further removed from the patterns of accountable life than when he first takes the money away, and this despite his religious conversion and all his achievements in constructing a simulacrum of a prosperous and comfortable life on the island. If Crusoe is ever to be incorporated in an accountable story, if there is ever to be a *Life* of Robinson Crusoe, he is going to have to be retrieved from this alienation. This is true in a very literal sense. He cannot give an account of his life, there can be no *Life*, because he has no ink: it ran out long since, when his Journal came to an end. It is not fanciful to make this point, and not something that flows only from a twentieth-century consciousness about the ontological status of text. Defoe's first-person narrators do not tell the stories of their lives from middle-age. They give an account of themselves in retrospect from old age. Obviously their *Lives* can not be complete because their lives are not yet ended, but they are approaching the end. (Some qualification about this in Crusoe's case will be made shortly, but he is none the less well over seventy-two – older than Defoe by more than a decade – at the time that the *Strange Surprizing Adventures* are composed.) It was part of Defoe's literary and spiritual inheritance that the only proper autobiography was a spiritual autobiography tracing the course of an individual's life from error through conversion to righteousness.[18] The account of a life was thus the kind of account that could be rendered up before God. Defoe's awareness of the relation between the life and the text of the life is amusingly if grimly signalled in *Captain Singleton*, where Singleton explains that one phase of his career 'brought me into contact with the most famous Pyrates of the Age, some of whom have ended their Journals at the Gallows'.[19] Crusoe, alienated in his unaccountable life, cannot perform the act of autobiography that could redeem him.

Hunter asserts that 'Travel books almost never have, or need, a sense of closure.'[20] This is true in much the same sense that it may be said of autobiographies, or biographies of living people, or histories that come up to the present, but even so, just as the travel in the travel account can only go up to the point in which it is transformed into text so the text itself is finite, is brought up to the point where it ends. Inevitably there is a closure of a kind. The project of the latter parts of *Robinson Crusoe* is to bring the unaccountable life to the point where an account of it can be given; it has to make apparent the acts of enablement that will bring the *Life* into being.

The deliverance of Crusoe from his unaccountable life begins with the prolonged crisis which afflicts him from the moment of his confrontation with one simple physical fact, his finding a human footprint on the shore. His account of this moment emphasises the undeniable actuality of the print. After being 'thunder-struck' by finding it, and running up a hill to look around, and going up and down the shore he comes back to see 'if it might not be my fancy'. There is no chance of this, however: 'for there was exactly the very print of a foot, toes, heel, and every part of a foot' (162). Crusoe, who has learned to be capable about so much, is quite unable to deal with this mark of human presence. His mind is flooded with 'wild ideas' and 'strange unaccountable whimsies'. He scuttles back to his castle not like a man, but like a 'frighted hare . . . to cover, or a fox to his earth'. Something extraordinary happens at this moment. His memory fails him: 'whether I went over by the ladder as first contrived, or went in at the hole in the rock which I called a door, I cannot remember; no nor could I remember the next morning' (162). At this critical moment the mechanism on which the entire narrative and ultimately the *Life* depends ceases to function and leaves a lacuna that is absolutely unfillable. This is a measure of the crippling effect which the discovery of the print has on Crusoe, and also of the distance which he must be brought before he can become author of the account of his life.

There is no need here to trace in detail the process of Crusoe's retranslation into the world of text. One aspect of it is his rescue of Friday and the effect of not just having a companion but of establishing a relationship with him. Crusoe seeks to define this relationship in the language of European order and social relationships, with himself as 'Master'. This is important, but also limited as it grows entirely out of island experience, belongs to an island context, and so only imitates rather than reproduces European structures:

> in a little time I began to speak to him, and teach him to speak to me; and first, I made him know his name was Friday, which was the day I saved his life; I called him so for the memory of the time; I likewise taught him to say Master, and then let him know, that was to be my name.   (209)

On the positive side of Crusoe's retrieval from the unaccountable world is his naming the man Friday, 'for the memory of the time'. The word Friday is accordingly the germ of a text that will recover and record the past and so supplant the fallibilities of personal memory. Less positive is the application of the term 'Master'. This is only an intelligible term for the transaction of relationships if both sides know what it means, just as is the case with money; Friday is taught to utter the sound 'master' and is told it is Crusoe's name (which it is not); Crusoe at this stage is master in name only. It is on a par with his description of himself as head of 'my little family', and as 'the prince and lord of the whole island':

> I had the lives of all my subjects at my absolute command; I could hang, draw, give liberty, and take it away, and no rebels among all my subjects.   (157)

This is all very well, but it is a fantasy or a whimsy to apply these terms to Crusoe's predicament. It is child's play; a pastiche of the real world, not an instance of it. Crusoe goes much further to turning the phonic utterance 'master' into a real signifier for Friday when a few days after naming him he demonstrates to him the power of his gun. Friday is deeply impressed, 'and I believe, if I had let him, he would have worshipped me and my gun' (214).

The acquisition of Friday is an early stage in Crusoe's recuperation, but it is limited. The process is rounded out and completed through the much more extended and perplexed story of his encounters with the cannibals. These shake him to the core. He is not only confronted with a concretisation of all his floating anxieties, a focus and perhaps a vindication for his paranoia, but also with a wonder, an extreme other, infinitely more alarming than a pineapple, in the compass of human nature. The cannibals are an aspect of what Chambers calls the 'demonized geography'[21] of Crusoe's island world. They are the kind of imagined creatures who were used to fill up the blank white paper on incomplete maps. Ian Bell argues that 'Crusoe's attitude towards the natives is consistently that they are part of the hostility of the environment, and so must be conquered',[22] but the truth of the matter is that Crusoe is so shaken that he does not really know what to do about them. Proof of their existence has led him to ask why 'the wise Governor of all things should give up any of his creatures to such inhumanity' (201). He is led into what he calls fruitless speculations. When he first comes across the cannibals he is precipitated into a 'murthering humour' (189) and thinks of various ways of attacking and killing them, and of the difficulties involved. He is 'in great perplexity and anxiety of mind' (189) about his own safety. For well over a year his 'perturbation of mind' disturbs his sleep and gives him 'frightful dreams' about killing the savages 'and of the reasons why I might justify the doing of it' (190). After the diversion of his visit to the second ship the mental disturbance returns, and during one night of extreme agitation he has the dream of a violent encounter with the savages and the romantic rescue of their victim that anticipates his rescue of Friday. On waking he speculates about getting 'a savage into my possession', but is troubled by the extent of the bloodshed that would be involved: 'I . . . greatly scrupled at the lawlessness of it to me; and my heart trembled at the thoughts of shedding so much blood.' He then argues that it might be justifiable as a case of 'self-preservation in the highest degree' but though this argues for it, 'the thoughts of shedding humane blood for my deliverance were very terrible to me' (202–3).

When the major crisis comes, and Crusoe and Friday encounter the cannibals at their feast, Crusoe is filled with 'abhorrence' and 'indignation' and tells Friday, 'I was resolv'd to go down to them, and kill them all.' In this 'fit of fury' he makes preparations for the assault, but on his way to effect it, 'my former thoughts returning, I began to abate my resolution', not out of physical fear but because he is afraid he may be encroaching on God's providence. God had left the savages in this inhuman state and 'whenever he thought fit, He would take the cause into His own hands, and by a national vengeance punish them as a people for national crimes'. However much Friday might be justified in attacking his enemies, Crusoe decides that 'it was none of my business', and that he will simply go and place himself near the savages, observe their feast, and leave the rest to God, concluding, 'unless something offered that was more a call to me than yet I knew of, I would not meddle with them' (233). The call, if that is what it is, comes when Crusoe discovers that one of the intended victims is not a naked savage like Friday, an inhabitant of the unaccountable world, but a white, bearded, clothed European. This discovery 'fired all the soul within me' (233) and it precipitates rapid, violent and unreflective action:

'Are you ready, Friday?' said I; 'Yes,' says he; 'Let fly then,' says I, 'in the name of God.'   (234)

Immediate slaughter follows, but this is the moment of Crusoe's retrieval for the accountable world. Finessing, doubt, alienation, are all over, Crusoe has enacted his culture: he has become again one of us. It is striking confirmation of this that as soon as the narrative of the assault is over Crusoe, for the first time since he drew up his 'accompt'

of Evil and Good, now presents in tabular form an 'account' (237) of
the savages he has attacked:

3 killed at our first shot from the tree.
2 killed at the next shot.
2 killed by Friday in the boat.
. . . . .
4 escaped in the boat, whereof one wounded if not dead.
—
21 in all.

The most preoccupying thread of *Robinson Crusoe* is now ready to be
wound up. Crusoe discovered that the savages were 'my business' and
now he gives an account of how he conducted it. His 'unaccountable
life' is behind him, and he is on the way towards the point at which, at
the conclusion of *Robinson Crusoe*, he will have given an account of his
life. Michael McKeon makes clear what happens through the concluding episodes of the novel as Crusoe proceeds towards rehabilitation in
an orderly, accountable, commercial and capitalistic culture. Defoe, he
says, is

> engaged here in the tangible externalisation of Robinson's now
> securely internalised utopia, in the representation of the psychologi-
> cal state of being a principled possessive individualist, fully recon-
> ciled to the naturalness and morality of the pursuit of self-interest.[23]

Returned, his wealth secured, married, a father of three children, bringing up his nephew as a gentleman and equipping him to make profitable merchant voyages, the errant Robinson Crusoe aged sixty-two or
a little more is finally turned into the normative text *Robinson Crusoe*.
An account has been given of the unaccountable.

This is almost true, but not quite. *Robinson Crusoe* actually ends with
a reopening of the wonder-world in its last four paragraphs. Crusoe
leaps ahead to tell us how he made another voyage and 'visited my new
collony in the island' and found out how the Spanish he had left behind
there had fared, 'a history, if it were entered into, as full of variety and
wonderful accidents as my own part' (298). He pours into these paragraphs a cornucopia of excitement and incident, including, yet to be
told, 'an account of how 300 Caribbees came and invaded them, and
ruined their plantations' (299). The orderly world of capital and
empire, of knowledge and progress, had been in the ten years or so
since the apparent end of the *Life* disrupted yet again by the wild and

unaccountable. But the story will have to wait for another publication: 'all these things, with some very surprising incidents in some new adventures of my own, for ten years more, I may perhaps give a further account of hereafter' (299). In these paragraphs Defoe is trailing further profitable publishing ventures if *Robinson Crusoe* succeeds, and he is at the same time positioning himself in that flux of the wonderful and the familiar that makes him one of the quintessential conscious-nesses of his era. For all that he was preoccupied with quantification and the workings of a political economy, one of Defoe's deepest aware-nesses was that on earth no account is ever truly closed.

Gulliver's Travels

The travels of Lemuel Gulliver are much more 'strange' and 'surprising' than those of Robinson Crusoe. They go beyond not simply what was known but beyond what we know could possibly exist. When Gulliver first encounters the Brobdingnagians he advances a proposition that might legitimise the fantastic narrative:

> Undoubtedly Philosophers are in the Right when they Tell us, that nothing is great or little otherwise than by Comparison: It might have pleased Fortune to let the *Lilliputians* find some Nation, where the People were as diminutive with respect to them, as they were to me. And who knows that even this prodigious Race of Mortals might be equally overmatched in some distant Part of the World, whereof we have yet no Discovery. (2.1.87; see note 3)

Gulliver's may be a mentality that can entertain such an idea, but the satirical burden of the passage is to insist that in promulgating such relativism 'Undoubtedly Philosophers are in the Wrong.' Creation was not a matter of free-wheeling possibility but of established fact: man is as God made him. Commentators on Swift now properly insist on the destabilising effects of his satire and the way in which it inhibits reso-lution. Nokes sees this as a symptom of the radical freedom of thought informing Swift's writing: 'those teasing contradictions in Swift's writ-ings which pose such problems for his later commentators, are them-selves the symbols of freedom, dissent and liberty of thought'.[24] The crucial and central perception of Rawson's writing about *Gulliver's Travels* is to enforce our inability to distinguish lucidly and absolutely between Gulliver's mentality and Swift's attitudes, so that 'we are made curiously insecure as to how, exactly, to take the joke'. Of the work as a whole he asserts, 'Swift's whole ironic programme depends on our not being taken in by the travel-book element, but it does require us to be infected with a residual uncertainty about it.' And, in a sentence which itself recreates some of the perplexing maze of thought through which Swift leads his readers, Rawson concludes that,

> The tense hovering between laughter and something else, the struc-tural indefiniteness of genre and the incessantly shifting status and function of the parodic element, the ironic twists and countertwists, and the endless flickering of local effect suggest that one of the most active of Swift's satiric weapons is bewilderment.[25]

These formulations are all excellent, but they also reflect a kind of earnestness, a will to understand, that may not take complete account of, to use a word which Henry James appropriated – maybe surpris-ingly – for his own late fiction, the 'fun' of Swift's satire.[26] John Traugott, talking admittedly mainly of *A Tale of a Tub*, recognises in Swift's satirical manner something that we might now identify as the Bakhtinian carnivalesque, a kind of licensed literary anarchy in which all the capacities of language to subvert and disrupt the traditional authority of conventional utterance and genre are exploited.[27] Despite the tragic strain in the writing, Traugott says, 'Swift's satire is so festively inventive, so raucous in its humour that the reader's experience of its harlequinade is far more euphoric than lugubri-ous.'[28] The image of Swift's writing as a stylistic harlequinade char-acterises it as marked by both clowning and disguise. In her study of the masquerade in eighteenth-century culture Terry Castle draws parallels between satire and masquerade: 'Like the world of satire, the masquerade projected an anti-nature, a world upside-down, an intoxicating reversal of ordinary sexual, social, and metaphysical hier-archies.'[29] She also establishes the link between the masquerade mode and narrative:

> True to its magical-seeming, transformational nature, the carniva-lesque episode characteristically provides the mimetic disequilibrium on which plot itself depends.   (21)

And she develops this to assert that the carnivalesque episode 'reveals itself as part of the hidden, life-giving machinery of narrative pleasure' (124).

All these responses coincide in recognition that *Gulliver's Travels* as a voyage narrative cannot be discussed in the same way as *Robinson Crusoe* and that each author apprehends the topos of the exotic voyage quite differently. Despite what Defoe later says in the Preface to the third part of *Robinson Crusoe* about the whole story of Crusoe having been a 'Riddle' which is 'now expounded' as an allegory of his own life, the entire narrative and thematic structure requires that it be taken at face value. By contrast, *Gulliver's Travels* depends completely for all its effects on continually renewed recognitions that it is not true, or that it embodies truths in disguise. The developmental effects of *Robinson Crusoe* are slow and cumbersome, with transitions only from one steady state in Crusoe's experience to another, which is one way in which it establishes its difference from the episodic adventurousness of literary romance. *Gulliver's Travels* is much more like romance: the publication comprises four fully accountable voyages to remote and extraordinary places; the personality of Gulliver is ostensibly stable and he appears to function primarily as the vehicle and recorder of his own adventures; he sees and observes all those things which Bacon says the traveller should seek out; his is a story of disaster, survival and rescue repeated in each voyage. The narrative is volatile and its tempo rapid as *Robinson Crusoe* never is. But there is this difference: the reader of romantic adventure suspends disbelief. The reader of *Gulliver's Travels* cannot. (Some qualification of this will be made later.) The apocryphal eighteenth-century reader who put down *Gulliver's Travels* in disgust, saying that he did not believe a word of it, was the wrong sort of reader: it was not that he did not know how to take the joke, but that he did not know there was a joke. His reading constructed a book Swift did not write. Swift's book is a narrative of fast episodic adventure for the mind: its volatility is conceptual and it has an extraordinarily rapid intellectual tempo, not matched even by the wayward unpredictabilities of *Tristram Shandy*. In terms of intellectual pace its nearest equivalent might be the *Dunciad*, but for all its difficulties that work is less testing than *Gulliver's Travels* because we always know where Pope stands. Swift leads us into the wood but keeps hiding behind the trees.

The raw material of Swift's narrative is of course the manifold features of the culture which Gulliver leaves behind and to which we readers belong: its politics, education, national feeling, relations between men and women, its vanity, its technology, especially as it is applied in warfare, its intellectual, philosophical and spiritual preoccupations, its professions, habits, follies and virtues, its fashions and its common sense.

Of all these the last is perhaps the most important: not because it is conspicuous or is given a steady voice in *Gulliver's Travels*, but because it goes almost entirely unspoken. We do, however, occasionally hear it. It is difficult to dissent, for instance when the king of Brobdingnag advances the opinion that,

> whoever could make two Ears of Corn, or two Blades of Grass to grow upon a Spot of Ground where only one grew before; would deserve better of Mankind, and do more essential Service to his Country, than the whole Race of Politicians put together.
> (2.7.135–6)

Normally, however, the voice of common sense remains mute (and it does not follow that because the king is right here he is always right), as it is for instance when Gulliver visits the Grand Academy of Lagado and witnesses the two principal experiments being conducted by '*the universal Artist*'. One is to sow the land with chaff in the belief that it contained 'the true seminal virtue'. The other is

> by a certain Composition of Gums, Minerals, and Vegetables outwardly applied, to prevent the Growth of Wool upon two young Lambs; and he hoped in a reasonable Time to propagate the Breed of naked Sheep all over the Kingdom.   (3.5.182)

Common sense, the attitudes and experience of most ordinary people, indicates that this is a very bad idea; not that this takes us the whole way into the satire. The '*universal Artist*' is an imitation of the true Universal Artist, and he is parodically engaged on a work of uncreation, and as a scientist seeking to modify the conditions of creation he is encroaching blasphemously on the divine prerogative and disposition. Common sense is by no means a sufficient guide to the satirical strategies of the *Travels*, but it is indispensable, and it needs to be always alert. If it lapses the reader may for instance accede in the proposition advanced by Gulliver on seeing the Brobdingnagians that 'Philosophers are in the Right' in arguing for the relativity of all things.

Common sense can lapse in *Gulliver's Travels* not just because it has limits and is liable to inattention but because in this book it is under siege. Gulliver's translations to other cultures are so extraordinary that he can lose hold on what he knows, and in this the reader may go with him. For example, in the land of the houyhnhnms Gulliver's master compares Gulliver's human physique unfavourably with that of the yahoos, who have stronger nails, tougher feet, and so on. He also observes, 'That I could not walk with any Security; for if either of my hinder Feet slipped, I must inevitably fall' (4.4.242). Under the sway of the complacent houyhnhnm's rhetoric the reader may feel that this is a fair point, but it is wholly theoretical and one which observation of Gulliver should have repudiated. Human beings may not be, like houyhnhnms, 'the perfection of nature', but what cannot be denied is that they are very accomplished bipeds. If one foot slips we do not 'inevitably fall'. We hardly ever fall; we recover our balance. As the comparison goes on it becomes clear that Gulliver's master is no longer measuring him against a yahoo, but against a horse, and finding fault with,

> the Flatness of my Face, the Prominence of my Nose, mine Eyes placed directly in Front, so that I could not look on either Side without turning my Head; That I was not able to feed my self, without lifting one of my fore Feet to my Mouth . . .   (4.4.242)

The horse's equicentricity is as absurd as Gulliver's human pride, but it is under the influence of this point of view that Gulliver comes to believe, as many readers have done, that there is no difference between himself and a yahoo. If, however, he were to cast his mind back to his first encounter with the yahoos he would recollect that 'I never beheld in all my Travels so disagreeable an Animal, or one against which I naturally conceived so strong an antipathy' (4.1.223–4). Human beings and yahoos may share some physical similarities and certain characteristics, but they are not identical, even if it requires a very vigilant common sense to sustain the discrimination, especially when it is being continually contested by the domineering ideology of the houyhnhnms. The isolation of the traveller in an alien or difficult environment makes it difficult for him to maintain sight of what he knows. When Robinson Crusoe sees the footprint he initially spends much longer on the elaborate and unlikely hypothesis that for some strange motive it had been set there by the devil than on the much greater likelihood that it had been made by a human being.

If common sense is liable to subversion in the narrative of the travels then it is also part of Swift's satirical strategy that in the society the travels mimic, Europe and England in particular, the common sense of men has been undermined, seduced or betrayed by a myriad follies and delusions. (And one thing that complicates this in some parts of the narrative at least is that Gulliver is an author whose common sense has surrendered to delusion, as the paranoia of the prefatory Letter to his cousin Sympson and the preposterous misanthropy of the last chapter of Book Four make clear.) The reader, even the academic reader, should not be too complacent. Common sense tells the reader that there is no such place as Lilliput, on this planet at least, where there is a race of men six inches high. On the other hand, is there a reader who has not wondered whether the Lilliputian temple would in fact (whatever that may mean) have a door four feet high and be long enough for Gulliver to lie down in, or not been tempted to do the calculation that would establish whether six hundred Lilliputian beds sewn up in four layers would make Gulliver a tolerable mattress, or to wonder whether his daily consumption of 'six Beeves, forty Sheep . . . with a proportionate Quantity of Bread and Wine' might not be an appalling burden on the economy of a small kingdom? Being prepared to read the narrative at all is in a way a surrender or willing suspension of common sense, and it is part of the whole sardonic project to expose the reader to the true nature of the curiosity that fostered the popularity of voyage narratives in the early decades of the eighteenth century.

Nokes's characterisation of the destabilising perplexities of Swift's writing as symbols of his 'freedom, dissent and liberty of thought' precisely identifies Swift's stance in relation to the culture out of which he is writing in *Gulliver's Travels*. Freedom is, as Isaiah Berlin established, not only freedom to, but freedom from.[30] *Gulliver's Travels* is a text that concretises liberation in both senses: in its extravagance, waywardness, eccentricity, obscenity and extremity it establishes a territory of unconstrained literary conduct, as it were going beyond the known world of convention – Swift takes not just the voyager but the voyage narrative where he wants. While in the last chapter of *Gulliver's Travels* Gulliver deprecates colonial practice and excuses himself for not having sought to 'enlarge his Majesty's Dominions by my Discoveries' (294) Swift has in a sense established a colony of his own, a colony of the mind, where he can 'hang, draw, give liberty, and take it away, and no rebels.' The absoluteness of his apprehension of this authorial liberty is the key to the carnivalesque licence of the style, where his 'harlequinade' of follies can have free play. The masquerade world of the narrative is not the real world, the world in which Swift is a friend, a political agitator, a clergyman of disappointed ambitions, a defender of Ireland, an associate of men of influence and abilities. That real world is the world he represents in the disguise of the harlequinade. The masquerade is an episode of freedom to do as he likes, but also of freedom from the fashions, follies and vices of the culture of eighteenth-century England. The voyage

experience in *Robinson Crusoe* allows Crusoe to recreate the world in his
own image, but no more; he is never free of the self he takes with him.
In *Gulliver's Travels* Swift recreates the people of his world in their image
as he sees it; by absenting himself from the narrative he establishes freedom from them and thereby allows the reader to exercise whatever freedom he or she can.

The principal mechanism of *Gulliver's Travels* is very simple. Gulliver
travels to exotic places and the people and practices he discovers there
initially appear as wonders, even though he reports them in a matter-
of-fact way. Developing experience promotes recognition, and what
seemed wonderful becomes familiar as European practice. The recognition is disturbing because what has been taken as familiar at home is
now identifiable as a wonder. The masquerade and the real world thus
exist in a constant oscillation with each other. It is as if the separate
modes of Defoe's narrative, the unaccountable and the accountable,
have become almost indistinguishable. They can only be separated by
an alert and vigilant common sense reinforced by all the better religious, moral and humane values to which European society can lay
claim. If no such claim could be made *Gulliver's Travels* would be meaningless. In a very crude formulation, the textual phenomenology of
Gulliver's Travels is that man at his best reads about man at his worst,
and they are the same person.

There is no need to enumerate and distinguish all the fields of activity and thought, all the beguiling fashions and foolish practices, Swift
replicates *en travesti* in *Gulliver's Travels*, but they do go to the core of
the preoccupations which were described as underlying the vogue for
travel literature in the first section of this chapter. Some are none the
less worth rehearsing, if only summarily.   ·

Firstly, the enterprise of travel itself is challenged in this book.
Broadly, Gulliver is trying to improve his lot, or his fortune: he is trying
to modify and improve the circumstances and situation allotted to him
by divine providence, and thus his voyaging can be construed as an
attempt to interfere with or subvert God's dispensation. The impulse to
travel is also something which Gulliver sees as lodged in his personality. Misfortune, hardship and lack of success in his voyages are overrid-
den by a kind of wilfulness. At the beginning of the second voyage, the
only motive Gulliver gives for setting out again is that he was
'condemned by Nature and Fortune to an active and restless Life'
(2.1.83) and at the start of the third voyage he explains his accepting
the post of Surgeon on a ship, saying 'the Thirst I had of seeing the
World, notwithstanding my past Misfortunes, continuing as violent as

ever' (3.1.153–4). Before the fourth voyage he stays with his family at
home for five months, 'in a very happy Condition, if I could have
learned the lesson of knowing when I was well' (4.1.221). But tempted
by 'an advantageous Offer' he is off again. Gulliver's travelling is thus
determined by self-interest and wilfulness, a perversity in the face of
fortune and experience.

Better, however, as an index of Swift's critique of voyaging is to look
at what Gulliver brings back. On one level at least it is the trophies that
vindicate the travel. In the last chapter of the voyage to Brobdingnag
Gulliver displays to the captain who rescued him the 'Cabinet' which
contains 'the small Collection of Rarities' he has with him; his words
echo Bacon's 'Cabinets, and Rarities'. The collection includes

> the Comb I had contrived out of the Stumps of the King's Beard;
> and another of the same Materials, but fixed into a paring of her
> Majesty's Thumbnail ... Four Wasp-Stings, like Joyners Tacks;
> Some Combings of the Queen's Hair: ... a Corn that I had cut off
> with my own Hand from a Maid of Honour's Toe; it was about the
> Bigness of a *Kentish* Pippin.   (2.8.146)

Rare and curious they may be, but they are also disgusting and worthless. From his last voyage Gulliver's trophies are not even the rejected
body-parts of his hosts; they are all in his mind – extreme misanthropy,
impossible pride and obvious madness. Gulliver concludes his voyages
unfit for human society. He has even lost the word for us: we are, as he
calls us in the Letter to Sympson, Yahoos. The world Gulliver left, the
world he once belonged to, has become in his mind the untranslatable
other, unaccountable.

Voyaging was partly a scientific activity, and there is a rattle of small-
arms fire directed at the gracelessness and inutility of scientific attitudes
and practice throughout *Gulliver's Travels*.[31] The worthlessness of the
Brobdingnagian scientists' conclusion that Gulliver is only 'Relplum
Scalcath' has already been mentioned, as has the travesty of the Royal
Society in the Grand Academy of Lagado. When Gulliver visits the
Struldbrugs he fantasises about living long enough to see 'the
Discovery of *Longitude*, the *perpetual Motion*, the *universal Medicine*,
and many other great Inventions brought to the utmost Perfection'
(3.10.210). Scientific practice and the detailed recording of marine
experience are parodied in the first two paragraphs of Book Two.
Mathematical science is ridiculed in Book Three, along with the preoccupation with music and harmony.

The British obsession with party politics is mocked throughout the *Travels*, in most detail in Book One, and equally pervasive is caustic commentary on the quest for, and exercise and abuse of power. It is an indication of how profoundly Swift was affected by his experience of power in action, in Ireland during the period when *Gulliver's Travels* was being composed, and earlier when he was working as a journalist and propagandist for Prime Minister Harley and Secretary of State Bolingbroke during the Tory administration of 1710 to 1714, that the abuse of power is a more prominent and more fiercely presented theme than the theme of money, recurrent though that is. During the Tory ministry Swift had directed his best energies against the apparently war-mongering Whigs and their great general the Duke of Marlborough, as the Tories tried to manoeuvre Europe towards an end to the War of the Spanish Succession, an effort which finally concluded in the Treaty of Utrecht of 1713. Swift had written the two most influential peace tracts of those years.[32] The savage indictments of the practice of European warfare in *Gulliver's Travels*, and of the corrupt and selfish interests that prompt it, have their roots in that experience, as does the repeated sniping against the Dutch, whom Swift saw as having manipulated and deceived their British allies in promoting and prolonging the long war against Louis XIV. An interesting small example of Swift's hostility to the Dutch is seen in Book Four, Chapter three, when Gulliver describes the houyhnhnm language as approaching 'nearest to the *High Dutch* or *German*' but 'much more graceful and significant'. He cites the Emperor Charles V saying 'That if he were to speak to his Horse, it should be in High Dutch' (4.3.234). What gives especial force to this satirical jibe is that of all the languages Gulliver meets on his travels the houyhnhnm language is by far the most difficult, hard to pronounce and remote from ordinary human speech. It is likely that the generally favourable light in which the Portuguese are presented in *Gulliver's Travels* also comes from that time. Portuguese and British interests were united in the Methuen Treaty of 1703. The most striking example is the Portuguese captain, Pedro de Mendez, who brings the reluctant Gulliver back to Europe after his departure from the land of the houy-hnhnms. His persistent kindness and tolerance in the face of Gulliver's unaccountable rudeness and lack of sociability contrast with the testy misanthropy which becomes Gulliver's final state of mind.

If religious experience is one of the great presences of *Robinson Crusoe* it is one of the great absences from *Gulliver's Travels*. Gulliver is not impious or atheistical, but the experience he recounts is physical, social and emotional, not spiritual. He does not resort to prayer in his adventures or to the Bible. Institutional religion has no evident part in his life. Religious wars are satirised in Lilliput in the account of the wars between the Big-Endians and the Little-Endians, disputing the text in 'their *Alcoran*' 'That all true Believers' shall break their Eggs at the convenient End' (1.4.49–50), and describing warfare in Europe Gulliver tells his houyhnhnm master that 'Difference in Opinion hath cost many Millions of Lives: For Instance, whether *Flesh* be *Bread*, or *Bread* be *Flesh*: whether the Juice of a certain *Berry* be *Blood* or *Wine*.' He adds that 'Neither are any Wars so furious and bloody, or of so long Continuance, as those occasioned by Difference in Opinion, especially if it be in things indifferent' (4.5.246). There is perhaps one moment at which a sense of true religious values comes close to the surface of the text. In Brobdingnag Gulliver is 'very desirous to see the chief Temple' (Bacon's list of worthwhile curiosities included 'Churches and Monasteries'), but it is clear that his principal interest is not religious but to see how high it was. He comes away disappointed as it is 'not above three thousand Foot', which, given the size of the Brobdingnagians, 'is no great matter for Admiration, nor at all equal in Proportion . . . to *Salisbury* Steeple'. He does go on to add in fairness to his hosts, 'that whatever this famous Tower wants in Height, is amply made up in Beauty and Strength. For the Walls are near an hundred Foot thick, built of Stone' (2.4.114). So here for the reader, though not it appears for Gulliver, is the emblem of a true and substantial church.

Gulliver is a man of his times. His insensibility to religious and spiritual questions marks him out as the representative of a culture which has lost all grounding in steady ideas and constant belief. It is this that makes him so vulnerable to the practices and ideologies of the nations he visits, especially and terminally those of the houyhnhnms. It is a vulnerability that ultimately costs him his mind.

The experience of voyaging and discovery, and the matter of giving an account of that experience as well as of living in alien and exotic environments, became in the hands of Defoe and Swift levers to prise up the lid of the culture in which, from which and about which they wrote. The voyage narrative brought together the wonderful and the familiar, the unaccountable and the accountable, in texts that translated the modern consciousness beyond all that was known, and then reclaimed or took possession of all discovered or transacted there, by a process of retranslation into the known, just as the exotic and untranslatable *anana* was appropriated for our language and culture as a pineapple.

2
Wit and Virtue: *The Way of the World* and *Clarissa*

In the second act of Sheridan's *The School for Scandal* (1777) the Scandalous College is in full flight, running through the names of their acquaintances and criticising them by turns. Even though the College consists of imaginary characters in a play talking about other people who are as it were even more non-existent as they are never more than names, the scene is entertaining, but slightly disconcertingly so: it is witty, but it essentially trades in the impure pleasures of improper gossip, and strictly, the absent victims are not so much criticised as anatomised:

> *Mrs. Candour*:   Well, I will never join in ridiculing a friend; and so I constantly tell my cousin Ogle, and you all know what pretensions she has to be critical on beauty.
> *Crabtree*:   Oh, to be sure! She herself has the oddest countenance that ever was seen; 'tis a collection of features from all the different countries of the globe.
> *Sir Benjamin Backbite*:   So she has, indeed – an Irish front –
> *Crabtree*:   Caledonian locks –
> *Sir Benjamin*:   Dutch nose –
> *Crabtree*:   Austrian lips –
> *Sir Benjamin*:   Complexion of a Spaniard –
> *Crabtree*:   And teeth *à la Chinoise* –
> *Sir Benjamin*:   In short her face resembles a *table d'hote* at Spa – where no two guests are of a nation –
> *Crabtree*:   Or a congress at the close of a general war – wherein all the members, even to her eyes, appear to have a different interest, and her nose and chin are the only parties likely to join issue.
>
> (2.2)

This is powerful not simply because it is an instance of freewheeling malice: it seems to realise a vision of existence as deconstruction, or one which echoes a larger political world understood as meaningless, ugly and fragmented. Sir Peter Teazle, an outsider in the Scandalous College, cannot stand it. His aside 'Mercy on my life! – a person they dine with twice a week!' implies a quite different understanding of the meaning of social relations, but when he protests against the abusive tenor of the conversation he only draws Lady Sneerwell's fire on himself:

> Well said, Sir Peter! But you are a cruel creature – too phlegmatic yourself for a jest, and too peevish to allow wit in others.

In response he takes up her words and protests,

> Ah! Madam, true wit is more nearly allied to good-nature than your ladyship is aware of.

The School for Scandal was first presented in 1777 but it is a piece that in many ways evokes the manners and spirit of earlier comedy, and Sir Peter's words crystallise one of the central vexations of the first fifty years or so of the eighteenth century, that wit and good nature did not seem to be 'nearly allied' and that bringing them into coexistence was not at all easy. What Sir Peter says is not a truism but a highly problematic assertion.

It seems like an axiom because Sir Peter speaks not of 'wit' but of 'true wit': Lady Sneerwell's wit cannot be true wit as it has no good-nature in it. The phrase 'true wit' had been prominently canvassed. In 1711 Addison devoted six consecutive *Spectators* (58–63) to an analysis of the distinction between False Wit and True Wit, and the phrase had attained cultural authority in Pope's formulation:

> *True Wit* is *Nature* to Advantage drest,
> What oft was *Thought*, but ne'er so well *Exprest*.
> ('An Essay on Criticism', 297–8)[1]

But even this constatation is revealed as vulnerable when in the opening chapter of *Tom Jones*, which draws an extended sardonic analogy between the phenomenon of reading and the physiology of eating, Fielding insists that Pope's metaphor of being 'to Advantage drest' is not a sartorial image but one drawn from cookery, where 'the difference between the food of the nobleman and the porter', eating parts of the same animal, is not in the substance 'but in the seasoning, the dressing, the garnishing, and the setting forth'.[2]

It may have been verbally acceptable and attractive for Sir Peter or Pope or Addison to speak of 'True Wit', but the problem was to know whether the concept reflected any social or psychological reality. In a letter Richardson takes up a proposition of Addison's in *Spectator* 51 that it is possible for a man to be both witty and virtuous:

> I allow, that it is possible, as the Spectator says . . . that a man who is *temperate*, *generous*, *valiant*, *chaste*, *faithful* and *honest*, may, at the same time, have Wit, Humour, Mirth, and Good Breeding.

But the possibility is not realised even in his own imagination. He speaks of the long-suffering Mr Hickman, suitor to the spirited Anna Howe in *Clarissa*, and says that had he made him such a man (both virtuous and witty), 'the Ladies *more than half-liked* Lovelace, would, compared to him, have made a sorry Figure'.[3] But he did not make such a man, and the appalling rake Lovelace remains the principal representation of the culture of wit in the novel and, despite his moral character, at least partly attractive. (It is worth remembering how scarce a commodity wit is among the principal characters of canonical eighteenth-century imaginative narratives, many of which are properly recognised and relished as witty novels. Defoe's main characters – and Defoe himself – are scarcely witty. The satirical comedy of *Gulliver's Travels* turns very much on Gulliver not being so. Neither Joseph Andrews nor Tom Jones, except perhaps when Tom is at his most compromised and nearly degenerate in London, are wits. Amelia is not. Of Smollett's leading characters only Ferdinand Count Fathom could be thought of as a wit, and he is a thoroughly bad hat. Sterne's narrators are rather wry and droll than witty.)

What can be posed as the tension between wit and virtue is the subject of this chapter. Whether wit and virtue could coexist was not simply a philosophical question of largely speculative interest. It was important because it was lodged in the historical position of eighteenth-century literary culture. Wit was the dominant mode of the late seventeenth century, specifically the period of what might be called the long Restoration, from 1660 to 1700, and it was not just a cultural fashion but an aggressive and assertive articulation of the aristocratic, quasi-aristocratic and 'wannabe' aristocratic élite that, with increasing precariousness, held centre-stage in public life. Wit dominated in the re-opened public theatres, and it was the celebrated quality of private verses. The presses were fertile in witty poems on affairs of state, and images of witty sophistication lay behind the lineaments of both male

and female role models. Even a figure as complex and serious as Dryden
was in the fullest sense witty: his earnestness, when he is earnest, is
made pungent by his wit, and his game is a gleeful celebration of wit.
It is significant that when Martin Battestin took as the title for his study
of order in Augustan art the phrase 'the Providence of Wit' he gleaned
it from Dryden's commendation in 1660 of Sir Robert Howard's verse
as manifesting exactly that.[4]

Eighteenth-century culture necessarily began in the shadow, or light,
of Restoration culture and it had to establish and define itself in that
context, or against it. This was difficult as the qualities which were
beginning to emerge as important if the culture were to avoid lapsing
into the perceived political, religious and moral chaos of the Civil War,
Commonwealth and Restoration periods were just those for which the
immediately precedent culture had little or no regard: they were the
values of civic humanism, religious morality, personal integrity and
financial prudence. They were seen as the bulwarks of the emergent
polity of the new century and they were valorised in its literature. But
that literature had in a sense learned its manners in the Restoration, and
hence the tension, as it has been rather crudely put here, between wit
and virtue in the literary culture of the first half of the eighteenth
century.

This chapter will deal with two instances exhibiting a complex negotiation of the wit/virtue dilemma from the beginning and end of the
period: Congreve's subtle working of the modes of Restoration stage
comedy in *The Way of the World* (1700) and Richardson's profound
searching of cultural and spiritual values in *Clarissa* (1748).

Congreve's play and Richardson's novel told in letters both accentu-
ate the uncertainty, fluidity and susceptibility to change of the societies
from which they emerge by removing from the literary product one of
its possible points of reference. In speaking of the assumptions about
class that are inscribed in eighteenth-century literary and critical
discourse, David Nokes argues that the 'class-consciousness of eighteenth-century vocabulary corresponds to the social preoccupations of
the literature itself. A dignified tone and polite style were the hallmarks
of a civilised culture in which manners and morality went hand in
hand.'[5] The dramatic and epistolary forms exclude any such supervising
style. Matters of 'manners and morality' are left as it were in the hands,
or voices, or pens, of the characters themselves. This is of course a
simplification, as no literary work, or any other text or utterance, exists
independently of the provenance, presuppositions and habits of its
author and the culture to which he or she belongs, but it is none the

less significant that both works eschew the stabilising influence of an explicitly present authorial voice.

Even before the play starts *The Way of the World* marks instability as its tone. The Prologue tells us that poets (that is, playwrights) are 'a sort of fools' who are first made by fortune and then forsaken by her. By contrast the witless, 'Nature's oafs', enjoy her life-long favour. The Prologue goes on to say that although this author knows that he has enjoyed the public's approval hitherto, he also knows that his tenure of it depends on his latest production:

> This author, heretofore, has found your favour,
> But pleads no merit from his past behaviour;
> To build on that might prove a vain presumption,
> Should grants to poets made, admit resumption:
> And in Parnassus he must lose his seat,
> If that be found a forfeited estate.[6]

What is notable here is that the imagery chosen associates the world of wit with insecure tenure of property – 'resumption', 'lose his seat', 'forfeited estate'. Although the characters of Restoration comedy ape the manners and attitudes of the old aristocracy, the old securities are gone or disappearing. Its place in the world is in jeopardy. It is very notable in *The Way of the World* especially that the tissue of the dominant culture is becoming distinctly threadbare. The wits are not very witty; the lovers are desperate and querulous; plots are sustained, if at all, only by luck and frantic efforts; hardly anyone has a title; and there is precious little money around – the whole story turns on the disposition of a fortune of £6,000, which, invested at five percent (and that would be lucky) would generate an income of only £300, perhaps the equivalent of a middling living for an eighteenth-century country clergyman. The prologue reflects an atmosphere of political and class instability, of uncertain tenure, of discontinuity, and a sense that the world's system is now a volatile meritocracy.

The Prologue goes on to say that the author does offer 'Some plot', 'some new thought', 'Some humour', 'no farce', and no 'satire' – 'For so reform'd a town, who dares correct?' This phrase registers an anti-wit mood that had been focused in the attacks of Jeremy Collier and others on both the brittle amorality of Restoration comedies and the immorality of the theatres as places of resort.[7] A tide was beginning to set in that would see the comic stage in England increasingly marked by moralism and sentimentality. *The Way of the World* is historically and culturally perfectly poised to attempt a negotiation between the old world of the Restoration and the emergent culture of the new century.

The play begins with a dialogue between two figures whom we might identify as wits or rakes, but there is a distinction between them. Mirabell and Fainall have been gambling, but Fainall wants to stop, as Mirabell seems unconcerned at losing. 'I'd no more play with a man who slighted his ill fortune,' says Fainall, 'than I'd make love to a woman who underrated the loss of her reputation.' This is a perversion of desire which Mirabell does not repudiate but from which he distances himself with a cool observation:

> You have a taste extremely delicate, and are for refining on your plea-
> sures.

This description would equally fit the complex deviationism of the elab- orately-minded Lovelace in *Clarissa*. The appeal from the distortion of desire in Fainall is implicitly to something more natural, and its exis- tence in the world is made clear in ensuing exchanges.

Mirabell confesses that he is out of humour because he has been slighted by Millamant. On the previous evening he had intruded on a gathering of ladies, including Millamant, who had sought to ease him out by all joining in 'an invective against long visits.' When Mirabell had indicated to Millamant that it was easy for him to know when his visit had begun to get troublesome, 'she reddened and I withdrew'. A blush is the sign of awkwardness or embarrassment, and of its nature it is natural, involuntary, unsophisticated. Millamant's blush arises in the tension between the social role she is playing in Lady Wishfort's 'Cabal-night' and her natural feelings for Mirabell. Blushing is referred to twice more in the play, with similar significations. Mirabell refuses to join Witwoud and Petulant for a walk in the park:

> . . . walk by yourselves, – let us not be accessory to your putting the
> ladies out of countenance, with your senseless ribaldry; which you
> roar out loud as often as they pass by you; and when you have made
> a handsome woman blush, then you think you have been severe.
>
> (2.6)

Petulant seeks to reveal the natural or underlying sexual consciousness of women by bringing colour to their cheeks. With a little more subtlety, in a cynical misanthropic conversation between Mrs

Marwood and Mrs Fainall about men, love and marriage, Mrs Marwood's true feelings are revealed when she changes colour at Mrs Fainall's malicious wish, 'Would thou wert married to Mirabell.' The blush is reinforced in what seems like an equally involuntary exclamation from Mrs Marwood of 'Would I were', which she tries to retrieve by adding (mendaciously) 'Because I hate him' (2.1). The witness of the blush is confirmed when Fainall tells Mrs Marwood, who is his mistress, that he knows she loves Mirabell because 'I have seen the warm confession reddening on your cheeks, and sparkling from your eyes' (2.3).

In these instances the natural, though not necessarily virtuous, feelings whose existence the blush bears witness to are feelings the characters are ashamed of or embarrassed by, and which they would rather hide. In the world of the wits the blush therefore doubles as a token of shame.

What is not being set up in *The Way of the World* is an opposition between perverse wit and natural virtue. The first mention of virtue in the play is in fact rather disconcerting. Mirabell explains to Fainall how he has been conducting a flagrant flirtation with Lady Wishfort as a smokescreen for courting her niece Millamant. He explains how far he had gone in this, even to spreading rumours that she might be pregnant by 'a young fellow', but also where he had stopped:

> The devil's in't, if an old woman is to be flattered further, unless a man should endeavour downright personally to debauch her; and that my virtue forbade me. (1.1)

It is difficult to know just what Mirabell's 'virtue' consists in, not least because his motives for courting Millamant are themselves equivocal: he is enacting a stratagem to avoid losing half Millamant's fortune if she marries without Lady Wishfort's approval. It is none the less significant that Mirabell chooses the term virtue to indicate what check there was in his conduct of his witty plot, a check that might not have operated in Fainall's case.

At this point in their conversation there is a small verbal ambivalence that reveals the cultural tensions Mirabell embodies. Fainall comments on his conduct:

> You are a gallant man, Mirabell; and though you may have cruelty enough, not to satisfy a lady's longing, you have too much generosity, not to be tender of her honour.

The ambivalent concept of 'gallantry' here articulates the tension between wit and virtue as Congreve inscribes in it both the Restoration sense of 'gallant' as rakish, and the chivalric sense of 'gallant' as courteous.

The state of Mirabell's feelings about Millamant register the unstable poise of the play, not so much because he is attracted by both her personality and her portion but because her personality itself, with all its whirling witticisms and indirectnesses, both allures and frustrates him. He is irritated by her affectations, but he thinks he can accommodate them, as she has assimilated them to the point where they have been transformed into 'nature' or are 'art' at a level high enough to be gratifying:

> I like her with all her faults; nay, like her for her faults. Her follies are
> so natural, or so artful, that they become her.   (1.3)

The speech from which this is taken is in itself a species of assimilation of nature and art, or wit and virtue: it is a speech in a dialogue between two wits, or rakes, and it is very witty, but at the same time it is a confession of the natural feelings of love.

It is, however, the habit of this play to discover all the terms with which it negotiates to be perplexed and uncertain. Even what might be thought of as so incontestable a value as 'nature', so often elevated to metaphysical levels in eighteenth-century discourse, as in the theorising poems of Pope, is not simple. Mirabell's inability to distinguish art and nature in Millamant's behaviour is, of course, one example. Another occurs when a comparison is made between the would-be urban sophisticate Witwoud and his coarse rustic brother. Fainall uses images from the world of unnatural growth to enforce it. Are the follies of the brothers in any way similar? asks Millamant. 'Not at all', responds Fainall,

> Witwoud grows by the knight, like a medlar grafted on a crab. One
> will melt in your mouth, and t'other set your teeth on edge; one is
> all pulp, and the other all core.
>
>   (1.5)

It may be characteristic of Fainall that he can exploit the unpleasantnesses of the natural world for his images of putrescence and bitterness, but it is also of a piece with this play's persistent instability that it can draw on nature-not-at-its-best to indicate the defects of a species as readily as it can use nature as an index of integrity.

Love certainly is not offered in *The Way of the World* as a simple counter to the reductive untenderness of wit, though the playwright might seem to be preparing for this in such passages as the fatuous Witwoud's denial that it is any criticism of Petulant to say that he is 'insincere':

> . . . what if he be? 'Tis no matter for that, his wit will excuse that: a wit should no more be sincere, than a woman constant; one argues a decay of parts, as t'other of beauty. (1.6)

It is true that Witwoud's is now an anachronistic construction of wit, and his crassness about human values and moral virtues is one index of that, but the play's conceptual schema offers nothing which will readily displace it. Love as it is evinced in the action certainly will not.

When women characters are first discovered they are talking about men and love, and while each is faking an indifference and cynicism she does not feel there is an inevitable sense that they are speaking from experience. Mrs Fainall, the discarded lover of Mirabell, speaks:

> . . . if we will be happy, we must find the means in ourselves, and among ourselves. Men are ever in extremes; either doting or averse. While they are lovers, if they have fire and sense, their jealousies are insupportable: and when they cease to love (we ought to think at least), they loathe; they look upon us with horror and distaste; they meet us like the ghosts of what we were, and as such, fly from us.
> (2.1)

If this is the story of love in the world of wit, it is not much of a resource. Shortly after this comes a real love scene, or better, a reality-of-love scene. It consists of a foolish jealous tiff between Fainall and his mistress Mrs Marwood, and a patched-up reconciliation. It carries extraordinary conviction as Fainall finds himself sarcastically reproaching Mrs Marwood for abusing her friendship with his wife by having an affair with him. This tangled quarrel itself epitomises the distorted condition of love in this world, but it is when Mrs Marwood really (and understandably) flares up at the accusation that the extension of its confusion of values is fully revealed:

> Do you reproach me? You, you upbraid me! Have I been false to her, through strict fidelity to you, and sacrificed my friendship to keep my love inviolate? And have you the baseness to charge me with the guilt, unmindful of the merit! To you it should be meritorious, that

I have been vicious: and do you reflect that guilt upon me, which should lie buried in your bosom?   (2.3)

Mrs Marwood here arrogates to her own adultery the language of virtue – 'strict fidelity', 'sacrifice', 'love inviolate', 'merit', 'meritorious'. The world of wit has devalued and distorted the very words with which the quality of existence is made intelligible. If there is to be a way out of this world it will have to be negotiated in new terms. This is precisely what Mirabell and Millamant attempt in the 'Proviso' scene (4.5) when they negotiate the 'terms' on which they might be able to live together as man and wife.

What needs to be made clear is that a simple conservative reversion to the old terms will not do. There are those who use the language of the past, most notably Lady Wishfort and Sir Wilfull Witwoud, but this fact displays its own limitations because both of them are, as it were, out of the game. The habits and what one can call the ideology of wit have become ingrained, and have qualities that need to be incorporated into any better culture and not simply rejected. Lady Wishfort cannot do this because she is too old and too exclusively physical in her desires, and Sir Wilfull cannot because he is too coarse.

This is not to say that either is without merit or value. It is refreshing when Sir Wilfull first arrives at Lady Wishfort's house and is aghast to find that the servants are all so new that they do not know who he is, or even properly recognise their mistress. When Sir Wilfull asks a footman how long he has been in the household and receives the reply, 'A week, Sir; longer than anybody in the house, except my lady's woman', the instability of the world of wit seems raised to the level of caricature and our sympathies lie with the provincial world of relative order and permanence from which Sir Wilfull comes. Similarly, Lady Wishfort can represent a world of truer human relations than most of her circle offers. For instance, when Witwoud is brought into contact with his rustic elder brother he pretends he does not recognise him, calls him a 'vile dog', and invites Petulant to 'smoke him' – bring him into ridicule (3.15). By contrast, when Lady Wishfort joins the group she immediately addresses Sir Wilfull with the words 'Nephew, you are welcome.' She repeats them, and says to him, 'Will you drink anything after your journey, nephew, before you eat? Dinner's almost ready.' She has her own reasons for treating him well, but at least she goes through the motions of the proper politeness of hospitality rather than the artificial politeness of wit.

The limitations of each code of manners are seen in the brief exchange when Petulant seeks to 'smoke' Sir Wilfull. Prompted by Witwoud, Petulant focuses on Sir Wilfull's muddy boots and then looking him all over pointedly says, 'It seems as if you had come a journey, Sir; hem, hem.' When Sir Wilfull starts to bridle at his insistence, Petulant explains, 'I presume upon the information of your boots', Sir Wilfull responds aggressively,

> Why, 'tis like you may, Sir: if you are not satisfied with the information of my boots, Sir, if you will step to the stable, you may enquire further of my horse, Sir.

Petulant's supposed wit generates only impoliteness and affectation; Sir Wilfull's directness offers in its place a coarse animalism. If the balance seems to fall on Sir Wilfull's side, it is worth remembering that what is seen on stage is a brutish, frequently inebriated country squire stamping around an elegant London drawing-room in muddy travelling boots.

What, however, enforces the inability of either Lady Wishfort or Sir Wilfull to offer terms that might displace or correct the linguistic and behavioural distortions of wit is the fact that each is totally unsuited to the person with whom they seek an alliance. The notion of Lady Wishfort as Mirabell's lover is grotesque, and there is no comfort in the thought that the light-hearted Millamant might become the bride of heavy Sir Wilfull. Neither Mirabell nor Millamant is perfect, but each deserves better.

The truth is that Lady Wishfort has not really got any language to live with. When she does see the possibility of a love-match for herself, with the supposed Sir Rowland, she struggles to assert that her sexual forwardness should not be construed as what it is. Devoid of modesty in demeanour, she is also barren in the language of appropriate modesty and so gets lost in the mazes of a barbarous jargon that is nobody's language:

> Sir Rowland, you must not attribute my yielding to any sinister appetite, or indigestion of widowhood; nor impute my complacency to any lethargy of continence – I hope you do   not think me prone to any iteration of nuptials.   (4.2)

'I do not,' says the disguised Waitwell, 'fair shrine of virtue'. Lady Wishfort's words do not form an alternative discourse to the discourses of wit and of virtue. They constitute a kind of anti-language, whose intended function is to disguise meaning and whose effect is to frustrate comprehension. The sardonic description of her as a 'shrine of virtue' by Waitwell underscores the blatancy of her artifices and their ineffectiveness.

If *The Way of the World* is to discover any redemption for the world of wit in a union between Mirabell and Millamant it cannot be articulated in any of the languages the play has to offer outside the Proviso scene. In that scene the pair of them have to discuss the terms of their marriage agreement without any mention of its supervising condition, that they love one another: the language of love has been so inverted, distorted, abused and misappropriated in the play that it cannot safely be used in a dialogue between lovers. Millamant and Mirabell none the less evolve between them a practical survival plan for their unspoken relationship.

Pat Gill reads this plan as 'a conservative counterpoint to the ever-changing way of the world'.[8] It is certainly an attempt to attain a kind of stability, but not really of the past. They are looking for a new way forward into the future; there are no satisfactory anterior models. Their whole dialogue is forward-looking, dominated by the future tense and by verbs which imply continuation or development, even when they are used ironically, as when Millamant says, 'if I continue to endure you a little longer, I may by degrees dwindle into a wife' (4.5). The fact that they, at Mirabell's insistence, talk about having children refers to a future which includes development. This of course distinguishes this relationship from Mirabell's earlier one with Lady Wishfort's daughter, whom he married off to Fainall when there was a possibility that she might be pregnant. Procreation with Millamant is to be welcomed; with the other it was to be feared.

As far as the terms of the negotiation are concerned, Millamant's first interest is to preserve 'My dear liberty', which is first of all a freedom of the mind: she links it with 'my darling contemplation'. Especially she thinks of lying in bed alone and drowsy in the mornings: 'my morning thoughts, agreeable wakings, indolent slumbers, all ye *douceurs*, ye *sommeils du matin*, adieu'. In this context she speaks of 'My faithful solitude'. It is significant that in the whole scene she only uses the language of love, 'dear . . . faithful . . . darling', to speak of her single condition. She knows herself, and can therefore use the language that has otherwise been degraded. Gill argues that in seeking to preserve this kind of liberty 'she asks for the private space women of her class generally obtain without question'.[9] What is striking, though, is how happy a space it is for Millamant. For the other women in the play solitude is desolation. What Millamant seeks is the liberty to be herself, which is why she will not 'be called names' such as 'wife, spouse, my dear, joy, jewel, love, sweetheart, and the rest of the nauseous cant'. Terms of endearment are repellent to Millamant as they are so often false, but also as they are limiting and reductive – precisely why she talks of 'dwindling' into a wife.

Mirabell does not contest this desire for the liberty of the mind and the self. If Millamant lies in bed as long as she wants, then he'll get up as early as he pleases. Gill properly points out that

> Less than a hundred years later, women's attempts to maintain invi-
> olate closets would preoccupy writers such as Samuel Richardson,
> Fanny Burney, and Ann Radcliffe, but the threat posed by the closet
> later in the next century – that of women's writings and private
> meditations – did not obtain as yet.   (119)

It does not obtain for Mirabell at any rate. The world of private meditation is not contested territory for Mirabell and Millamant because,
though it cannot be spoken, they trust one another. Later heroines will
be in different situations, embattled and besieged by men who do fear
what is going on in their heads. They will need the closet as the space
in which they can defy the encroachments of their oppressors and
say, like the Lady in *Comus*, 'Fool . . . thou canst not touch the freedom
of my mind' (Milton, *A Masque Presented at Ludlow Castle*, 1634,
ll. 661–2).

Millamant's further stipulations are for liberty to conduct her own
social life, to write and talk as she wishes, and so on. It is in part a joke
list, such as a husband used to the contrariness of wives might draw up
– 'Come to dinner when I please, dine in my dressing-room when I'm
out of humour, without giving any reason' – but essentially it is a rational request for a moderate degree of personal freedom. Again, Mirabell
does not challenge it, but he does start making conditions himself.
These seek to ensure that Millamant will not abuse the freedoms that
are properly hers. Again, it is a man's list, comically proscribing the
devices and stratagems women in the world of wit use to betray their
husbands. Millamant does not contest these conditions, but she does
not agree to them: it is not that she opposes them, but that she resents
the imputation that they might apply to her: 'O horrid provisoes! Filthy
strong waters! I toast fellows, odious men! I hate your odious provisos!'

Millamant, as well as wanting to preserve her liberty of mind and action, wants Mirabell to stay polite to her, to be in a sense a true wit. Mirabell wants to ascertain the conditions that will preserve her virtue. But one should not concentrate on the apparent substance of this scene, the provisos, and ignore its tone, because the true substance of the scene is what goes unspoken – that they love and wish to marry each other. The tone of the conversation is lively, amusing, teasing, provocative and flirtatious. It is a kind of duet in which we hear voices that are well matched; it is a good scene because they make a good pair. The comparison the play offers is with the querulous dissatisfactions of the scene between Fainall and Mrs Marwood (2.3), which is full of the language of love but miserable and desperate in tone. Throughout the play Millamant is charming and articulate. She is fluent in the language of wit, though impatient when it is squandered or abused, as when Witwoud pesters her with a string of foolish similies. Witwoud is witty by rote. Millamant by contrast can invent and improvise. Why was she late? She had letters, Mincing prompts her:

> O ay, letters – I had letters – I am pestered with letters – I hate letters – nobody knows how to write letters; and yet one has 'em, one does not know why. – They serve to pin up one's hair.

All one's letters? 'Only with those in verse, Mr Witwoud. I never pin up my hair with prose. I tried once . . .' (2.5). She finds her way into the wit, develops it, enjoys it, draws in others. This is one reason why we know she does not mean it (much) when she says 'I love to give pain'. She is human; she does enjoy her power as a beautiful and witty coquette; she seems almost a free spirit, much freer certainly than most others on the social carousel. She is not unlike Pope's Belinda, but with brains as well as bosom. She expresses herself as a wit, and she is also in love – and perhaps more nearly than Mirabell a true wit. If she were to enter into the explicit discourse of love with Mirabell she would not only be using a degraded and untrustworthy ideolect: she would be surrendering the style that is her own. She may be prepared to marry Mirabell but she will not exchange the language of her own wit for a factitious language of sentiment. She cannot bring herself to say more to him than '. . . well – I think – I'll endure you' and 'I suppose you have said something to please me' (4.6). Immediately she is alone with Mrs Fainall, however, she comes right out with it, and needs no prompting:

> Well, if Mirabell should not make a good husband, I am a lost thing;
> – for I find I love him violently.   (4.7)

The story of Millamant and Mirabell's relationship is not yet over, but it has gone as far as it can in the sphere of the emotions. They have shared the stage together and performed well; they have spoken a lot, but not to each other of what matters most. They retain their individuality and neither has compromised their liberty. Inarticulate about their virtuous love they have managed to attain the stage of 'proximity talks': they have spoken of their love, but in separate rooms. The play has now to keep its mechanisms running until Millamant and Mirabell are free to become man and wife. The mechanism is the plot. As the Prologue said of the author, 'Some plot we think he has.' Devising plots is something wits are good at, and one of the ways by which Mirabell is registered as a wit is his contriving and manipulating of stories: he pretends to court Lady Wishfort as a cover for courting Millamant; he makes up stories about her, implying that she has an active amorous life; he marries his manservant and hers, disguises Waitwell as the expected suitor Sir Rowland, and launches him into courting Lady Wishfort. The skill and elaboration of Mirabell's plotting marks him out as a wit superior to, for instance, Petulant, whose ingenuity (if Witwoud is to be believed) does not rise above disguising himself as a woman and pretending to call for himself at a chocolate house to suggest that he is a favourite with the ladies. There is one last piece to Mirabell's plotting: he has contrived to secure a Deed of Trust for Mrs Fainall's property that will prevent Mr Fainall getting his hands on it, and this also disarms the threat that Fainall represents to Lady Wishfort and her daughter.

What is particularly striking about the resolution of *The Way of the World* is the way it turns on documents, written tokens of transactions. Trust having proved unreliable in the world of wit, it is now inscribed as a document, a Deed of Trust. The last scenes of the play are marked and governed by a new discourse with a new vocabulary – penalty, settle, maintenance, endowed, will and testament, contracting, provided for, instrument, sufficient deeds, papers, sign, estate, management, 'pursuant to the purport and tenor of this . . . covenant', subsistence, compensation, conveyance, elder date. This is the language of law and commerce, displacing the language and the manners of the play's world with the terminology and instruments of bourgeois administration.

It is tempting to say that Congreve has contrived to break the link between wit and viciousness in two ways, firstly by offering a heroine who combines wit and virtue, and secondly by resolving his plot through bourgeois expertise in handling and transmitting property: this

would resolve those insecurities that were encoded in the metaphors of
the Prologue, insecurities about grants, seats and estates. The play
would thus smooth the transition from the instabilities of the
Restoration world into a world of, on the one hand, Addisonian possibility, where wit and virtue can consort happily together, and on the
other of reliable bourgeois transaction, where trust is inscribed in
Deeds and uncertainty displaced by Securities. The way of the world
is more perplexed than this, however. The continuance of the love
between Mirabell and Millamant is still a hypothesis. Millamant at the
end of the play is no more able to speak of love or make further concession to Mirabell's enthusiasm than she has done already; when
Mirabell declares his love he seems to be hedging slightly ('heaven
grant I love you not too well, that's all my fear'); his closing lines,
moralising against allowing mutual falsehood to stain the bridal bed,
do not sort particularly well with his own amatory history (though he
has not been an adulterer, only a fornicator), and in tone they are out
of keeping with not only his own utterances but with everything in the
play up till the moment when they are spoken; and his last two lines,
using as they do the new language of bourgeois transaction, '. . . each
deceiver to his cost may find, / That marriage frauds are oft paid in
kind', are not altogether reassuring as they indicate that this new world
will as readily afford metaphors for the abuse as for the ascertaining of
relationships. And as if to confirm this renewed instability, it must be
recorded that the resolution of the plot does not turn on the production of a single document but on a contest between two documents.
Mirabell is only just able to trump Fainall's document making his
wife's fortune over to himself, together with half Millamant's, because
Mirabell's has a prior date. At the last moment the play offers a battle
not of words but of wits, and the victory goes to the more artful plotter. The play may not be opening up a way out of the world as much
as securing a temporary respite while the rules are transcribed into new
terms.

The terms in which Millamant and Mirabell negotiate their marriage
are behavioural: they regulate how they will behave to each other and
how they will behave in society. Relations between men and women as
they are inscribed in eighteenth-century fiction are also governed by
terms, but the terms are now increasingly financial, and are negotiated
less between individuals than between families, estates and fortunes. As
the Harlowe family becomes increasingly infatuated with the notion of

marrying Clarissa to the rich but odious Mr Solmes Clarissa describes the atmosphere in the family: 'They drive on here at a furious rate; The man lives here, I think. He courts them, and is more and more a favourite. Such terms, such sentiments! That's the cry.'[10] Whether or not the arranged or dynastic marriage was increasingly precluding the affective or companionable marriage, novelists were increasingly inter-' ested in it and voices of protest of various kinds are raised against it. To take an example chronologically about halfway between *The Way of the World* and *Clarissa* (I also refer to this in Chapter 4), Moll Flanders overhears the sisters in the Colchester family talking about her, whom their brother has just described as 'the Handsomest young Woman' in the town:

> I wonder at you Brother, *says the Sister*; *Betty* [Moll] wants but one Thing, but she had as good want every Thing, for the Market is against our Sex just now; and if a young Woman have Beauty, Birth, Breeding, Wit, Sense, Manners, Modesty, and all these to an Extream; yet if she have not Money, she's no Body, she had as good want them all, for nothing but Money now recommends a Woman; the Men play the Game all into their own Hands.[11]

When Moll reflects on this later she acknowledges that 'Money alone made a woman agreeable' and she adds, 'That Men chose Mistresses indeed by the Gust of their Affection, and it was requisite for a Whore to be Handsome . . . but that for a Wife, no deformity would shock the Fancy, . . . the Money was always agreeable, whatever the Wife was' (67). Whether or not such a harsh materialism in fact governed the world (the rise of mobile and transferable wealth and the kinds of insecurity which it occasioned are discussed in chapter three), a novel like *Clarissa* needs to be construed against an awareness that it might. The first frame in which the Harlowe family see their attractive and virtuous daughter is that she is heiress of part of her grandfather's estate.

Although the Colchester sisters include 'Modesty', which Moll in her version of their list renders as 'Vertue' (67), among the qualities made irrelevant by the values of the marriage-market, virtue in various aspects is a preoccupation of eighteenth-century reflection and narrative. In one simple sense it mattered for women to be virtuous: women were indispensable to the process of heredity. Documents could channel and direct wealth, but only women could provide true heirs. The virtue of the wife was the essential condition of the line of heredity. Although married women could not hold property they could pass it on.[12] Virtue

translated into the social currencies of Reputation and Honour. If either
of these were lost a woman's value in the marriage-market immediately
depreciated. This is why Belinda wants her lock back: she does not
want the Baron displaying it to all his coffee-house cronies with the
implication that it is either a token or a trophy of conquest. (See also
Chapter 4.)

At the same time, and perhaps as the alternative face of the same
phenomenon, virtue gradually seems to have acquired a more metaphysical status than it had had before in English letters. It became not
just an attractive feature of a personality, but the defining one for some
writers, in a sense the depository of all the values imperilled by the
hectic material adventure of the world, a stable quality in a world in
flux. Thomson, admittedly not himself a figure of striking worldliness,
writes about it like this:

> . . . Ah! Whither now are fled,
> Those Dreams of Greatness? Those unsolid Hopes
> Of Happiness? Those Longings after Fame?
> Those restless Cares? Those busy bustling Days?
> Those gay-spent, festive Nights? Those veering Thoughts,
> Lost between Good and Ill, that shar'd thy Life?
> All now are vanish'd! VIRTUE sole survives,
> Immortal, never-failing Friend of Man,
> His Guide to Happiness on high.

('Winter' 1033–41)

This is fine for the reflective poet, more problematic for the novelist.
Narratives, novels especially, tend to deal in all the stuff that fills the first
part of this quotation, because it is out of it that stories flow and plots
are made. One could construe Thomson's lines as an eighteenth-century
yearning for stability and permanence confronting the turbulence,
volatility and degeneracy of a lingering Restoration culture: a phrase
like 'gay-spent, festive Nights' evokes the world of Rochester more than
that of Walpole.

It is on such an opposition that Richardson structures *Clarissa*, and
it is worth reflecting that Richardson himself was born into the
Restoration world – he was eleven when *The Way of the World* was first
produced – and, although his own lifestyle could hardly have been less
like Rochester's, the manners of the Restoration world marked his
imagination. His villain Lovelace is clearly modelled on the Restoration
rake/wit: Lovelace dramatises himself as a rake and in the persistent

theatricality of his manners and mental habits he seems to belong more to the high Restoration stage (both tragic and comic) than to the bourgeois novel.

Lovelace's persecution of Clarissa obviously affords Richardson his plot: vice persecutes virtue; virtue is defeated, but ultimately triumphs and in that triumph destroys vice. The aspect of this that is important here is that Lovelace is a wit, and so tends to confirm the unholy alliance between wit and vice that was the commonplace of Restoration culture and Augustan prejudice. There is no need to elaborate this at any length, but it is worth registering some of the ways in which he is identified with the culture of wit.

In the first place, he is a trifler. When Clarissa's sister Bella is piqued at Lovelace's ready acceptance of her refusal of his proposal, she decides he is 'A vain creature . . . A steady man, a man of virtues, a man of morals, was worth a thousand of such gay flutterers' (Letter 3: 1.9). The same phrase is used by Richardson in a letter to Aaron Hill (18 November 1748) explaining why in his narrative he had paired the lively Anna Howe with the stolid Mr Hickman. He intended, 'to shew Women that one man could not be everything; and that tho' the gay flutterer might be the Man for an Hour, the Solid-thinking, honest-hearted Man, was to be the Companion for Life.'[13]

Lovelace is also a wit in the intellectual sense: at university he had been known for the rapidity and extent of his acquisition of knowledge: 'for the swift and surprising progress he made in all parts of literature; for diligence in his studies in the hours of study, he had hardly his equal' (Letter 4: 1.14).

He is a wit too in that he is a facile writer. Anna, herself a witty writer, records that, 'He delights in writing . . . you and I, my dear, have observed on more occasions than one, that though he writes even a fine hand, he is one of the readiest and quickest writers' (Letter 12: 1.49). Apart from all the other more obvious ways in which he fits the lineaments of the rake/wit figure, one of the most important aspects of Lovelace's wit is that he is a lover of plots, ingenious in their conception, gleeful in their execution. He is a much more sophisticated plotter than the Harlowes: Anna talks of Clarissa's brother 'laying foolish plots' against her (Letter 43: 2.155). Lovelace triumphs in his superiority over them as a plotter – triumphs in outwitting them. Immediately after the abduction from Harlowe Place he write to Belford:

> I knew the whole stupid family were in a combination to do my
> business for me. I told thee that they were all working for me like so

many underground moles; and still more blind than the moles are said to be, unknowing that they did so. I myself, the director of their principal motions; which falling in with the malice of their little hearts they took to be all their own.   (Letter 97: 1.493–4)

At the stage in the narrative when Lovelace is about to make himself ill with the emetic ipecacuanha so that he can inspire and exploit Clarissa's pity for him, he tells Belford, 'Wilt thou believe me when I tell thee, that I have so many contrivances rising up and crowding upon me for preference, with regard to my Gloriana, that I hardly know which to choose? I could tell thee of no less than six princely ones . . .' (Letter 110: 2.425). And in the same letter he speaks of 'my gloried-in devices'.

'Some plot' was what the Prologue commended the author of *The Way of the World* for having; Mirabell was a great deviser of plots. Much of the wit of *Tom Jones* lies in Fielding's witty manipulation of an extra-ordinarily elaborate plot that can ultimately be seen to contain the apparently chaotic and circumstantial world of the novel. Battestin, arguing for 'the Providence of Wit' as manifested in Augustan art, and talking of Fielding's 'twin themes', calls Providence 'the theological argument of the book's design'; this in effect identifies plot and wit. The other theme is Prudence, which he calls 'the moral doctrine of its fable'. Thus the witty plot and the more sober moral fable, which Battestin says 'turns upon the meaning of "virtue" ',[14] run in parallel until Fielding brings them together in the artful contrivance of the ending.

Significantly, Richardson did not present himself as a plotter, and seems even to have thought that he was not one. In *Clarissa* the epistolary form, with its apparent exclusion of a supervisory author and the constant illusion of 'writing to the moment', militates against any consciousness of an overarching plot or any plotter between God and the characters. In his autobiographical letter to Johannes Stinstra (2 June 1753), speaking of his last novel *Sir Charles Grandison*, 'The History of my Good Man', Richardson presents himself as, whatever significance *Grandison* may have had in the large story of his fiction, characteristically undesigning:

I designed it as my last Work; & as the completion of my whole Plan – If a Man may be allowed to say *Plan*, who never was regular enough to write by one; & who when he ended one Letter, hardly knew what his next would be.[15]

Of course there is a tension here between awareness that there is plot and an illusion of surrender of the will, or of the wit, to the vagaries of circumstance and story. Even so, the effect of the ostensible exclusion of authorial plotting is that what plotting there is in the narrative appears to be the contrivance of the characters.

It is at this point that *Clarissa* takes on a degree of interest far beyond anything implicit in its simple vice versus virtue fable, because Clarissa has many of the characteristics of wit that distinguish her persecutor. In terms of the immediate point, she is herself a plotter. From very early on she reveals herself as capable of contrivance: forbidden to write to Anna Howe after her visit to her, at which she was known to have met Lovelace again, she does write to her, but sends the servant with two letters. One is the letter to Anna which we are reading; the other is a thank-you letter to Mrs Howe: 'The bearer, if suspected, is to produce *that* as the only one he carries.' And Clarissa notes that this subterfuge has been forced upon her: 'How do needless watchfulness and undue restraint produce artifice and contrivance' (Letter 9: 1.39). Throughout the novel Clarissa exercises circumspection and anticipation. She is forever devising stratagems to disarm, dissuade, circumvent, outwit or frustrate her persecutors. And her designing continues until and beyond the end of her life: she goes on seeking to produce effects.

For instance, the coffin which she orders and has brought into her room before her death, is replete with what Belford calls 'devices'. They have been executed according to Clarissa's 'draft by which all was ordered'. Belford offers Lovelace 'a sketch of the symbols'. These include 'a crowned serpent, with its tail in its mouth . . . the emblem of eternity', her name and age, an hourglass, an urn, texts from *Job* and the *Psalms*, an image of 'the head of a white lily snapped short off, and just falling from the stalk'. After his description of the coffin Belford records that Clarissa,

> excused herself to the women, on the score of her youth, and being used to draw for her needleworks, for having shown more fancy than would perhaps be thought suitable on so solemn an occasion.
>
> (Letter 90: 4.257)

Clarissa is not of course simply continuing a childish habit of elaborate decoration. Or if she is, it is a habit that has marked and defined her mature life. She is contriving that the text of her life will be read after her death as it has been in the period leading up to it. It is the ultimate *esprit d'escalier*, a construction of herself that Lovelace will never be able to trump in the battle of wits which has been the story of *Clarissa*.

If Clarissa is a plotter, she also has many of the other characteristics that were associated with the world of wit. This is Richardson's translation into the field of the intellect of the aspect of Clarissa that Lovelace finds so perplexing and frustrating – that she is beautiful, sexually alluring, in command of all the social skills that make women attractive in society, accomplished, but still virtuous. But *Clarissa* is not just a narrative about physical conquest; it is a novel of mental conquest. One wit is pitted against another, and whether or not Richardson formulated it to himself in such terms, Clarissa is a figure in whom an attempt is made to reconcile wit and virtue.

It is a very demanding project, and the measure of it is taken by comparing Clarissa with her confidante Anna. Anna Howe is plainly attractive, and to a reader often refreshing, by virtue of her wit. She is excitingly free of the piousness that so often seems to constrain Clarissa's spirit, and this emerges again and again in the freedom of her utterance, even just in the habits of expression. For instance, when she describes meeting Solmes socially she writes, 'I took great notice of him, as I do of all the noble lords of creation in their peculiarities' (Letter 27: 1.26). There is a spirited irreverence about this: Anna is evidently no respecter of persons, but this is also her limitation. She lacks discrimination and it is on precisely this point that Clarissa takes her up. Her wit is too promiscuous. After a letter in which Anna has become very sharp, about the Harlowes and even about her own mother, Clarissa rebukes her: 'Nor, my dear, does your *own* mother always escape the keen edge of your vivacity.' And she says that at times Anna's wit carries her beyond true judgement: 'I have known you . . . sit down resolved to write all that wit, rather than strict justice, could suggest upon the given occasion' (Letter 28: 1.133).

Wit exercised for its own sake and irrespective of context is precisely the fault of the vexatious Witwoud in *The Way of the World*. Anna's wit is a habitual mode. She is much closer than Clarissa to what Gill characterises the Restoration comedies' representation of women as being: 'wanton women who make wanton use of words'.[16] Richardson in his letters is studious to make sure that Anna is read in the right way. He suggests to Sarah Chapone (2 March 1752) that she thinks too highly of Anna's character: 'Surely it has great Blemishes, as well as Beauties.' He deplores Anna's lack of 'Generosity' to Hickman and summarises her as 'a blustering, bullying Girl; soon terrified.' But Richardson is at the same time urgent that Anna's faults do not impugn her morals: 'Yet Lovelace is vile to say . . . he could have had her in a fortnight.' There is, none the less, a difference between Anna and Clarissa: 'Clarissa is a

Heroine' and manifests '*that* Magnanimity, which will ever be the distinction of a true Spirit'.[17] Clarissa is also a wit, but unlike Anna's her wit is never wanton: it is always excited by context and circumstance.

Clarissa is, of course, like Lovelace a prodigious writer of letters. Lovelace's fertility in letter-writing is, however, even for Anna a cause of some suspicion. It is an equivocal facility:

> supposing it to be true that all his vacant nightly hours are employed in writing, what can be his subjects? . . . decent as he is in his conversation with us, his writings are not probably such as would redound either to his honour, or to the benefit of others, were they to be read.
> (Letter 12: 1.50)

Anna says that he is known to be very 'secret and careful' about his writings, and this makes them suspect. She says of herself and Clarissa, 'we can scribble upon twenty innocent subjects, and take delight in them because they *are* innocent . . . But that such a gay, lively young fellow as this, who rides, hunts, travels, frequents the public entertainments, and has *means* to pursue his pleasures' should spend so much time writing, 'that is the strange thing' (Letter 12: 1.50). Richardson's Mr B. and Lovelace have a corresponding suspicion about the writings of Pamela and Clarissa. They are fully alert to Gill's 'threat posed by the closet . . . that of women's writings and private meditations', and both extend their curiosity and anxiety to invasion, appropriation and intervention in the women's journals and correspondence.

Pamela and more especially Clarissa are in the position of the female narrators of the heroic epistle, which records the voices of abandoned, desolate and hopeless women. It reached its epitome in the eighteenth century, in the story of Yarico and Inkle (see Chapter 4) in the decade before *Clarissa*. The authors are male, but they have no voice in the epistles. Gillian Beer writes, 'Here . . . the women control pen, ink, and utterance.'[18] The men in Richardson try to wrest textual control from the women, and unable to succeed by wit they resort to subterfuge and violence.

The fact of Clarissa's writing as much and as readily as she does is a species of wit because of the form she is mostly writing in: she is often meditative, reflective, grave, solemn and even pompous, but it is always within the context of the familiar letter, and such seriousness is rather a change within the form than the primary mode. Clarissa's letters constitute part of a lively interpersonal exchange, not solitary meditation. The first is witty; the second need not be. But it is not the form alone that marks out Clarissa's letter-writing as that of a wit: it is how she writes and what she writes about. A few examples will have to serve, but they are available throughout, though with a frequency that varies with the pressure and nature of Clarissa's experience.

In the first place she has an instinctive vitality and spirit in her natural utterance that is both engaging and amusing. In her first letter she explains how her sister had found a reason for Lovelace's failing to come up with a marriage proposal sooner:

> It was bashfulness, truly in him. Bashfulness in Mr. Lovelace, my dear! Indeed, gay and lively as he is, he has not the *look* of an impudent man. But I fancy it is many, many years ago since he was bashful.   (Letter 2: 1.6)

In the same letter she also demonstrates what sounds like an aphoristic worldliness, when she comments on Bella's strategy of trying coldness to see if that will not bring Lovelace up to scratch. Bella cannot have 'considered the matter well . . . if love has not taken root deep enough to cause it to shoot out into declaration, there is little room to expect that the blighting winds of anger or resentment will bring it forward'. (It is notable that this image is well-founded, in experience of the natural world.)

When Lovelace is finally left with no alternative but to propose to Bella, and she gives him the initial refusal decorum demanded, Clarissa represents it in crisp oxymoron: it was 'A good encouraging denial' full of 'consenting negatives'.

At times Clarissa shapes judicious observations into more sustained but no less well-directed utterance. Here the context is what her mother has had to endure from her father's ill-temper:

> Our sex perhaps must expect to bear a little – *uncourtliness* shall I call it? – from the *husband* whom as a *lover* they let know the preference their hearts gave him to all other men. – Say what they will of generosity being a *manly* virtue; but upon my word, my dear, I have ever yet observed that it is not to be met with in that sex one time in ten that it is to be found in ours.   (Letter 5: 1.23)

This is, of course, a little bit stately and tending towards the Clarissa-voice that can be exasperatingly sententious and self-righteous. (It is not illicit to react to Clarissa at times like this: the entire moral strategy of the book rests not on a reader identifying with her but being persuaded by her, and this is bound sometimes to be by an effort, and sometimes reluctant. For all sorts of motives Clarissa at need can be *difficile*.) But her voice can be much broader and more comic. She talks of Bella's appearance as she joins in the family's condemnation of herself for having encountered Lovelace at Mrs Howe's house: 'The poor Bella has, you know, a plump high-fed face, if I may be allowed the expression.' The wit in this is revealed if the sentence is read without the opening definite article, which creates distance and turns Bella into a comic object. That Clarissa's animus is generated by her predicament (and not in any large degree by sisterly spite) is confirmed, and made sympathetic, when Clarissa adds to Anna, 'You, I know, will forgive me for this liberty of speech sooner than I can forgive myself; yet how can one be such a reptile as not to turn when trampled upon!' (Letter 7: 1.30) There is an attractive energy here and a demonstration of spirit that makes Lovelace's persecution of Clarissa all the more contemptible. It is an energy that is implicit in the very emphases of Clarissa's utterance. That her habitual discourse is strongly stressed is made apparent in the frequency of italics in Richardson's text, as when he italicises the key word in the sentence in which Clarissa describes how her family were proposing to get her married to Solmes: 'They ask not for my approbation, intending as it should seem, to *suppose* me into their will' (Letter 8: 1.32). This emphatic force of Clarissa's habitual utterance, which marks her out as one at ease in the dialogic human vitality of language, and able to exploit it, is even more apparent in the first paragraph of this letter. This has been quoted already: Richardson does not use italic emphases, but here it is with the stressed words italicised:

> They drive on here at a *furious* rate; The man *lives* here, I think. He courts *them*, and is *more* and *more* a favourite. Such *terms*, such *sentiments*! That's the cry.

That some of these italics could be placed elsewhere only confirms how energetic and highly charged Clarissa's writing is, and how it has the dynamics of witty interpersonal speech. Again, this force is not just a stylistic idiosyncrasy in Clarissa: it is precipitated by the circumstances she is pressed into, but it records a highly vital responsiveness.

Clarissa can become sharp to the point of satire. When in the period when the family is still trying to persuade her to accept Solmes her mother points out that there may be flaws in the grandfather's will which would prevent Clarissa from inheriting, Clarissa retorts, 'Permit me, good madam, to say that, if it were *unjustly* bequeathed me, I ought not to wish to have it. But I hope Mr. Solmes will be apprised of these flaws' (Letter 20: 1.96). 'That is very pertly said, Clarissa', her mother responds. Pertly, yes – and pertinently too. At an earlier point where Clarissa has responded sharply to her mother she has drawn on herself the rebuke 'This quickness on me . . . is not to be borne' (Letter 17: 1.78).

In the Restoration period Wycherley takes issue with women who bridle at apparently salacious material in his comedy:

> those who act as they look ought not to be scandalised at the reprehension of others' faults, lest they tax themselves with 'em and by too delicate and quick an apprehension not only make that obscene which I meant innocent but that satire on all which was intended only on those who deserved it.[19]

This identifies an unvirtuous mind in women who display too delicate and quick an apprehension: the witty woman is not virtuous. It is Pat Gill's argument that this attitude is characteristic not only of characters within Restoration comedy, like Petulant in *The Way of the World*, who says something very similar of women who blush at his 'senseless ribaldry' (1.9), but of its authors as well.[20]

A delicate and quick apprehension exactly characterises Clarissa's wit, with delicate here used in its proper sense. She embodies an attempt to render a personality which is both witty and virtuous and so to make available for the public consciousness an unexpected and unusual human type. It is not, I think, primarily a gendered endeavour, except in so far as the discovery of wit in a woman was thought to be a surer index of unstable morality than in a man; but the wits in *Clarissa* are chiefly men, and they are vicious. When (like Belford in the book's last volumes) they cease to be vicious, they cease to be witty. It is the women who provide the possible combination of wit and virtue. Anna Howe is almost an example but she has, in Richardson's conception of her, 'great Blemishes' and they are associated with the promiscuity of her wit. Clarissa is the successful example. She unites the sophistication of Restoration intelligence with the security of eighteenth-century virtue.

Something of a key to what Richardson attempted in his conception of Clarissa is apparent in a letter to Stinstra of 20 March 1754. Richardson commends English women:

I think, Sir, we in England may glory in numbers of women of genius. I in particular may – I could introduce you, Sir, to such a circle of my own acquaintance! – No man has been honoured by the fine spirits of the sex as I have been. I verily think, that the women of the politest regions are not to vie with ours. And the taste and numbers are every day increasing . . . [21]

This is a curious letter as it is cast very much in the manner one voluptuary might write to another praising the women of a particular nation, complete with an offer of introduction and the testimony of personal experience, but its crucial unspoken term is that it is not at all about sexuality. When Richardson speaks of these Englishwomen (and he did know many through correspondence and personal acquaintance) as 'fine spirits' he means it, and nothing more. Clarissa is a fine spirit, but she is also something more. Richardson's imagination in the fiction takes him beyond the modest enthusiasm of his letter to Stinstra. Clarissa is a fine spirit, but she is also attractive; and she is aware of her attractiveness; and she is attracted to a man of absolutely the wrong sort, an immoral and callous sexual predator. When she is worried that she has discovered to Lovelace (and to herself) too much of her feelings after he had deliberately made himself ill, she wrestles pitifully with the state of her heart. She writes to Anna, ' 'Tis true I have owned more than once, that I could have liked Mr. Lovelace above all men.' And she remembers what Anna wrote: 'You used to say, and once you wrote, that men of his cast are the men that our sex do not *naturally* dislike.' Clarissa's response was that, 'such were not the men . . . we *ought* to like.' 'For,' as she says with one of the most striking examples of litotes in English literature, 'Mr. Lovelace is not wise in all his ways.' And in a kind of agony she asks Anna,

> But, O my dearest friend, am I not guilty of a punishable fault, were I to love this man of errors? And has not my own heart deceived me, when I thought I did not? And what must be that love that has not some degree of purity in its object?
>
> (Letter 113: 2.438–9)

This is by no means the last word on Clarissa's feelings about Lovelace, but it does confirm that Clarissa's virtue is something maintained not just in the face of extreme external difficulties but of deceptions in the heart too. Clarissa's is not the fugitive and cloistered virtue that Milton says he cannot praise, but a virtue maintained in the full flow of worldly experience. In the elaborate contrivances of his fiction it is possible for

Fielding to keep a heroine virtuous simply by saying that she is so: Fanny, Sophia, Amelia (though she is a bit of a special case, conceived as she was in the wake of Fielding's tremendous admiration for *Clarissa*) are not put to the same tests as Clarissa. If Clarissa is virtuous her virtue has to be proven, in both senses – demonstrated, and tried.

Clarissa's virtue may be convincing, but it is also, as the letter to Stinstra goes on to reveal, exceptional. The good taste, and the numbers, of 'fine spirits' are increasing, even though, Richardson adds,

> in an age of such general dissipation. O that we had been able to keep our women of condition to ourselves; that we had not given way to their crossing the narrow seas into a neighbouring kingdom! Since we have very few instances of ladies returning thence improved, I may say, uncorrupted, by the levities of the nation I have in my eye. Don't you think, Sir, that women are generally more susceptible of levity than men, If they are, they should not be allowed to go abroad, and to places of entertainment so often as they do.

Clarissa was not susceptible, or if she was, she did not become corrupted by the world of levity Lovelace epitomises. But she is so exceptional that even her author can hardly trust her example: he would have women locked up! The negotiation between wit and virtue is extremely fraught, and Clarissa's victory is highly provisional.

Is she ultimately victorious? In conception she is: she does embody that desirable reconciliation of wit and virtue, and the embodiment is convincing. But in her story she is, as far as the world goes, defeated. She is violated, and though unbroken in spirit she is devastated and she dies. She takes her virtue to the grave, but of course 'The grave's a fine and private place, / But none, I think, do there embrace.' Hers is not unlike the condition of the pairs of lovers Romeo and Juliet, and Antony and Cleopatra. They have a conviction that their love will survive death – 'Where souls do couch in flowers, we'll hand in hand, / And with our sprightly port make the ghosts gaze' (*Antony and Cleopatra*, 4.14.51–2) – but in the world of real transactions they are utterly and undeniably defeated. Or, to take an example from nearer Clarissa's own time, she might share the formulation of Gray's bard, who escapes ultimate persecution by committing suicide, saying,

> To triumph, and to die, are mine.   ('The Bard', 142)

The tragedy of *Clarissa* can be seen as a cultural tragedy. It was the definitive endeavour of a culture to bring its heritage and the real world in which it had to do its business into alignment. Addison had felt that the reconciliation of wit and virtue should be possible. But that was a theoretical position. Richardson tried to put it into practice, testing it at the most profound level of his human imagination, but ultimately he could not convince himself and find a story his heroine could survive in. There was no resort for Clarissa, the most comprehensively accomplished heroine in the literature of his England with its women 'the politest regions are not to vie with', but her own articulate coffin.

3
Money and Government: *Roxana* and *The Beggar's Opera*

In his second *Moral Essay* on the subject of 'the Use of Riches' Pope describes how the unnatural and uncomfortable ostentatious grandeur of Timon's villa will in the course of time be repossessed by nature:

> Another age shall see the golden Ear
> Imbrown the Slope, and nod on the Parterre,
> Deep Harvests bury all his pride has plann'd,
> And laughing Ceres re-assume the land.[1]

The gold which Timon so lavishly squandered will be displaced by a more productive gold in the ears of corn. The villa is not going to revert to wilderness; it is going to be transmuted into a productive estate working in harmony with opulent nature. The process will be a kind of laundering of bad money.

Pope's vision is one way of coming to terms with the most spectacular and disruptive of all features of life in the first half of the eighteenth century, the translation of a society seen as traditional and stable, founded in the security of land, to a society determined by the possession and manipulation of money. Britain now seemed at the mercy of what Raymond Williams calls 'the new arbitrariness of money'.[2] Pope's response was alluring, and the polish and elegance of his verse is, as Cedric Watts says of its operation in a similar context, 'ideologically seductive'.[3] It was a way of retrieving and imaginatively reconstructing a damaged society.

The attractions of this vision remained seductive well into the era of sentimentalism, receiving indeed a new charge from the valorising of feeling. In 1784 the agricultural theorist and writer Arthur Young

describes the approach to Thomas Coke's Holkham Hall by way of the
orderly cottages and farms of the estate:

> This is the diffusion of happiness; an overflow of wealth that gilds
> the whole country, and tells the traveller, in a language too expressive
> to be misunderstood, *we approach the residence of a man, who feels for
> others as well as for himself* . . .[4]

Young's imagery – 'gilds the whole country' – performs the same
alchemy as Pope's 'golden Ear', as it were turning base metal into a
truer gold. Holkham Hall is in fact an instructive concretisation of the
extent and signification of wealth in the eighteenth century.

Holkham was built in the middle 1740s, the decade that saw the
composition of both the National Anthem and 'Rule Britannia!' –
hymns to the national self-confidence which was, as Sambrook says, the
'reflection of a real economic strength which was (largely) attributable
to what has been called the "financial revolution".'[5] The house is
substantial but not colossal, and its austere palladian exterior, largely
devoid of ornamentation, can be construed as a cultural and political
commentary on the overwhelming baroque extravagance of the most
prestigious and notorious building of the eighteenth century, Blenheim
Palace, built at prodigious cost by a grateful nation for the great Whig
general the Duke of Marlborough over twenty years from 1705.
Holkham's exterior is thus a construction of virtuous wealth. The
entrance to the house is made by way of a relatively plain ante-room,
but the effect of passing from this into the main hall is astounding.
There is an explosion of colour and expense. Huge columns in pink
marble reach from floor to ceiling; the walls are lined in the same material; a wonderful and elaborate staircase surges up to an ornamental
gallery richly filled with statuary and bas-relief brought from Greece
and Italy. This is an introduction into a world of extraordinary
opulence, of a seemingly limitless wealth and of a cultural appropriation
that reaches across a continent and extends through its entire history.
The architecture, the columns and the statuary relate Holkham to the
cultural supremacy of the Renaissance and classical worlds. The building thus exploits the riches which went into its construction by contex-
tualising itself in a world remote from the chaos of social mobility and
the money markets. It also demonstrates just what eighteenth-century
writers were talking about when they discussed 'riches': the contrasts
were enormous, not just between rich and poor but even between the
rich and the middle-class affluence that enabled Pope to create his coun-

try estate in miniature on five acres of land at Twickenham. It is also worth remembering that when Young visited Holkham the surrounding countryside, like the countryside everywhere in Britain, would have been far more built over with small dwellings and agricultural buildings than it is now. The contrast between estate dwellings and the Hall would have been far more conspicuous, and so Young's ability to read the scene as 'the diffusion of happiness; an overflow of wealth that gilds the whole country' is the more remarkable.

What Pope and Young were seeking to accommodate in their rural idealisations can be approached by way of an early print of William Hogarth, *An Emblematical Print on the South Sea Scheme* (1721). The South Sea Bubble, as it was called, was the epitomising and culminating manifestation of a series of speculative adventures running through a number of years in the second decade of the century and reaching a climax and exploding in 1720. In addition to buying in to a fantastical scheme for exploiting the imagined riches of the South Seas, speculators were invited to invest in a multitude of projects like importing jackasses from Spain to improve English mules, developing mulberry groves to create English silk, and the devising of a perpetual motion machine. All except the poorest sections of society were drawn into the speculative craze, whose fervour can be measured by the fact that South Sea Company stock rose from £128 per share in January 1720, to £550 in May, to £1,000 in July before the collapse.[6] Hogarth's print represents an ugly, crowded and chaotic vision of a London square. It is dominated by a large merry-go-round operated by various projectors under the banner 'Who'l Ride' and patronised by dupes ranging from a Scottish aristocrat to a boot-black. Faint and distant in the background is St Paul's Cathedral; in the foreground three divines, Catholic, Anglican and dissenting, are gambling on the pavement. In the centre a mass of greedy speculators are reaching up to catch lumps of the body of Fortune, who is being cut up and thrown to them by the Devil outside the Guildhall; the base of the Monument to the fire of London, topped with foxes, now bears the inscription 'Erected to the Memory of the Destruction of this City by the South Sea in 1720'; in the foreground in the shadow of the Monument the gaunt figure of Trade lies sprawled and neglected; the figure of Honesty is being broken on a wheel, and against the plinth of the Monument Honour is being scourged. The print is a representation of an entire community degraded and corrupted by greed: on a balcony women are queuing under a sign reading 'Raffleing for Husbands with Lottery Fortunes in here'. Like all Hogarth's prints, this is best seen in its original state:[7] in printed book reproduction the image loses some of the vivid contrast between dark etched lines and white paper that gives such drama and moral urgency to the scene, and so stresses the intensity of its contemporary significance.

Hogarth's print is not a literal representation of London, but a way of seeing it. It belongs to a mode of representing places that is called chorographic rather than geographic. Geography is modern, scientific, governed by the representational discipline of Mercator's projection. Chorography seeks to represent not where places are, but what they are like. What London was like in the 1720s mattered as in the quarter-century following the grant of a charter to the Bank of England in 1695 it had become the focus of national economic, social and administrative life in a way that it had never been before. In his study of contesting chorographic and geographic representations of the world in English writing in the late seventeenth and early eighteenth centuries, Douglas Chambers makes the point that is implicit in the Hogarth print, but which now needs to be reinscribed into it, that 'What London was not . . . was what Wren and John Evelyn hoped it might become after the Fire: a *tabula rasa* upon which an orderly baroque geometrical plan could be inscribed.'[8] David Nokes talks of how in eighteenth-century satire 'familiar landmarks of London topography, Drury Lane and Change Alley, Smithfield and Covent Garden, Newgate and Bedlam, take on the significance of mythological realms.'[9] London had become disconcertingly the metonym of the culture; if London were not the city designed after the fire then it was also apparent that, disturbed and transformed by the manifold madnesses of money, Britain was not running with the metronomic steadiness and the ever self-correcting equipoise, with its careful regulation of the relationships between different parts of the constitution, which had been intended in 1689.

This chapter will deal principally with two works which represent eighteenth-century culture or figures from it negotiating their lives in the flux of money transactions and exchanges, Defoe's *Roxana* and Gay's *The Beggar's Opera*, and also with two or three works that reflect in different ways on that negotiation. Before concentrating on these, however, one or two points should be made. The first is that there is a distinction between money and trade, as was apparent in the gaunt figure of trade lying neglected amid the monetary frenzy of Hogarth's South Sea print.

In general trade was one of the great cultural positives of the period. In Steele and Addison's *Spectator* the trading or merchant interest is represented by Sir Andrew Freeport and the landed interest by Sir Roger de Coverley. The friendship between the two men (despite their

disagreements) is an imaginative idealisation of reconciliation between
the old world and the new, but while Sir Roger is softened into an
engagingly old-fashioned eccentric, Sir Andrew is in tune with the tides
of the modern world. His attitudes are clearly those which are endorsed
in an exchange in *Spectator* 174 (19 September 1711) when Sir Roger
recommends a gentleman's charity to the poor above the selfish materialism of a merchant. This is an expression of the old hierarchical
conception of society, which might be instanced in Andrew Marvell's
favourable account of Fairfax's Appleton House as featuring a 'noble
frontispiece of poor'. Sir Andrew challenges and repudiates Sir Roger's
attitude, asking 'whether so many Artificers at work ten Days together
by my Appointment, or so many Peasants made merry on Sir ROGER's
Charge, are the Men more obliged' and concluding 'Sir ROGER gives to
his Men, but I place mine above the Necessity or Obligation of my
Bounty'.[10] Two years later the lines which bring to an end Pope's
Windsor-Forest (1713), his panegyric poem published to celebrate the
end of Britain's long war with Louis XIV's France, are essentially a
rhapsody on a world united and made prosperous by trade. Sambrook,
describing Burke's enthusiasm for the enterprise of the New England
whale fishery in 1775, notes how 'Burke, like Pope, Thomson, Dyer,
and many other poets of the century, is imaginatively excited by trade
and industry.'[11] For instance, this excitement enables John Dyer
(1669–1785), who is commonly associated with his landscape poem
Grongar Hill, to describe the cloth workers in 'busy Leeds', where 'all is
joy', like this:

> As when a sunny day invites abroad
> The sedulous ants, they issue from their cells
> In bands unnumber'd, eager for their work;
> O'er high, o'er low, they lift, they draw, they haste
> With warm affecxtion to each other's aid.[12]

The thought of trade and its percolation through all strata of the
nation's life set Defoe's prose rolling in the rhythms of the dissenting
religion in which he had been brought up:

> the Blood of Trade is mix'd and blended with the Blood of Gallantry,
> so that Trade is the Life of the Nation, the Soul of its Felicity, the
> Spring of its Wealth, the Support of its Greatness, and the Staff on
> which both King and People lean.[13]

This way of viewing trade promotes a construction of the nation as a unified and, as it were, an organic entity in which trade is a beneficent facilitator of harmony and affluence. But there were also less comforting perceptions, and it was to some extent against the grain of these, all focusing on the corrupting effect of credit and the disruptive effects of the new mobility of money, that such a vision had to be sustained. All major authors of the period sensed and addressed the issues that arose from the accelerating transformation of the life of the nation. Colin Nicholson argues that by as early as 1697, when Britain had at last managed to secure peace, 'England had become a trading nation and at a very rapid pace an entity known as Trade entered the political vocabulary to an extent that all writers engaged with its significance.'[14] He also explains how writers sought to evolve a discourse that would accommodate trade without abandoning more traditional values:

> Writers steeped in the cognitive ideals of civic humanism found it increasingly difficult to grant self-interested individuals enmeshed in credit-driven commercial enterprise the autonomy and breadth of mind necessary for civic virtue. Simultaneously it became possible for the argument to be put (by Addison among others) that market forms of sociability, sympathy and honesty might be developed to redefine citizenship, and this was the project of *The Spectator*. The virtues of sociability in this view are substituted for civic virtues in an attempt to provide ideological coherence for a developing political economy.[15]

'The virtues of sociability', as Nicholson calls them, came to be subsumed in a concept of 'politeness'. The historian Paul Langford explains how the construction of politeness as a social value evolved as a substitute for the honour codes of an obsolescent traditional society, and became accessible to a much wider section of the population:

> Politeness conveyed upper-class gentility, enlightenment and sociability to a much wider élite whose only qualification was money, but who were glad to spend it on acquiring the status of gentleman.[16]

The trouble was, as Hogarth's print and a multitude of other witnesses make clear, the harmonising benefits of Trade depended on the new technologies of money manipulation, of capital transactions and especially of credit, and this was not necessarily very polite at all, neither socially nor in its habits and tendencies. 'Blest paper-credit!' exclaims

Pope ironically, 'That lends Corruption lighter wings to fly!'[17] Credit was in a sense fantasy money, money that did not exist though everyone pretended it did, and its emergence and dominance seemed to excite and license the disruptively fantastical in human nature. Instead of composing a coherent and orderly system society risked becoming an aggregation of undisciplined phenomena. In 1711 Swift writes in the *Examiner*,

> through the contrivance and cunning of stock-jobbers there hath been brought in such a complication of knavery and cozenage, such a mystery of iniquity, and such an unintelligible jargon of terms, as were never known in any other age or country of the world.[18]

('Mystery' in this quotation means 'trade' or line of business, thus bringing 'iniquity' into the daily working life of the nation.) The alarm of traditionalists like Swift and their fear of the implications of the culture of credit for human behaviour and human relationships is summarised by Nicholson:

> The emergence of classes whose property consisted not of lands or goods, but of paper promises to repay in an undefined future, was seen as entailing the emergence of new types of personality, unprecedentedly dangerous and unstable.[19]

And he says that the texts produced by 'opposition' writers such as Swift, Gay and Pope 'repeatedly express a struggle for value and meaning in what was for them an era of devastating change'.[20] (One should not lose sight of the fact, though, in the face of Nicholson's rather apocalyptic reading, that what the Tory satirists may have deplored was also grist to their mills and fed the ebullient energy of Swift, the sophisticated wit of Pope and the engaging good-nature of Gay: theirs is not just writing in opposition, but writing in the oppositional mode.)

The new culture of cash and credit was alarming not just as it was socially disordering, but as it seemed linked with an increasing corruption in public life. A lexicon of terms such as bribe, perquisite and emolument came to a new prominence in the discourse of politics. And it was not just individuals who were open to corruption. Money from the city (and increasingly from British colonial territories) was buying its way into administration and government; parliament, formerly the preserve of land, found its doors opening to money; power and influence had become tradeable commodities. The long stability of

Walpole's Whig administrations through the 1720s and 1730s was achieved not by anything remotely resembling democracy but by the manipulation of influence. Cedric Watts speaks of Walpole as one 'to whom bribery and corruption were the natural modes of civilised government'.[21] What is more, the interpenetration of money and government was inevitable and permanent: since the establishment of the Bank of England to fund William III's wars the nation itself had been living on credit. The National Debt grew steadily with the cost and complexity of government. All administrations needed the resources and expertise of the city. City men traded in government stock and government was always devising schemes to raise money from the city. Corruption, or the opportunities for it, was not a matter of money alone. The other great commodity was government patronage – the distribution of official and semiofficial posts, places, appointments, sinecures. This had always existed, but with the increasing complexity of government and the increasing range of governmental activities at home and abroad, it mushroomed, as government had, as it were, more and more things to sell.

Seen in full Pope's lines on paper-credit in the 'Epistle to Bathurst' indicate how far the moral health of the nation could be represented as compromised by credit and the corruption of the national polity that went with it. It is significant that paper-credit places the modern nation at a remove from a golden age, but ironically a golden age not of the remote past but of more recent times, when the carelessly dropped golden guinea would reveal corruption at work:

> Once, we confess, beneath the Patriot's cloak,
> From the crack'd bag the dropping Guinea spoke,
> And gingling down the back-stairs, told the crew,
> 'Old Cato is as great a Rogue as you.'
> Blest paper-credit! Last and best supply!
> That lends Corruption lighter wings to fly!
> Gold imp'd by thee, can compass hardest things,
> Can pocket States, can fetch or carry Kings;
> A single leaf shall waft an Army o'er,
> Or ship off Senates to a distant Shore;
> A leaf, like Sibyl's, scatter to and fro
> Our fates and fortunes, as the winds shall blow:
> Pregnant with thousands flits the Scrap unseen,
> And silent sells a King, or buys a Queen.
>
> ('Epistle to Bathurst', ll. 65–78)

The lines transcend their primary function as a satirical indictment of a compromised polity. They are an imaginative apprehension of credit as a new, transforming and almost magical power. They are not just about the implications of a credit economy: they are a poetic enactment of credit itself, and constitute a poetry enabled by the topic it addresses. The lighter wings of paper-credit are also the viewless wings of poesy that translate the poet from the mundane world to another beyond it. The financial revolution did not transform only the economy: it entered and transformed the imagination.

The Fortunes and Misfortunes of the Famous Moll Flanders; *The Fortunate Mistress or, a History of the Life and Vast Variety of Fortunes of . . . the Lady Roxana*: the recurrence of the root 'fortune' in these extended titles of Defoe's novels does not refer just to the varying fates of his heroines; it points to the fluctuations in their finances too. The lives of Defoe's principal characters are not traced simply through a sequence of adventures: they are often literally accounts. Narrative drive is suspended while a computation is made of the character's worth in goods or specie (or cash-negotiable bills and other documents) at that point in time. Indeed the sequence of such moments can at times seem to constitute an alternative narrative, or even to become the narrative, so that the story the reader follows is not one of adventure in the first instance but of monetary arithmetic.

The most interesting case to take is *Roxana* (1724) because this fiction is ostensibly the least mundanely materialistic, in its outlines and some of its settings the most romantic, and in psychological terms the most complex and sophisticated of Defoe's major narratives. This is enforced in Bell's assertion that 'The increased sophistication of *Roxana* in terms of characterisation and technique makes it less of a popular text, and more of a literary one, and the book deserves to be read alongside Richardson.'[22]

Even so, the consciousness through which the narrative is mediated, Roxana's own, functions almost entirely along the spine of the loss, acquisition, securing and investment of money. This is not to say that Roxana's unconscious mind is not often wayward and in terms of the material values of Roxana's awareness transgressive, or to ignore the fact that her concern to secure wealth may be grounded in the insecurities of her early experience, or even to question the fact that her motivation sometimes seems to be as deeply lodged in the mysteries of human character as that of some of Shakespeare's figures; but money is

Roxana's main concern, and she does not represent her preoccupation with it as a psychological abnormality or peculiar obsession. (And it would be hard to argue that her text invites such a reading.) Money is represented in the text as Roxana's proper concern, and as a topic about which the reader will welcome detailed information.

This information can be very detailed indeed. It is difficult to find another central character in the canon of English fiction about whose money management so much information is supplied. For instance, when Roxana is living in London and lodging in expensive apartments in Pall Mall she seeks the advice of Sir Robert Clayton (a historical figure, a well-known economist admired by Defoe) about how to manage her money. In recording his advice Roxana is offering a narrative not just of cash accumulation, but of investment and capital growth by way of interest and interest compounded. There is no essential stylistic difference between the way Roxana recounts this and the telling of any other episode in her life:

> Sir *Robert*, a Man thorowly vers'd in Arts of improving Money, but thorowly honest, *said to me*, Madam, I'm glad you approve of the Method that I propos'd to you; but you have begun wrong; you shou'd have come for your Interest at the Half-Year, and then you had had the Money to put out; now you have lost half a Year's Interest of 350*l.* Which is 9*l.* For I had but 5 *per Cent.* on the Mortgage.
>
> Well, well, Sir, *says I*, can you put this out for me now?
>
> Let it lie, Madam, *says he*, till the next Year, and then I'll put out your 1400*l.* Together, and in the mean time I'll pay you Interest for the 700*l.* So he gave me his Bill for the Money, which he told me shou'd be no less than 6*l. Per Cent.* Sir *Robert Clayton*'s Bill was what no-body wou'd refuse; so I thank'd him, and let it lie; and next Year I did the same; and the third Year Sir *Robert* got me a good Mortgage for 2200*l.* at 6 *per Cent.* Interest: so I had 132*l.* a Year added to my Income; which was a very satisfying article.[23]

In Swift such a passage would be harshly satirical, composed to ridicule the jargon of monetary transaction and to condemn the values it inscribes. In Defoe it is just part of Roxana's story, which is also a story of sexual adventures, of personal relationships, of chances (such as storms at sea, or unexpected encounters), of social advancement, and of intermittent religious experience; but it is no more any one of these than any other, and there is no supervisory authorial moralisation that directs the reader's attention to one more than another. Roxana is highly materialistic, and her materialism focuses on cash and cash values, but she is not flagged up as distinctively or reprehensibly so. Signification, moral message, even theme, seem almost removed from Roxana's narrative. There is of course a moralising Preface almost certainly written by Defoe. This does point to the 'Noble Inferences' of her story:

> even in the highest Elevations of her Prosperity, she makes frequent Acknowledgments; That the Pleasure of her Wickedness was not worth the Repentance; and that all the Satisfaction she had, all the Joy in the View of her Prosperity, no, nor all the Wealth she rowl'd in; the Gayety of her Appearance; the Equipages, and the Honours, she was attended with, cou'd quiet her Mind, abate the Reproaches of her Conscience, or procure her an Hour's Sleep, when just Reflections kept her waking. (2)

It might be attractive to think these things, but in fact this Preface misrepresents the narrative in both substance and tone. Besides which, like the full title-page, which contains information completely unmentioned in the text (such as Roxana's various names), it has other functions: it both hints at the sexy and glamorous material the book contains and legitimises the prurient reader's interest. The episodes of Roxana's life may be extraordinary, but her consciousness is essentially the transparent consciousness of her culture, albeit modified by her background and predicaments. One might say that if she often thinks about money, counts it, is interested in it and tells her reader about it, then that is only natural.

Roxana's father was a prosperous businessman who, as a Protestant, fled to Britain to escape persecution in France. He was able to give her a dowry of '25000 Livres, *that is to say,* two Thousand Pounds' (7) when she was fifteen, and married her to an eminent brewer. Throughout her life Roxana admires successful and honest businessmen and merchants. Her husband loses her money and his own, and Roxana's tirade against marrying a fool is directed as much against his incompetence as it is against the social embarrassment of a wife being 'oblig'd to Blush for him every time she hears him speak' (8). Her father deprecates his son-in-law's business habits and leaves Roxana only 5000 livres (£400) at his death: 'Thus I lost the last Gift of my Father's Bounty, by having a Husband not fit to be trusted with it; there's one of the Benefits of marrying a Fool' (9). Roxana never again places herself in the hands of anyone so financially foolish, except in so far as they give her large sums of money – if this is folly, and she always takes both care and practical measures to look after her money as far as she can herself.

Roxana's monetary predicaments are grounded in the reality of early eighteenth-century life. Deserted by her improvident and bankrupt husband she will become destitute once her immediate resources run out. She tells her relatives,

> if I had but one Child, or two Children, I would have done my Endeavour to have work'd for them with my Needle, and should only have come to them to beg them to help me to some Work, that I might get our Bread by my Labour; but to think of one single Woman not bred to Work, and at a Loss where to get Employment, to get the Bread of five Children, that was not possible, some of my Children being young too, and none of them big enough to help one another. (15)

Roxana's husband in abandoning his family has disabled them as an economic unit.

When two years earlier Defoe had presented Moll Flanders in a comparable situation the narrative blended the discourses of emotion and of money. Moll at forty-eight is left with two children and few resources when her husband dies. Even his death, which is precipitated by a financial breach of trust, is a story of the inner life. Moll tells him 'his Credit was so good' he would easily recover the lost money, but

> It was in vain to speak comfortably to him, the Wound had sunk too deep, it was a Stab that touch'd the Vitals, he grew Melancholy and Disconsolate, and from thence Lethargick, and died.[24]

Moll represents the predicament in which this bankruptcy of enterprise leaves her in practical terms, but also and more forcefully in emotional terms: she is in 'a dismal and disconsolate case'; she is 'Friendless and Helpless'; 'Apprehensions' for the future 'doubl'd the Misery'; she is like 'a distracted Woman' and her 'Understanding was sometimes quite lost in Fancies and Imaginations' (189–90). Moll lives in this state for two years until, her 'Soul' made 'Desperate by Distress' (191) she commits her first theft, from the Apothecary in Leadenhall-street, and her second crime, the robbery of a necklace from the child returning from the dancing school, together with the alarming impulse to kill the child.

In *Moll Flanders* the representation of this episode is very much part of Defoe's explicit working of the theme of the relation of poverty to crime and the extent of the individual's culpability, and is thus part of the moral discourse of the narrative. This is much less the case with *Roxana*, although there are of course long and interesting passages which deal with the heroine's conscious and unconscious inner life, and with some of the moral implications of her actions. The reader is always aware that Moll is in a sense making out a case for herself. Roxana's address is much more habitually to the practical and the material: when in the last pitches of her destitution the landlord brings her some relief in the form initially of food, what Roxana reports first is the rather sharp transactions involved in buying the meat. The landlord

> call'd my Maid *Amy*, and sent her out to buy a Joint of Meat; he told her what she should buy, but naming two or three things, either of which she might take; the Maid, a cunning Wench, and faithful to me, as the Skin to my Back, did not buy any thing out-right, but brought the Butcher along with her, with both the things that she had chosen, for him to please himself; the one was a large very good Leg of Veal; the other a Piece of the Fore-Ribs of Roasting Beef; he look'd at them, but bade me chaffer with the Butcher for him, and I did so, and came back to him, and told him what the Butcher demanded for either of them, and what each of them came to; so he pulls out 11*s.* and 3*d.* Which they came to together, and bade me take them both, the rest, he said, would save another time.   (25–6)

There is at times about Roxana, who is probably Defoe's most complex, interesting and intelligent central character, a kind of metaphysical numbness that – to put it melodramatically – marks her out not so much as a fallen woman as a lost soul.

However, she is also constructed as a woman dealing with the business of living in the eighteenth-century world. Deprived of economic support by father and husband, she has to secure her existence. She is rescued from destitution by becoming the mistress of her landlord, the jeweller 'husband', and this sets her on the road to affluence. In essence it launches her on a career when no other is open to her, and her preoccupation from now on is less acquiring than securing wealth. This presents her with a series of practical and legal dilemmas, not all of which are spelled out in her text because she could have taken an appreciation of them for granted. These are dilemmas peculiar to women, and they relate to what Locke repeatedly emphasises as the principal and even the only concern of government, 'the preservation of Property'.[25] Swan takes Roxana as one of her chief examples for describing in detail the position of women in relation to money and the law; she notes that 'If Roxana were male, her interest in commerce would be unremarkable' and describes Defoe's (and others') treatment of women's financial relations in the period as 'sadly realistic'.[26]

The core of the problem was that married women could not hold property; whatever they had was ultimately vested in their husbands. (Before the age of twenty-one any unmarried woman's property was in the control of her father or other male relations.) This is why Roxana's first husband is able to throw away her substantial dowry as well as his own fortune and business. Widows and unmarried women over twenty-one could hold property. Roxana goes to great lengths after the death of her jeweller 'husband' in Paris to represent herself as his widow: this gave her a title to what he had left, even though of course she had no title to it in law. The 'Contract in Writing' (42) which he drew up had no real status, whatever her moral title, if any, to his property. The problem was accentuated because although independent women over twenty-one could hold property they could not very well enter contracts. This is why even when Roxana is very affluent she is dependent on men to manage her money for her. It is also the case that for much of the narrative Roxana does not know for certain that her first husband is dead or that he will not return; if he did he could legally take all her property, cash, jewels (probably), clothes, securities, gold and silver plate – everything. Hence she is extraordinarily circumspect and cautious in the enquiries she instigates after him, and it explains why she needs to know whether he is alive or dead. Furthermore, management of money is at the heart of the long and absorbing debate in the middle of the book (144–53) about the status of women in marriage which she has with the French merchant lover who wants to marry her, and who does eventually become her husband. The crux of the matter is, as Roxana puts it,

> That the very Nature of the Marriage-Contract was in short, nothing but giving up Liberty, Estate, Authority, and everything, to the Man, and the Woman was indeed, a meer Woman ever after, that is to say, a Slave. (148)

This is not rhetorical exaggeration on Roxana's part. It is legal fact. The husband did not simply assume ownership of his wife's property: she herself actually became his property. If she were attacked or raped by another man she could not prosecute him, but her husband could, for injury or damage done to his property.

In his eagerness to marry Roxana the merchant offers not only to allow her management of her own money, but management of his as well. They deal with this suggestion through the appropriate mercantile imagery of steering a trading ship. The merchant offers, 'if I desir'd the Management of our Estate, when put together, if I wou'd not trust him with mine, he would trust me with his; that we wou'd be upon one Bottom, and I shou'd steer.' Roxana responds, 'Ay, *says I*, you'll allow me to steer, *that is* , hold the Helm, but you'll conn the Ship, *as they call it*; that is, as at Sea, a Boy serves to stand at the Helm, but he that gives him the Orders, is Pilot' (150–1). The merchant protests his good intentions, and insists that Roxana should have absolute command: 'you shall conn the Ship.' In response Roxana is derisive, 'ay, *says I*, as long as you please, but you can take the Helm out of my Hand when you please, and bid me go spin.'

Roxana is not being unduly independent-minded or sceptical. She is simply voicing the fact that under the law in the eighteenth century (as was the case well into the nineteenth as well) it was effectively impossible to make any contract or agreement that would secure any part of a wife's property from her husband. Roxana knows what she is talking about and abandons the fanciful metaphor in order to specify legal fact: 'It is not you, *says I*, that I suspect, but the Laws of Matrimony puts the Power into your Hands; bids you do it; commands you to command; and binds me, forsooth, to obey' (151). She says that a humble wife will be 'infinitely oblig'd' for what mutual interest, affection, courtesy, and kindness she meets with in a husband, but she 'can't help herself where it fails' (151).

In the course of her story Roxana may make some very questionable decisions, she may be dishonest and seem heartless; she may go on adding to her wealth when she seems already to have enough to last her for life – '*What was I a Whore for now?*' she repeatedly asks herself (201–3), and it is also true that read carefully Roxana's arguments against the marriage are not altogether to the point. There is something in her that rebels against the only terms on which she *could* bring herself to marry the merchant: as for not giving him the management of her money, 'I thought it would be not only a little Gothick and Inhumane, but would also be a Foundation of Unkindness between us' (147). But overriding all these things is Defoe's representation of Roxana's story as that of a woman for whom money is not a peculiar psychological obsession, but the only thing she has. In the new world of the early eighteenth century money is the medium in which, willy-nilly, human life has to be negotiated and transacted. *Roxana* is the most complete presentation of the absoluteness of this fact in English fiction.

Despite the sudden catastrophe which seems to be visited on Roxana's fortunes at the end of the narrative, Defoe does not orchestrate the reader's attitudes to his narrative. The novel raises innumerable issues about existence in a cash-driven economy, but does not resolve them. Watts summarises Defoe's position *vis-à-vis* the oscillations between the expression of lofty moral or religious sentiments by his characters and their blatant materialism in this way:

> To a large extent Defoe seems to have shared his fictional narrators' double-standard – their untidy, inconsistent appeals to both God and Mammon; he voiced ideological contradiction without mastering it.[27]

The writer who most emphatically forced readers of the early eighteenth century to confront the ideological contradictions in the national life was Bernard Mandeville (1670–1733). In a highly provocative allegorical fable, *The Grumbling Hive: or, Knaves Turn'd Honest* (1705) and in further editions of it with extensive prose commentaries over the next twenty years, Mandeville crystallised and elaborated the argument that the prosperity of a nation depended on the vices, especially greed and luxury, of its individual inhabitants. The 1714 edition, entitled *The Fable of the Bees*, bore a subtitle that put what is often called the argument about luxury into epigrammatic form, *Private Vices, Publick Benefits*.

Mandeville, who became a successful physician in London, emigrated to Britain from Holland in his twenties. In his writing he sees British behaviour and culture with the raw clarity of the outsider and, especially in the 1705 fable, expresses himself with the simplicity and directness of an author with no linguistic finesse to refine or distract his ideas. He represents the economic nation as a beehive seething with vigorous activity, all members ministering to the greed of others, and seeking to cheat them out of their wealth. It is disorderly, almost chaotic, but it generates prosperity:

VAST Numbers throng'd the fruitful Hive;
Yet those vast Numbers made 'em thrive;
Millions endeavouring to supply
Each other's Lust and Vanity;

> While other Millions were employ'd,
> To see their Handy-works destroy'd;
> They furnish'd half the Universe;
> Yet had more Work than Labourers.
> Some with vast Stocks, and little Pains,
> Jump'd into Business of great Gains;
> And some were damn'd to Sythes and Spades,
> And all those hard laborious Trades;
> Where willing Wretches daily sweat,
> And wear out Strength and Limbs to eat:

The hive is full of Sharpers, Parasites, Pimps, Pick-Pockets, Coiners, and so on:

> These were call'd Knaves, but bar the Name,
> The grave Industrious were the same:
> All Trades and Places knew some Cheat,
> No Calling was without Deceit.[28]

In the frenzy of competition and self-interest the hive prospers hugely:

> THUS every Part was full of Vice,
> Yet the whole Mass a Paradise;
>
> . . . . .
>
> THIS was the State's Craft, that maintain'd
> The Whole of which each Part complain'd:
> This, as in Musick Harmony,
> Made Jarrings in the main agree.   (1.24)

This is a rough account of the economic principle which Pope later aggrandises into universal theory when in the 'Epistle to Bathurst' he explains how extremes of economic behaviour, miserliness and profligacy, are part of the Divine scheme of things operating throughout all nature:

> Ask we what makes one keep, and one bestow?
> That POW'R who bids the Ocean ebb and flow,
> Bids seed-time, harvest, equal course maintain,
> Thro' reconcil'd extremes of drought and rain.   (165–8)

The prosperity of the hive continues until Jove, irritated by the bees' persistent grumbling about vice and corruption, decides to make them honest. From that moment the economy of the hive collapses, activity diminishes, prices fall, the population shrinks, and eventually the tiny residue of the hive

> . . . flew into a hollow Tree,
> Blest with Content and Honesty.   (1.35)

The Fable of the Bees and his Remarks upon it, together with some other searchingly sceptical pamphlets, made Mandeville the most controversial author of the first three decades of the century. In 1723 the *Fable* was prosecuted by the Grand Jury of Middlesex as a public nuisance, and the author's surname opened him up to representation as a diabolical agent or Antichrist. Fully to understand this one needs to read the Remarks with their blistering sarcasm and often shocking imagery, and to become familiar with the mordant cogency of such essays as the attack on Charity and Charity Schools which was published in the 1723 edition of the *Fable*, but what Mandeville had done was to lay bare the silent conspiracy of hypocrisy that enabled a nation to enjoy the fruits of a prosperity that was grounded in the very vice, luxury, that had led to man's Fall and expulsion from Paradise. Luxury was a far wider concept than its modern meaning of extravagant materialism suggests: it connoted all yielding to the allure of the senses, lack of discipline, indulgence, excess. In *Paradise Lost*, Book Nine, Eve argues dangerously and revealingly with Adam that 'This garden . . . grows, Luxurious by restraint' (206, 209). Luxury's inevitable problematising of prosperity was a deep cultural anxiety, especially for 'low-church' and 'trade': the centrality of the debate about luxury is indicated in Langford's observation that 'A history of luxury and attitudes to luxury would come very close to being a history of the eighteenth century.' He elaborates:

> There is a sense in which politics in this period is about the distribution and representation of this luxury, religion about the attempt to control it and social policy about confining it to those who did not produce it.[29]

Money was at the heart of English life, and it was the key to the cultural transformations its literature registered. 'Britain in the eighteenth century', argues Langford, 'was a plutocracy if it was anything, and even as a plutocracy one in which power was widely diffused, constantly contested, and ever adjusting to new incursions of wealth . . .' (4–5). The controversies surrounding Mandeville's *Fable* and his highly contentious commentaries on it came to a head in the 1720s and forced the phenomenon of the new economy into the arena of moral debate in a way Defoe's self-denying ordinance as an author absent from his own text avoids. Affluence, insisted Mandeville, was bought at a moral cost. Hogarth's 1721 South Sea print represented this in the chaos and distortion of his urban landscape; Defoe in 1724 was tight-lipped about it and let the implications of *Roxana* speak for themselves; the prominence of Mandeville from 1723 onwards made his ideas the centre of discomfittingly fierce controversy. In 1728 Gay drew together the threads of Money, Luxury, Vice and Corruption in the most successful public entertainment of the first half of the eighteenth century.

The Beggar's Opera (1728) ran for a prodigious sixty-two nights in its first season. Most plays enjoyed a run of three, or, if successful, six nights. Running for so long, its audience comprised people who came to see it again and again, and a social range beyond that for most plays and operas. Like Hogarth's print and Mandeville's image of the thriving beehive, *The Beggar's Opera* is not so much an account of its culture as a way of seeing it, a satirical vision. The piece works by establishing an automatic, axiomatic and unembarrassed fluency of reference between the world in which it is set, the world of highwaymen, prostitutes, thief-takers, gang-leaders, fences and gaolers and the worlds outside, especially those of the beau monde and of government. Peachum and Walpole, Macheath and a gentleman, Mrs Peachum and an aristocratic matron, Polly and a society heroine are interchangeable. Their preoccupations and their conduct in pursuit of them are the same. Put all together they constitute a national community; they inhabit the same universe of values. Peachum's first Air emphasises the *Opera*'s vision – 'Through all the employments of life' practice is the same. 'All professions berogue one another.'[30] All the figures in the Air are generic – the neighbour, the brother, the Whore, the Wife, the Rogue (fancy-man), the Husband, the Priest, the Lawyer, the Statesmen. Just as in *The Grumbling Hive* 'Jarrings' were brought together in Musick so all these diverse figures are brought together in the simple melody of the Air.

Much satirical writing of the early eighteenth century works by the reader knowing the key that will unlock its references. In Arbuthnot's narrative satires collectively known as *The History of John Bull* (1712) the reader recognises John Bull as England, Lord Strutt as Charles II of Spain, Nicholas Frog as the Dutch, Lewis Baboon as the Bourbon King of France, Louis XIV, and the ruinously expensive lawsuit in which they are all engaged as the War of the Spanish Succession (1702–13). Reading is thus a process of simultaneous translation from the explicit discourse of the narrative to the discourse of power it represents. There are parts of *Gulliver's Travels*, and perhaps more parts than can now be recognised, that are open to a similar satirical mechanism, though that narrative works in many other ways as well. With *The Beggar's Opera* there is no translation necessary because it is simply assumed that the whole world speaks the same language. In fact, the power of that assumption is such that no translation can be thought even possible, because translation implies difference, and the axiom of this piece is that there is no difference between a highwayman and the Prime Minister. Robin of Bagshot, alias Bob Booty (1.3) is also that other Robin, Sir Robert Walpole, Lord Treasurer of the Robinocracy Britain had become. He attended the first night and the complete reflexivity of the piece was manifested in his both laughing and being the object of laughter. As Nicholson puts it, 'Gay was laughing literate London into forms of self-recognition.'[31]

There is no field of activity in *The Beggar's Opera* which is not governed by money (or by the vice, corruption and luxury which are its other faces). Marriage is, of course, an avenue of monetary transaction. Peachum is incensed by the possibility that Polly may have transgressed the code and secretly married for love: he knows the marriage laws as well as Roxana and in his angry flow his discourse automatically blends profit, pleasure, power and crime:

> Married! If the wench does not know her own profit, sure she knows her own pleasure better than to make herself a property! My daughter should be to me, like a court lady to a minister of state, a key to the whole gang. (1.4)

Love is of course what would seem to come nearest to contesting the supremacy of money in the play, but it does not have an existence distinct from the world in which it is transacted. When Polly sings of her relief at hearing that her lover Macheath is not to be hanged she concretises her feelings in the imagery of commerce, although amusingly, and true to her upbringing, when she figures herself as a ship it is one carrying a contraband cargo:

> I like a ship in storms was tost;
> Yet afraid to put into Land;

For seiz'd in the port the vessel's lost,
Whose treasure is contreband.
  The waves are laid
  My duty's paid
O joy beyond expression!
  Thus, safe a-shore,
  I ask no more,
My all is in my possession.   (1.10)

Although it may seem portentous to say so in the context of the amusing charm of Polly Peachum's love-life, her Air reveals the extent to which the percolation of a monetary consciousness through all areas of life has modified the way we construe and imagine ourselves and others. Of course in the *Opera* almost everyone's worth is open to monetary calculation. At the beginning of the play Peachum is writing down the names of criminals he could impeach in a large Book of Accounts:

> For *Tom Gag*, forty pounds. Let *Betty Sly* know that I'll save her from Transportation, for I can get more by her staying in *England*.
>   (1.1)

Mrs Peachum is circumspect about her daughter marrying a highwayman for financial reasons, which make his probable bigamy important:

> I am very sensible husband that captain *Macheath* is worth money, but I am in doubt whether he hath not two or three wives already, and then if he should die in a Session or two, *Polly*'s dower would come in dispute.   (1.9)

When Macheath is trying to explain away Polly to Lucy he tells her, 'You see *Lucy*, in the account of Love you are in my debt' (2.15). It is common for rakish figures in literature to address women in a rather out-moded amatory style, as Lovelace frequently addresses and speaks of Clarissa. Here, however, Macheath simply deploys the imagery that comes so readily to hand in the play and that everyone understands, the imagery of financial transaction. The language of money needs no translation: the entire culture from the Prime Minister to the Child-Getter (in fact both had a certain aptitude for the same activity) has internalised the discourse of money to the extent that in the play one could say that the financial condition has become the human condition.

This is confirmed in the words of Macheath as he faces the prospect of the gallows. His philosophy amounts to a simple credit transaction: he has borrowed life and now he must pay it back. His statement is, however, not personal but universal. We are all debtors, we all have to pay on demand:

> 'I go undismay'd. – for death is a debt
> A debt on demand. – So, take what I owe.'   (3.11)

Nicholson argues, a trifle heavily, that *The Beggar's Opera* 'pursues a sense of money transformed from its role of the circulation of goods into the Lord and God of the world of commodities, autonomously arising out of circulation to become the arbiter of value, and its acquisition the aim of all endeavour'.[32] This is over-interpretation. There is no such mystification of money in the play, where although money is universally desired it is not deified. In fact it is common, available to all, readily got and readily lost, something that passes from hand to hand. Taken from the pocket of a gentleman it can pass into the purse of a drab, overnight. It facilitates the wonderful promiscuity of the play, which is its most striking thematic feature: its comprehensive fluency of reference between high society and low society, between government and crime, between prison and Parliament. Money generates the instability which is a function of the play's promiscuity, but which also makes it extraordinarily liberating. It frees up categories and encourages a play of the mind, as when Matt of the Mint reflects on his own profession:

> Of all mechanics, of all servile handycraftsmen, a gamester is the vilest. But yet, as many of the Quality are of the profession, he is admitted amongst the politest company. I wonder we are not more respected.   (3.4)

The remarkable ranging here between points of cultural definition – mechanics/gamester; handycraftsmen/profession; servile/Quality; vilest/politest – is not baffling because it is predicated on a perception shared between author and audience that the new world is not the old world and all relationships are changed. In her consideration of the masquerade mode, Terry Castle discusses the opportunism which attaches to disguise, and goes on,

> Disguise, when unveiled, is perceived as profoundly anti-social;

witness the persistent association between the mask and criminality, travesty and treachery. The cheek of the masquerade was that it both sanctioned such deceit and suffused it with a kind of euphoria.[33]

In *The Beggar's Opera*, however, there is no disguise; it is a carnival without masks. It offers an unhypocritical world of desires free and understood, and the euphoria is generated in the frankness which the universal appreciation of the centrality of money-value licenses. Of course, it is a play, but the frequency and accuracy of reference to the real world outside the play disarms the fiction and authenticates *The Beggar's Opera* as a true vision of the social world rather than just a dramatic illusion.

It is now generally recognised that Gay's success with the piece is in discovering a form as varied and inclusive as the promiscuity at its thematic heart, though it should perhaps be thought of as an authorial mode rather than a form, as it has no real precedent except in the cultural inventiveness which Gay and his fellow Scriblerians (Pope, Arbuthnot and Swift) had relished from around 1713. They enjoyed playing with, inventing and misappropriating established literary forms and kinds and re-presenting them in entertaining travesty. Gay's play is an opera which makes fun of the contemporary fashion for opera. An élite form is turned into something like popular entertainment. Operatic airs are displaced by ballads with familiar tunes. High-life plots are shouldered aside by low-life narrative. Realism obliterates aspiration. And the other way round – the thief-taker's daughter becomes a heroine; the highwayman is the dashing romantic lead.

Taking his cue from Peachum's assertion that the lawyer and the thief-taker both act 'in a double capacity' (2.1), Ian Donaldson calls the *Opera* 'a triumph of the counterfeiter's art'[34] in which Gay is able to keep alternative meanings in continuous suspense, making the piece both earnest and playful, comic and tragic at once. In a brilliant observation Donaldson notes how the tolling bell in the hanging scene echoes the famous tolling bell at the end of Otway's heroic tragedy *Venice Preserv'd* (1680), a stunning effect which is then turned around with the cry of a reprieve for Macheath, itself a parody of the absurdly contrived happy endings of romantic narrative.[35] He says that Gay's interweaving of literary kinds – heroic tragedy, pastoral, popular ballads, sentimental comedy, 'gently challenges the old neo-classical premise that insists that the kinds be kept pure and distinct', and adds that the mingling of echoes and varieties of literary experience nevertheless forms 'a whole which is in some ways curiously life-like'.[36] He sees the overall effect of this as 'puzzlement'.[37] It is not, however, really puzzling. The rigidity of the old formal conception of literary kinds was being contested by responses to the metamorphoses taking place in society. The financial revolution and all that went with it rendered the cultural distinctions of neo-classical taxonomy irrelevant. If *The Beggar's Opera* seems life-like, it is not really 'curiously' so. It is naturally so, as it follows the promiscuous fluidity which now characterised national life, and of which all writers – and particularly the group of 'opposition' writers with which Gay was associated – were uncomfortably aware.

If Gay devises a mixed and undetermined literary form for his representation of a promiscuous society then it is equally true that the *Opera* is not readily accommodated within any ideological structure, and this is one reason for Nicholson's assertion that 'there is no easy point of rest in Gay's text'.[38] Donaldson sees the work as reflecting an essentially Hobbesian view of society in which all are driven by self-interest and society as a whole is the aggregation of a universal competition, and he adduces in support Gay's use of animal imagery; but he also argues that in accordance with some of its fundamental ambivalence, the play sustains at the same time a more benign competing vision of human existence, that of Shaftesbury's *Characteristicks of Men, Manners, Opinions, Times* (1711). Broadly, Shaftesbury argues that humans do have a moral sense, that all things being equal they will tend to do good by their fellows, and that they recognise their own good in the promotion of the common good. In the explicit material and incidents of *The Beggar's Opera* it is easier to detect the Hobbesian than the Shaftesburian tendency, but its tone, its lightness of touch, playfulness, witty toleration of human weakness, and its fun – and the fact that there is an unmotivated reprieve at the end, enabling everyone to join in a cheerful dance – savours more of Shaftesbury than Hobbes. Nicholson in *Writing and the Rise of Finance* does not take issue with Donaldson's sense that Gay both proffers and holds in suspense these two interpretations of human society, but he also adds a suggestion that Gay reveals a scepticism about Locke's widely received understanding of society as a form of contract between rulers and ruled to secure tenure of property. If this is so, then we have to recognise that the play does not seek conclusively to endorse any of the three major secular readings of social organisation that directed cultural understanding in the period.

We have become accustomed to see that all cultural products reflect the presuppositions and ideologies of their social and historical provenance. The ideological indeterminacy of *The Beggar's Opera* does not contest this. The play is perhaps best understood through that favourite Romantic image of the Aeolian harp, the stringed instrument that produces notes called forth by the breezes that play through it. The opera is highly sensitive to the moods and feelings, values and prejudices of the society it represents; it resonates to money, luxury, corruption and vice, but in its easy fluency through the whole register of human experience it comes closer to discovering a convincing harmony in post-financial revolution British society than any other work of the period.

4

Men and Women – Love and Marriage: *The Rape of the Lock, Roderick Random* and *Tom Jones*

Mrs. Waters had in truth, not only a good opinion of our hero, But a very great affection for him. To speak out boldly at once, she was in love, according to the present universally received sense of that phrase . . .   (Fielding, *Tom Jones*, 9.5)[1]

The sense in which the phrase 'in love' is used is, Fielding goes on, that it is 'applied indiscriminately to the desirable objects of all our passions, appetites, and senses'. This clearly being insufficiently precise, he then explains how 'love' has different effects in different circumstances:

how much soever we may be in love with an excellent surloin of beef, or bottle of Burgundy; with a damask rose, or Cremona fiddle; yet do we never smile, nor ogle, nor dress, nor flatter, nor endeavour by any other arts or tricks to gain the affection of the said beef, &c.

It is not the same with love between men and women, where it becomes 'our principal care to engage the affection of the object beloved', and the focus of our young people's education 'in all the arts of rendering themselves agreeable'. Without this aim in love much of Britain's trade and commerce might collapse:

Nay, those great polishers of our manners, who are by some thought to teach what principally distinguishes us from the brute creation, even dancing-masters themselves, might possibly find no place in society. In short, all the graces which young ladies and young gentlemen too learn from others, and the many improvements which, by the help of a looking glass, they add to their own, are in reality those very *spicula et faces amoris* so often mentioned by Ovid; or, as they are sometimes called in our own language, the whole artillery of love.

It emerges from these passages that the language we use for the experience of love is inexact and misleading; there may be a real experience of love and a real language for it, but neither is likely to be found in the real world – nor in these extracts, which do not so much clarify questions of love as signal them as problematic. Fielding does not even establish a distinction between the love for a piece of beef and love for a fellow human being. It is appetite in the first case, and for all the polish gained from dancing masters and looking-glasses, it may be only appetite in the second, as the reference to the erotic writing of Ovid indicates. It seems that the only way to write about love is comically or ironically. Love in the world, as Fielding represents it, is not only compromised in linguistic practice but in social practice too, and this is one reason why the relations between men and women, the social structures in which they are fostered, and the social forms – such as marriage – through which they are articulated, are so often the topic of eighteenth-century writing.

It was not that there was a dearth of examples of previous writing about love and the relations between men and women, but that the literary tradition for all its diversity did not seem to match the contemporary condition. This is what drives the shocking ironies of Swift's obscene verse in which the pastorally-named Strephon encounters the realities of a modern lady's dressing-room. One can get a sense of the gap to be bridged by use of a contrast. In number nine of his love-sonnets, *Amoretti* (1595), Spenser seeks for a suitable simile to describe the eyes of his lady. He runs through and rejects a series of possibilities – the sun, the moon, crystal, and so on, and eventually concludes that the only thing they can be properly compared with is God himself:

> Then to the Maker selfe, they likest be,
> Whose light doth lighten all that here we see.   (13–14)

The comparison beautifully expresses the lovely transcendence of spirit he discovers in the eyes of his future wife. But the language of the English renaissance sonnet tradition will not readily handle the circumstance of the early eighteenth-century marriage market. When (in a passage cited in Chapter 2 above) the elder brother in *Moll Flanders*

(1722) observes to his sister that Betty (Moll) 'is the Handsomest young Woman in *Colchester*' he elicits this response:

> I wonder at you Brother, *says the Sister*; *Betty* wants but one Thing, but she had as good want every Thing, for the Market is against our Sex just now; and if a young Woman have Beauty, Birth, Breeding, Wit, Sense, Manners, Modesty, and all these to an Extream; yet if she have not Money, she's no Body, she had as good want them all, for nothing but Money now recommends a Woman.[2]

Even discounting the narrative moment, which includes the sister's pique at having the maid commended above the mistress, the passage reflects a social reality that discourses available in past literature did not treat.

No-one had written about love and marriage in the way they needed to be discussed now. They had to be placed in the narrative of modern life. Of course, Shakespeare had written matchlessly about the relations between men and women, but perhaps it is easier now than it was in the past, because of our own cultural preoccupations as well as those we have inherited from eighteenth- and nineteenth-century novels of bourgeois realism, to see *Macbeth* and *Othello*, for instance, as plays about marriages. But the cultural ideolect of Shakespeare was not amenable to accounts of love in the world of Defoe. The love-poetry of the sixteenth and seventeenth centuries, diverse as it was in its scope from the idealism of Spenser to the vexed obscenity of Rochester, had a lot to say about passion but comparatively little about the evolution of gender relationships through time. There was nothing in them that would help Richardson.

Even so, there was perhaps one narrative which did help to enable a new way of writing about men and women, a work of almost incalculable cultural pervasiveness, and that was *Paradise Lost*. It is not the place here to argue that *Paradise Lost* made possible a whole new way of conceptualising love and marriage, but it is worth remembering that it is a narrative about a *couple*. We see Adam and Eve living together, eating together, praying together, working together, making love with one another, making mistakes and enduring the consequences of them together, as we do in no precedent narrative in English. In Book Nine, where Eve is tempted by the serpent and eats the fruit, and Adam joins her, the episodes of the narrative are embedded in the context of a highly realistic representation of the relationship of the human pair. Eve is piqued at having been sidelined by Raphael in Book Eight, when he

was discoursing with Adam on elevated cosmic matters. She determines
to get away from Adam for a while and to do some gardening by
herself; Adam is alarmed and tries to prevent her, talking in a rather
priggish and patronizing way. When he gives his consent it is with a
sullen grudgingness: 'Go; for thy stay, not free, absents thee more'
(372). As Eve begins to yield to the serpent's tempting she is influenced
by the glamour, sophistication and fluency of this plausible creature, by
the possibility of being made superior to Adam through the operation
of the fruit, and by the fact that it is getting near lunch-time – she is
hungry after working in the garden and the fruit smells delicious; and
so on. It is also worth adding that Adam and Eve, for all their prelap-
sarian nobility, are not grandees. They live in comfort without luxury;
they have none of the trappings of affluence such as a magnificent
house, horses and carriages, servants in livery, or elaborate costumes for
themselves. They are thus in a sense bourgeois lovers, and the narrative
of their relationship is closer to the world of the eighteenth-century
reader-to-be than to the worlds of romance, so distant in culture, values
and idiom.

For all the possibilities that *Paradise Lost* opened up, none were
realised in the immediate future at least. For one thing, although
Paradise Lost told the story of the Fall, it was not really a narrative of
love in the fallen world, a narrative, that is, of the journey on which
Adam and Eve embark as they leave Paradise in the last lines of the
poem. Nor was that journey the topic of *Paradise Regain'd*. In a sense
it had been visited by Milton in his representation of the relationship
between Samson and Dalila in *Samson Agonistes*, but in his imaginative
writing, outside the Divorce Tracts, that is, he left it essentially untold.
A second reason why this aspect of *Paradise Lost* was not immediately
productive was that the poem was deliberately composed against the
dominant culture of the Restoration court, which found its image in a
stage comedy of brittle caricature, artificial manners and obtrusive sexuality, in everything unlike Milton's careful charting of interpersonal
negotiations. But with the revolution of 1688 and the gradual emergence of a counter-aristocratic and more moralising culture the atmosphere was changing and becoming more receptive to the sensibilities
and values that inform *Paradise Lost*. Johnson in a little excursion in his
Life of Milton imagines how the poet 'surveyed the silent progress of
his work, and marked his reputation stealing its way in a kind of subter-
raneous current through fear and silence'.[3] None of this is designed to
establish a direct link between *Paradise Lost* and eighteenth-century
treatments of the relations of men and women, though its influence is

everywhere and references to it frequent; it is simply to say that there was one influential precedent rendering of the theme, and that the coincidence of the poem's rise in prestige and influence with an emergent interest in the narrative representation of the lives of men and women may have been productive in ways that were, even if in Johnson's word only subterraneously, facilitating.

This chapter will examine a number of eighteenth-century ventures into the theme with a view to seeing how writers of the period explored its various problematics in the context of the culture of their own times. The works principally discussed are *The Rape of the Lock* and two mid-century narratives, Smollett's *Roderick Random* (1748) and Fielding's *Tom Jones* (1749), though of course many of the works discussed in other chapters, such as *Clarissa*, deal with and sometimes concentrate on similar material.

The spirit of scientific and philosophical enquiry which characterised the later decades of the Restoration period and the early decades of the eighteenth century naturally addressed the topic of human behaviour, and in doing so came up against the phenomena firstly that, although mankind was capable of reason, human conduct was not therefore always reasonable, and secondly that human beings appeared to be endowed with a moral sense, and yet able to act both in accordance with and in defiance of it. A simple version of the problems these things raise is seen in Thomson's treatment of the stirrings towards procreation in the poem with which he began *The Seasons* when he first assembled its component poems in 1730, 'Spring'.

Thomson is concerned with the harmony of natural process and presents the theme of sexuality and procreation in this context. He wishes to celebrate 'The Symphony of Spring', and begins with the vernal behaviour of birds – 'a Theme / Unknown to Fame, *the Passion of the Groves*'.[4] There is a great deal of natural imagery and lore, but Thomson's language persistently anthropomorphises the birds' conduct. When 'the Soul of Love' enters 'the Heart' the 'gay Troops' begin to plume themselves; 'their Joy o'erflows / In Musick unconfin'd'; the lark in the morning 'Calls up the tuneful Nations'; the thrushes are most melodious, but the nightingale plans to outdo them at night-time, 'in Thought / Elate, to make her Night excel their Day'. 'This Waste of Musick is the Voice of Love' (582–615). The birds' 'Courtship to their Mates' is interpreted in the language of human social behaviour: the male birds try 'by a thousand Tricks to catch / The cunning, conscious, half-averted Glance: Of their regardless Charmer' (622–4). Eventually, 'CONNUBIAL Leagues' – marriage contracts – 'agreed', the birds in pairs hasten off to the deep woods 'That NATURE's *great Command* may be obey'd' (631–4).

And so it goes on through the process of laying, brooding on the eggs, when the hen's 'sympathizing Lover' sings away the 'tedious Time' (665, 667) on the opposite bank, self-sacrificingly feeding the 'helpless Family' (673) of chicks when they arrive, protecting them from danger, and seeing the fledglings fly from the nest, when 'Th' acquitted Parents' rejoice to see 'their soaring Race' take off and away (753–4).

This anthropomorphising discourse is less fantastical than it might appear: it is certainly a reading into natural phenomena of human experience, but it is also a mode of interpretation that is a mode of understanding made more legitimate as it exemplifies the birds' obedience to the '*great Command*' of Nature, which, if it is universal, must govern human conduct as well. Describing birds as 'the feathered tribe', fish as 'finny people' or sheep as the 'woolly nation' is not just what used to be called 'elegant variation': it is the linguistic expression of a process of accommodation that brings the diversity of the world into a single view. (And it is remarkably persistent: in what senses do spiders have the cruelty, cats the independence, foxes the cunning, racehorses the elegance or small rodents such as guinea-pigs the sweetness we habitually attribute to them?)

As his account of the spring continues Thomson describes the rougher loves of animals and even of sea-creatures: these last, comically as they are presented, are worth mentioning because while the loves of the birds and animals is something the poet could have witnessed in process, he could not have seen the mating of whales and squids, and so his account of them is pure deduction from the theory that he finds to obtain in the land-world:

> NOR undelighted, by the boundless Spring,
> Are the broad Monsters of the foaming Deep:
> From the deep Ooze and gelid Cavern rous'd,
> They flounce and tumble in unwieldy Joy.   (821–4)

Thomson gradually works towards a representation of human sexual feeling in the spring, but before he does so he confirms that the energetic universal urge towards sexuality and reproduction is not just sanctioned by God but is an actual manifestation of God's spirit:

> What is this *mighty Breath*, ye Curious, say,
> That, in a powerful Language, felt not heard,

Instructs the Fowls of Heaven; and thro' their Breast
These Arts of Love diffuses? What, but GOD?
Inspiring GOD! Who boundless Spirit all,
And unremitting Energy, pervades,
Adjusts, sustains, and agitates the Whole. (849–55)

In full awareness of this universal regime Thomson represents 'this *mighty Breath* . . . powerful Language' as it is expressed in humanity. He first presents a girl responding to the feelings of the spring, which are registered in changes to the body and instinctual sensations:

FLUSH'D by the Spirit of the genial Year,
Now from the Virgin's Cheek a fresher Bloom
Shoots, less and less, the live Carnation round;
Her Lips blush deeper Sweets; she breathes of Youth;
The shining Moisture swells into her Eyes,
In brighter Flow; her wishing Bosom heaves,
With Palpitations wild; kind Tumults seize
Her Veins, and all her yielding Soul is Love. (963–70)

The desire all this inspires in her lover is almost too much for him: 'Full of the dear exstatic Power' he is 'sick / With sighing Languishment' (971–2). These young persons are clearly fully in tune with the universal harmony and are a hair's-breadth away from obeying nature's '*great Command*' in 'powerful Language'. But just at this moment they are interrupted by a different discourse designed to stop them in their tracks, right in mid-line:

. . . Ah then, ye Fair!
Be greatly cautious of your sliding Hearts:
Dare not . . .

. . . Let not the fervent Tongue,
Prompt to deceive, with Adulation smooth,
Gain on your purpos'd Will. Nor in the Bower,
Where Woodbines flaunt, and Roses shed a Couch,
While Evening draws her crimson Curtains round,
Trust your soft Minutes with betraying Man. (973–82)

Why not? All that has been represented as benign, generative and natural is now perilous and deceptive: it calls for caution; the will purposes against it; it renders the young woman liable to deception and betrayal. The discourse of love has been displaced by the discourse of treason, but Thomson does not explain why. There is apparently a command in human life that overrides nature's *'great Command'*. There are dangers for the young man too. He is now 'th'aspiring Youth' who has to 'beware of Love' and of the 'smooth Glance', or his 'Wisdom' will lie prostrate, while his 'fading Fame / Dissolves in Air away.' His 'fond' (foolish, or doting) soul, 'Wrapt in gay Visions of unreal Bliss', is at risk from 'Th'inticing Smile; the modest-seeming Eye' (983–90). In fact the female sexuality that draws him, and that Thomson had represented in such warm terms is now impious, inscrutably designing, bewitching, deceptive and deadly. Beneath the 'beauteous Beams' of that modest-seeming woman's eye

> . . . belying Heaven,
> Lurk searchless Cunning, Cruelty, and Death:
> And still, false-warbling in his cheated Ear,
> Her syren Voice, enchanting, draws him on,
> To guileful Shores, and Meads of fatal Joy.   (991–5)

This reconstruction of sexuality, and of female sexuality in particular, goes on from bad to worse, detailing the unmanning passions of sexual fantasy, the debilitating and melancholic effects of frustration, and the poison of jealousy, until finally we see 'the warm Youth, / Whom Love deludes into his thorny Wilds' (1107–8) in a condition of spiritual and social entropy:

> His brightest Aims extinguish'd all, and all
> His lively Moments running down to Waste.   (1111–12)[5]

All this misery lies in wait for the human beings who yield to the passions that invigorate and restore the rest of the world. The narrative of Thomson's treatment of sexuality has one last turn. He develops a vision of the happiness available to the couple 'Whom gentler Stars unite, and in one Fate / Their Hearts, their Fortunes, and their Beings blend' (1114–15). This is clearly a marriage, but a marriage that draws its justification not from the laws that establish it but from the harmony that underlies it:

> 'Tis not the coarser Tie of human Laws,
> Unnatural oft, and foreign to the Mind,

That binds their Peace, but Harmony itself,
All their Passions into Love.   (1116–19)

What Thomson has in mind is the ideal companionate or affective
marriage, featuring 'Friendship', 'Perfect Esteem enliven'd by Desire',
'Sympathy of Soul', 'Thought meeting Thought' and 'boundless
Confidence' (1120–4). Such harmony, Thomson adds, will not be
secured by a marriage contracted in the market-place. He wishes only
ill to the man who buys a bride:

Let him, ungenerous, who, alone intent
To bless himself, from sordid Parent buys
The loathing Virgin, in eternal Care,
Well-merited, consume his Nights and Days.   (1126–9)

Thomson's account of sexuality and the relations between the sexes
is interesting in two main ways: firstly, in its methodology it teases out
into their separate components many of the factors which constitute the
complex discourse of gender relations in the wider body of eighteenth-
century writing; secondly, it leaves completely unexamined the fact that
while sexuality itself is unproblematic and an articulation of the divine
spirit, in the human context it is problematised by social and ethical
factors. Whatever may go on in the natural world, gender relations in
human society are the outcome of a negotiation between natural
impulse and social structures, to the point where they can be recon-
structed almost entirely in social terms. This is perhaps most evident in
the contrast between the perils sexuality presents to each sex. For the
young woman the danger is not specified as it is too obvious. She will
lose her virtue if she indulges her instinctive feelings. In the case of the
young man, succumbing to the wiles of the woman will subvert his
aspirations and his fame, all his worldly ambitions and potential for
achievement. Adam and Eve have now clothed themselves, and in
dressing they have become different, not creatures of nature but of society. This is how the eighteenth-century imagination continued the
narrative Milton had set in train.

Adam and Eve are both generic Man and Woman and distinctive
individuals, both type and personality. The same is true of most render-
ings of human beings in eighteenth-century representation when the
sexes are seen in relation to one another: characters are distinctive, but
they are also made to conform to a mould shaped by the desire to establish or at least accept generalised types. This is readily seen in Hogarth's

six prints representing *Marriage-à-la-Mode* (1745). A City heiress and the son of Lord Squanderfield are the subjects of an arranged marriage: as such they are types derived both from literary tradition and from contemporary experience, where the financial vigour of the City is brought to the aid of a decaying traditional aristocracy. It is an appalling marriage with a dreadful outcome. The young viscount is not interested in his bride, and wastes his money on debauchery. Left to herself Lady Squanderfield takes her middle-class lawyer for a lover. Finding them together at night, Lord Squanderfield, who has himself got a child-mistress for whom he has tried to procure either an abortion or a cure for venereal disease, attacks Lawyer Silvertongue, but is killed by him. The lawyer is apparently hanged for the murder, and Lady Squanderfield expires in poverty and squalor, her crippled child (the heiress of her father's disease) hanging round her neck. As Lady Squanderfield dies her merchant father coolly retrieves her costly wedding ring from her finger. In terms of moral and social typology this is a plain story, awful as it is in its melodramatic terseness, but the figures in each vignette are all individualised in their attitudes and expressions, from the ingratiating lasciviousness of Lawyer Silvertongue as he makes up to the bride-to-be, through the despairing resignation of Lord Squanderfield's steward as he tries to make his debilitated master attend to his bills, to the amused glee of the negro servant handing round chocolate at Lady Squanderfield's graceless soirée. But the expressions of the principals above all tell the story in terms of its individual human rather than just its typological implications. The face (and body and dress language) of each person changes from plate to plate in sequence, so that each is explained by the preceding plate and anticipates the next. A collection of symbolic vignettes thus performs as a narrative. In the first plate the reluctant young heiress wears an expression of rather vulgar petulance and deliberate grumpy withdrawal, looking down, meeting no-one's eye, studiously avoiding looking either at her husband-to-be (her back is turned to him though they share the same couch); she toys indifferently with her wedding ring, not wearing it, but pulling her handkerchief through it. The young viscount looks bored; he is turned away from the whole scene and gazes vacantly at his foppish reflection in a dark mirror. An entire narrative instantly comprehensible in terms of types and troublingly intimate in terms of individual lives is implicit in this scene.[6]

The representational manner of Hogarth is essentially that of the imaginative literature of the early eighteenth century in its handling of gender relations, though the mood is not always as caustic or tragic.

Pope's Belinda in *The Rape of the Lock* is perhaps of much the same age as the young city heiress in Hogarth's print. She is certainly like her in that she is entering a new phase of her existence. She is not in herself an important person: she is perhaps just one of the myriad 'young *Coquettes*' who are taught by social ambition to roll their eyes alluringly, and to blush at will, and whose 'little Hearts' 'flutter at a *Beau*'.[7] But hers is an important story, not because she has a lock of her hair cut off, but because in the course of the poem she embodies a universal narrative of transition from which no-one is exempt: she moves from the childhood world of toys, trinkets, dreams and lap-dogs to the adult world of the court, with its business, recreations, obsessions and betrayals. She moves from the private world of home to the public world; she makes the transition from innocence to experience (it has been suggested that this first major poem in the heroic manner since *Paradise Lost* is the story of the Fall of Woman in answer to the story of the Fall of Man); she moves from the world of natural daylight, when she wakes at noon, to the artificial world of artificial light in the evening party at Hampton Court.

Belinda's rites of passage, universal as they may be, are none the less concretised in the specific culture of Queen Anne's court; she is a product of its values and she has to negotiate her adventure in its terms. And this is where Pope's poem reaches into the problematics of gender relations in a sophisticated society. This is limned out in the ironies of the invocation to the muse at the start of the poem:

> Say what strange Motive, Goddess! Cou'd compel
> A well-bred *Lord* t'assault a gentle *Belle*?
> Oh say what stranger Cause, yet unexplor'd,
> Cou'd make a gentle *Belle* reject a *Lord*?　　　　　(1.7–10)

There is nothing 'strange' about the Lord's motive if the assault is to be of the kind the word 'Rape' in the title indicates: it is the universal impulse that Thomson celebrates. But it really would be strange if a woman with the role of a 'belle' were to reject advances from a Lord. There are other ironies in this passage too, but in broad terms Pope identifies the forces that drive the intricate clockwork of the beau monde as desire and ambition, nature and culture.

Belinda awakes into the poem from a 'Morning-Dream' of a young man. It is a dream with at least some erotic component as 'ev'n in Slumber' it 'caus'd her Cheek to glow', but the glow might not be just sexual awareness. The youth she dreams of is not exciting because he is naked, but because of how he is dressed. He is 'A Youth more glitt'ring than a *Birth-night Beau*' (1.23). Belinda's imagination is already shaped by the culture of which she is becoming a part. It is a culture in which her vocation will be to exploit her sexual allure in order to attract a socially glamorous husband. On the other hand, while she must attract a man she must not become his lover or her reputation, and with it her chances of marriage, will be lost.

Belinda seems fortunate to be comparatively untroubled by the moralising about women that would increasingly during her century compromise her role as a coquette. This is partly Pope's way of registering the insouciance of the beau monde to which she belongs, and it is also an index of her ignorance and naivety. Furthermore, although books offering all kinds of advice on religious, social and moral behaviour – conduct books – were a publishing staple, in 1717, when *The Rape of the Lock* reached the state in which we know it, they had not yet reached their peak of popularity or insistence. To give one example, in 1740 Wetenhall Wilkes in his *Letter of Genteel and Moral Advice to a Young Lady* is rhapsodising about the spiritual beauty of chastity in woman, 'a quick and delicate feeling in the soul, which makes her shrink, and withdraw herself from any thing that is wanton, or has danger in it'.[8] According to Wilkes, she would even have to be careful about her dreams: 'If wanton dreams be remembered with pleasure, that, which before was involuntary, and therefore innocent, becomes a voluntary and sinful transgression of virtue' (30). More particularly pertinent is the fact that the one accomplishment Belinda really has is a talent for making herself look attractive to men, and this, according to Wilkes, is tantamount to adultery:

> That girl, who endeavours, by the artifice of dress, to attract the admiration, to stir up the languishing desires, and to provoke the wanton wishes of her gay beholders, is as guilty of breaking the seventh commandment, as the woman in the *Gospel*, that was taken in the fact. Therefore be not industrious to set out the beauty of your person; but, as I said before, let your dress always resemble the plainness and simplicity of your heart.   (30)

By these standards the Belinda who wears on her white breast 'a sparkling *Cross* . . . / Which *Jews* might kiss and Infidels adore' (2.8–9) would find it hard to avoid stoning. There is, however, one point in Wilkes's admonitions that bears directly on the predicament in which the poem places Belinda. He says that chastity 'is the great point of female honour, and the least slip in a woman's honour, is never to be recovered' (29).

'Honour' is 'What guards the Purity of melting Maids / In Courtly Balls, and Midnight Masquerades' (1.71–2). Honour is the guarantor of reputation in a gossipy court where 'At ev'ry Word a Reputation dies' (3.16). It is Belinda's honour that the virago Thalestris foresees as being lost as a result of the seizure of the lock. She claims to

> Already hear the horrid things they say,
> Already see you a degraded Toast,
> And all your Honour in a Whisper lost.   (3.108–10)

Preservation of her honour, or reputation, is the absolute condition of success in Belinda's career as a coquette, and this is why in her moment of victory over the Baron in the battle of the sexes in Canto Five her repeated demand is that he '*Restore the Lock!*' (5.103) In itself it has no value: it cannot be reattached to restore the symmetry of Belinda's coiffure. But it does have symbolic value – to the Baron. Why did he want it in the first place? Cutting it off might simply have been a mischievous *jeu d'esprit* prompted by the malice of Clarissa, who supplied the scissors and later speaks a hypocritical and wounding 'Moral' (5.9–34), towards a new rival, but Thalestris indicates how he wants to use it. He will have 'th'inestimable Prize' set under crystal on an expensive finger-ring and will show it off as a token of love or conquest. ' 'Twill then be Infamy to seem your Friend' (4.112–15). There has been neither love nor conquest, but that is immaterial. Whether the Baron appears to have won Belinda 'By Force . . . or . . . Fraud' (2.34) will also be immaterial. A public display of the lock will make it appear that Belinda has yielded to him, and her value in the marriage-market will evaporate. For all that chastity was as Wilkes was to see it, a condition of spiritual purity, it was in terms of eighteenth-century marriage of much more practical importance as warranty for the preservation of the true line of inheritance of property, and as Vivien Jones puts it starkly, 'women are objects of exchange within a mercantilist discourse which conflates self-interest and moral rectitude'.[9] One of the eighteenth-century tracts on marriage which she extracts in her anthology is candid about the double standard which condemns the female adulterer more than the male:

> it is generally supposed a greater Crime in the Woman than the Man. Because she not only imposes a spurious Breed on her Husband's Family; makes a Foreigner Heir to his Estate; depriving sometimes

his own real Children begotten afterwards, of their just Inheritance; or, at least, his right Heirs and next Relations; but makes the Son of a Man his Heir, who has done him the greatest Injury.[10]

Belinda wants the lock back in order to forestall any use of it that would impugn her reputation. That it could have damaged her less if the Baron had actually seduced her and no-one had known, than it will if he publicly 'flaunts the token of a conquest that never took place is the realisation that lies behind her exclamation at the end of Canto Four:

> Oh hadst thou, *Cruel!* Been content to seize
> Hairs less in sight, or any Hairs but these!   (4.175–6)

That she says this is, of course, an index of how far Belinda has travelled into the adult world of hypocritical protocols about gender relations since she woke in comparative innocence at noon.

The paradox for Belinda is that while she must never admit violation she is committed by her only role in society to excite the feelings that might prompt it. Her treasured locks have no function but to 'attract admiration' and 'stir up languishing desires'. She wears them 'to the Destruction of Mankind' and in the knowledge that 'Fair Tresses Man's Imperial Race insnare' (2.19, 27). Belinda is empowered by her beauty alone. She is like the pathetic Venus in Shakespeare's *Venus and Adonis* who is distraught when Adonis rejects her, 'Poor Queen of Love, in thine own lore forlorn' (251), trapped by her own nature. But in Belinda's case it is not so much her nature that traps her as the only character in which society has provided for her to act.

Although there is nothing in the poem to suggest that Belinda brought her mishap wholly on herself, still less that she deserves to have her reputation ruined, there is no doubt that she was aware of what a game she would be entering on going to Hampton. The military imagery when she is at her dressing-table, 'Now awful Beauty puts on all its arms' (1.139), the fact that she is inspired by 'Thirst of Fame' when she approaches the card-table where she 'Burns to encounter two adventrous Knights' and 'swells her Breast with Conquests yet to come' (3.25–8), attest to her awareness. And this is confirmed when at the critical moment Ariel is disabled in his attempt to protect the lock because he spies 'An Earthly Lover lurking at her Heart' (3.144).

Reading Pope's narrative like this allows for quite a dark interpretation, which is signalled as apt in Canto Three, lines 19–20, when the sun sets on Hampton and the light of nature disappears from the poem's world:

> Meanwhile declining from the Noon of Day,
> The Sun obliquely shoots his burning Ray.

That we may at this point be entering a discourse of more serious moral implication seems to be confirmed by the next couplet ('The hungry Judges soon the Sentence sign, / And Wretches hang that Jury-men may Dine'), registering the injustices of the outside world disregarded by a trivial élite among whom

> *Snuff*, or the *Fan*, supply each Pause of Chat,
> With singing, laughing, ogling, and all that.   (3.17–18)

But this is not the whole of the poem; the irritable moralism that dominates *Marriage-à-la-Mode* does not prevail in *The Rape of the Lock*. Moralism is there, and occasional couplets reach into the world of gender relations in modern society and discover something like tragedy. It is there, for instance, in the paragraph in Canto One which describes how the gnomes lure some nymphs into rejecting ordinary and appropriate love in the hope of realising a marriage of fantastic grandeur (1.79–90). The images of mental emptiness supplied only with chimeras of splendour, and of the corruption of childhood innocence, are genuinely disturbing. The lines have been referred to already:

> 'Tis these that early taint the Female Soul,
> Instruct the Eyes of young *Coquettes* to roll,
> Teach Infant-Cheeks a bidden Blush to know,
> And little Hearts to flutter at a *Beau*.   (1.87–90)

Moments like these deepen but do not determine the tone of the poem, and they consort with other voices and moods.

The description of Belinda at her dressing-table is funny, charming and sensitive to beauty in a way that largely disables the moralism that would condemn Belinda for pride and vanity. It may be absurd that the whole globe contributes to her toilette, but it does so to some effect:

> This Casket *India*'s glowing Gems unlocks,
> And all *Arabia* breathes from yonder Box.   (1.133–4)

Belinda is certainly putting on her war-paint, but she is not putting on a mask. She is enhancing a beauty that is already hers:

> The Fair each moment rises in her Charms,
> Repairs her Smiles, awakens ev'ry Grace,
> And calls forth all the Wonders of her Face.   (1.140–2)

Her dressing-table is the site of an ideal collaboration between art and nature. It features nothing like the cosmetic process Thalestris, the hardened and cynical woman of the court, outlines after Belinda has lost her lock:

> Was it for this you took such constant Care
> The *Bodkin*, *Comb*, and *Essence* to prepare;
> For this your Locks in Paper-Durance bound,
> For this with tort'ring Irons wreath'd around?
> For this with Fillets strain'd your tender Head,
> And bravely bore the double Loads of Lead?   (4.97–102)

Pope is able to present the world Belinda enters as engaging even when it is trivial and ridiculous. The coffee ceremony performed after the card game is described in a language which both highlights its absurdity and redeems it with images of a delicious richness and beauty:

> From silver Spouts the grateful Liquors glide,
> While *China*'s Earth receives the smoking Tide.   (3.109–10)

The poem is full of moments of beauty, comic absurdity, knowingness and joke which are not simply ornamental. They are part of the narrative, as they belong in the narrative context and articulate event. It is not funny in itself to call a pair of scissors a 'glitt'ring *Forfex*', but the couplet in which Pope does it becomes so as it foregrounds its own poetic elaboration in order to highlight the petty and unheroic action of the Baron in cutting the lock:

> The Peer now spreads the glitt'ring *Forfex* wide,
> T' inclose the Lock; now joins it, to divide.   (3.147–8)

Although *The Rape of the Lock* traces Belinda's passage from childhood into the adult world it has also another function. Epic poems are about great and heroic events: here is a heroic poem in which nothing happens. Part of its point is to demonstrate that nothing happened to Belinda. She has entered the court, but she has not come to much harm. She has certainly not been raped. She will be the beautiful Belinda again. All that has really happened is the poetry. The insult to Arabella Fermor has been transformed into a charming myth that immortalises her:

> When those fair Suns shall sett, as sett they must,
> And all those Tresses shall be laid in Dust;
> *This Lock*, the Muse shall consecrate to Fame,
> And midst the Stars inscribe *Belinda*'s Name.   (5.147–50)

Valerie Rumbold records the shock of going through the Blount family papers and suddenly recognising in the 'Cosen Bell' referred to there the Belinda of Pope's poem, but that is of course the shock of *not* having recognised her immediately.[11] Cosen Bell/Arabella Fermor/Belinda is transformed into a narrative text in which she is not a nonentity but a star. It is a transformation effected by Pope, but only made possible by the reality of the social world out of which the poem arises. The heroine finds her identity through her engagement in the elaborate structures her culture has evolved to mediate, and make the most of its fulfilment of nature's '*great Command*'.

Pope is only able to bring the narrative to its beautiful and touching conclusion by a narrative or generic trick. The lock of hair disappears from a realistic narrative – no-one can find it – and reappears in a quasi-Ovidian myth in which it becomes a star. It is an elegant, and one hopes it was for Arabella a consoling, fiction. Most early eighteenth-century narratives were, however, earthbound and had to stick to the conventions of realistic representation which made fantastic escape from the problematics of sexuality and the social relations that shaped it much less easy.

One instance of this is an uncomfortable little narrative which is referred to in *Spectator* 11 (13 March 1711) and appeared in several versions through the middle of the century. One might almost say that it came back to haunt English culture again and again. In a full form it appears in an anonymous heroic epistle called *Yarico to Inkle* in 1736. This is a story with a colonial Caribbean setting and it takes the form of a verse letter from a native Indian woman called Yarico. She has had an English lover called Inkle whom she has looked after and protected for a period on her island. They have enjoyed an idyllic love affair together, and he has taught her English and how to read and write.

Eventually he resolves to abandon her and to sell her into slavery. She naturally protests at this heartless treatment, and tells him that she is expecting his baby. When Inkle hears this he responds by raising the price he is asking for her.[12] There is no comforting resolution of this narrative, no generic escape from the problematics of sexuality: its only issue is in the woman's voice that conveys it, and she has no power except the power of protest and complaint.

The story of Yarico and Inkle has all kinds of resonance, some of them about the implications of British colonial exploitation, but one of them was that the position of Yarico was not legally worse than that of the majority of women, married women especially, in Britain throughout the century. However men and women negotiated their relationships they did so under a legal regime which left women in absolute subjection to men. A pamphlet of 1735, *The Hardship of the English Laws in Relation to Wives*, argues that the condition of married women is 'of all others in his [Majesty's] Dominions the most deplorable' and advocates 'an Alteration or Repeal of some Laws, which, as we conceive, put us in a worse Condition than *Slavery* itself'. The author notes,

> That Wives may be made Prisoners for Life at the Discretion of their *Domestick Governors*, whose Power, as we at present apprehend, bears no Manner of Proportion to that Degree of Authority, which is vested in any other Set of Men in *England* . . .

and that, 'Wives have no Property, neither in their *own Persons*, *Children* or *Fortunes*.'[13] A slave had some rights of redress against a cruel or unjust master. An English wife had none. She was her husband's chattel and had no existence in law, which was why she could not hold property. As Beth Swan says in her very detailed account of the law in eighteenth-century fiction, especially as it applied to women,

> the very basic rights of personal security, liberty, property and redress of injuries, used by Blackstone [Sir William Blackstone, author of *Commentaries on the Laws of England*, 1753] to argue that English law protected people's interests, often excluded women in practice.[14]

All accounts of the relations between men and women in the eighteenth century need to be read in the light of a recognition that all authors and all readers knew this, as well as a great deal more in detail about the law. Swan asserts that 'One of the most important blind spots in literary criticism concerns the legal knowledge of eighteenth-century readers' (12). Even episodes that seem outlandish or fantastical were often grounded in actual practice. As Janet Todd points out acidly, in fiction 'a woman might be in a madhouse not as metaphor and symbol . . . but because the laws of England allow her sometimes to be shut up by her husband'.[15] Divorce was in effect impossible. For the very few wealthy enough to embark on the process it involved a public exposure that was itself ruinous. The Marquis of Halifax writes in *Advice to his Daughter* (1688), 'The causes of *Separation* are now so very coarse, that few are confident enough to buy their *Liberty* at the price of having their *Modesty* so exposed. And for *disparity of Minds*, which above all other things requireth a *Remedy*, the *Laws* have made no provision.'[16]

It is not surprising that the law as it was applied tended to reinforce social practice, especially when it is remembered that what Locke repeatedly calls 'the protection of property' was more central to legal practice and to statute than any chimerical concerns with freedom, equality or justice. The law, in other words, tended to be applied in favour of men and of the rich. This is why, for instance, Lovelace has so little fear of prosecution whatever he does to Clarissa. Daughters were almost totally in the power of their fathers, and servant girls at the mercy of their masters; what are described as seductions are often what we would call rapes; even independent women, unmarried daughters over twenty-one or widows, needed men to manage their property, and had virtually no chance of respectable employment. In these circumstances it would seem that the happy, mutual, companionable marriage envisaged by Thomson as the resolution of natural and social pressures would be a virtual impossibility.

The witness of much imaginative writing is, however, rather different, and eighteenth-century fiction in particular again and again manipulates the circumstances of the world so that they may reach a culmination in the happy and stable union of a man and a woman. It does this with varying degrees of ingenuity and plausibility, but on the whole attempts it within the conventions of its own discourse, as if to assert that this is the way things *can* be in the world. A novel that ends in a happy marriage thus carries a double charge. It has an ending that the reader, alert to the circumstances and practices of the prevailing culture, knows is not the norm, but also one that implies that if things work out as they should this should be the norm. (It is true that this is the case more with novels written by men than those written by women, which tend to be more romantic and fantastical, perhaps as women were less sanguine about the likelihood of a companionable marriage being realised in actuality.)

At the end of *Roderick Random* the egotistic, wayward, impulsive, unreliable serial fornicator of a hero is restored to his paternal estate in Scotland and, after numerous adventures and hardships, due in equal measure to the wickedness of the world and his own folly, is at last affluent, and is married to an angel called Narcissa, who is pregnant. He has cause to go to London, but will not, because

> my dear angel has been qualmish of late, and begins to grow remarkably round in the waist; so that I cannot leave her in such an interesting situation, which I hope will produce something to crown my felicity.[17]

This ending has not been contrived through the operation of a just providential plot that apportions rewards and punishments according as the characters merit them. Nor is it the culmination of an elaborate mechanism that knits together innumerable threads in a coherent pattern, though there is some gesture in this direction. Nor, though *Roderick Random* is often thought of as picaresque, is it the lucky last resting-place in a career governed by chance, circumstance and contingency. There is some sense in which the conclusion is presented as fitting – or so at least the first-person narrator seems to think, and with Smollett it is absolutely impossible to detect a coherent authorial viewpoint behind the narrator.

Roderick is not a true amorist or a rake or a determined seducer, but from the time that he leaves his austere grandfather's home for university in Edinburgh he has no scruple in availing himself of whatever opportunities come his way, and many of the episodes that animate his story involve sexual encounters. When he finds himself in favour with the ladies in Edinburgh he says that this was 'an intoxicating piece of good fortune to one of my amorous complexion!' (27). The circles, many very humble, in which he moves feature frequent sexual escapades of a rather unglamorous kind, and are marked by plotting, recriminations, jealousies and revenges. In a fairly typical episode early in the novel Roderick gets the maid-servant of his employer, Mr Crab, pregnant. Knowing, however, that she has been sleeping with Crab, he persuades her to tell Crab the baby is his. Mr Crab, foreseeing troublesome consequences, 'was far from being overjoyed at this proof of his vigour'; it was not 'that he dreaded any domestic grumblings and reproaches from his wife, whom he kept in perfect subjection', but that he feared it would give a rival practitioner an advantage. He therefore tries to persuade the maid that she is not pregnant but suffering from some female disorder, which he gives her pills to cure. The pills are in fact designed to procure an abortion. The maid, knowing she is pregnant, rejects the pills and threatens to publish Crab's disgrace if he does not provide for her. Crab's resource is not to do this, but to persuade Roderick to embark on a career as a ship's surgeon, which should be profitable in view of the likely war with Spain, and to give him the money for the journey to London. Roderick, who wanted to leave the bullying Crab anyway, accepts even though 'I was very well apprised of his motive, which was no other than a design to lay the bastard to my charge after my departure', and thus be rid of the maid (Chapter 3).

Episodes of a similar harshness, self-interest and opportunism recur throughout the novel in a representation of a sexual culture that is degraded and nihilistic, and in which women exhibit a spirit or ruthlessness equal to or greater than that of the men. It is a culture of mutual and universal exploitation.

Any gesture in the direction of a more sincere or idealistic passion is demolished and ridiculed in the narrative. When Roderick is in London and waiting to be examined in his professional competence at Surgeon's-Hall a young friend tells him about 'a certain lady', 'a five thousand pounder . . . besides expectations' whom he hopes to marry. He was introduced to her by a footman, who has been paid for his good offices, and now,

> I have proposed marriage, and the day is fixed; she's a charming creature; writes like an angel. O Lord! She can repeat all the English tragedies as well as e'er a player in Drury Lane! And indeed is so fond of plays, that, to be near the stage, she has taken lodgings in a court hard by the theatre. (87)

In other words she is a failed actress now working as a prostitute in the notorious precincts of Drury Lane. Her lover shows Roderick a love-letter she has written to him. The language of elegant romantic love has been degraded into ludicrous and ignorant travesty, in which the vocabulary of the real world shoulders out the locutions of elevated passion:

> DEER KREETER, – As you are the animable hopjack of my contemplayshins, your aydear is infernally skimming befoer my kemerycal fansee, when Morfy sends his puppies to the heys of slipping mortals; and when Febus shines from his merry-dying throne.

> Wherupon, I shall canseeif old whorie time has lost his pinners, as
> also Cupid his harrows, until thou enjoy sweet propose in the loaf-
> seek harms of thy faithfool to command.   CLAYRENDER

Clarinda's misspellings constitute an alternative – and truer – lexicon in
which to describe the world Roderick finds himself in: puppies, slip-
ping mortals, merry-dying, Cupid's harrows, and loafseek harms.
Indeed, as was suggested at the outset of this chapter, the world of the
eighteenth-century realistic novel is one in which it is effectively impossible to discover a language for genuine feeling. At moments of genuine
emotion Roderick, who is normally voluble, is often struck dumb.

The project of the narrative must nevertheless be to effect a negotiation out of this culture of violently degraded gender relations towards
the personal and social gratifications of its conclusion. An intermediate
episode comes about a third of the way through the novel, when
Roderick contracts an acquaintance with a young woman,

> who found means to make a conquest of my heart, and upon whom
> I prevailed, after much attendance and solicitation, to give me a
> promise of marriage. As this beautiful creature passed for a rich
> heiress, I blessed my good fortune . . .   (113)

This move towards love and prosperity, signalled in the studious rectitude of the language, is halted abruptly when Roderick enters her chamber and finds her in bed with a man. Matters seem to become only worse
when shortly afterwards he discovers her almost dying of venereal
disease and starvation in a room neighbouring his own. Her condition
'filled my heart with compassion' (120) and he tries to help her. She
expresses her gratitude in refined terms: 'You are too generous! – I wish
I could live to express my gratitude; but, alas! I perish for want' (121).
Roderick manages to restore her to life, and as he himself is suffering
from a venereal condition they decide to share a room and lead one
another back to health: 'I found in her not only an agreeable companion, whose conversation greatly alleviated my chagrin, but also a careful
nurse, who served me with the utmost fidelity and affection' (121). This
relationship cannot issue into the kind of conclusion the book eventually
offers because Miss Williams, for all her refinement, is a prostitute, and
neither she nor Roderick has any money. It is, none the less, a witness
that better relationships between men and women than have been met
hitherto in the narrative are possible. This is confirmed when Miss
Williams tells Roderick her 'history'. A prosperous young woman, and

an enthusiast for fictional romances and poetry, she was saved from a rapist by a handsome young man who subsequently seduced her, got her pregnant, and abandoned her in order to marry another woman. By exploitation and deception she was forced into a career of ever more squalid prostitution until she ended up in the condition from which Roderick rescued her. Miss Williams is largely victim, forced into degradation by circumstances that are only partly her own fault (giving herself to her first lover). She is not innately wicked; she is saved by Roderick's compassion; she proves companionable and helpful; and she does, on her recovery, secure employment at least marginally more respectable than her last.

The possibilities opened up in this episode do not have any immediate sequel in terms of personal relations or of any developing narrative because Roderick is press-ganged, and the next sixth of the novel comprises a blistering account of his experiences in the navy and on the Carthagena expedition. Eventually he is left destitute and injured on the seashore in Sussex. He is taken into the household of an eccentric and slatternly blue-stocking whose pretensions to learning de-feminise her, but who has a beautiful niece, Narcissa. Narcissa inspires very fervid emotions in Roderick: her 'whole person', which includes her 'aspect noble, ingenuous and humane', was 'so ravishingly delightful, that it was impossible for any creature endued with sensibility, to see her without admiring, and to admire without loving her to excess': 'when she spoke to me, my soul was thrilled with an ecstasy of tumultuous joy!' (220). As may be guessed from these reactions Narcissa is an interesting construction of femininity because she is very attractive sexually, and sexually responsive to Roderick, as well as being attracted by his sensibility and intellect, which have an opportunity to emerge in her company as they have not in his career up to this point. She is also virtuous and accomplished in a way that enhances rather than diminishes her femininity. She also has what Roderick has not, money.

Narcissa is in fact designed for a different plot from that which eventually embraces her. She lives with a coarse brother whose best friend is a gross country squire, Sir Timothy. She is to marry Sir Timothy, while her brother marries Sir Timothy's sister, 'by which means, as their fortunes were pretty equal, the young ladies would be provided for, and their brothers be never the poorer' (221). This is the quintessential eighteenth-century arranged marriage, but it is a story that *Roderick Random* must thwart if it is to make its way to its ideal conclusion, and Narcissa's distaste for a match with Sir Timothy would not itself be potent enough to thwart it.

What *is* potent enough is that Sir Timothy, who had 'a good deal of the brute in him' attempts to rape Narcissa. Roderick intervenes, knocks Sir Timothy senseless, and catches the fainting Narcissa in his arms. This is a moment of high emotional and sexual excitement for Roderick:

> My soul was thrilled with tumultuous joy at feeling the object of my dearest wishes within my arms; and while she lay insensible, I could not refrain from applying my cheek to hers, and ravishing a kiss.
>
> (229)

This is a narrative we have visited before: being seduced by her rescuer was what precipitated Miss Williams's career of degradation. It cannot be replicated. Narcissa wakes; Roderick manages to restrain himself from declaring his passion, and the immediate crisis passes, but not without a great deal of mutual emotional recognition. This is one recuperation of a narrative that had had a tragic outcome, but even so the story of *Roderick Random* has not yet been manoeuvred into a position where a union between Roderick and Narcissa could be plausibly acceptable, and so there is another violent reversion of fortunes. Roderick is abducted by Sir Timothy's agents, finds himself in France, and is soon in bed with an innkeeper's daughter:

> In vain did my reason suggest the respect that I owed to my dear mistress Narcissa; the idea of that lovely charmer rather increased than allayed the ferment of my spirits; and the young paysanne had no reason to complain of my remembrance.   (240)

The elevation of his passion for Narcissa has not allayed the pressure of his 'amorous complexion'; a marriage with Narcissa will somehow have to accommodate it.

When Roderick eventually returns to England he sets himself up in the clothes and with the air of a gentleman, in the hope of attracting an heiress. In the course of various adventures, all abortive, he meets Narcissa again at Bath. He is thrown into violent agitation, and she too exhibits strong psychosomatic symptoms: 'the roses instantly vanished from her polished cheeks, and returned in a moment with a lovely glow that overspread her lovely neck, while her enchanting bosom heaved with strong emotion' (333). Roderick is soon exposed as a fortune hunter, and eventually imprisoned in the Marshalsea for debt. His good-hearted uncle, Tom Bowling, rescues him and proposes a trading voyage. Even though it means abandoning hopes of Narcissa, Roderick agrees, but does manage one brief meeting before leaving. His language lacks the resources to describe this event, and he yearns for the expressive powers of another art: 'O! That I were endowed with the expression of a Raphael, the graces of a Guido, the magic touches of a Titian . . .' (399). Few readers would have seen even in reproduction any paintings of the Italian renaissance, and so this desire functions entirely rhetorically in pointing up the inadequacies of any available discourse to convey the experience.

The voyage prospers, largely through slaving, and in South America Roderick meets up with his long-lost father, himself now prosperous. His father learns of Narcissa and says he will help secure a marriage. They return to England, and a wedding is arranged, even though Narcissa has now been disinherited by her brother. Prosperous social circumstance, sexual fervour and virtuous passion are now aligned, and combined in Roderick's words as he looks at his bride-to-be:

> her looks glowed with modesty and love; and her bosom, through the veil of gauze that shaded it, afforded a prospect of Elysium! I received this inestimable gift of Providence as became me.   (422)

The stunning lack of specification in the last phrase again registers the insufficiency of the language available to Roderick to treat the actual experience of love, and something similar happens when he describes the wedding night itself. His language rises tumescently to render the experience of frantic expectation: after the wedding breakfast,

> I cautioned my Narcissa against exposing her health by sitting up too late, and she was prevailed upon to withdraw with her maid to an apartment destined for us. When she left the room, her face was overspread with a blush that set all my blood in a state of fermentation, and made every pulse beat with tenfold vigour! She was so cruel as to let me remain in this condition a full half-hour; when no longer able to restrain my impatience, I broke from the company, burst into her chamber, pushed out her confidante, locked the door, and found her – O heaven and earth! a . . .

Found her a what? 'found her . . . a feast a thousand times more delicious than my most sanguine hope presaged!' He cannot go beyond this appetitive metaphor, or not with Narcissa – 'but let me not profane the chaste mysteries of Hymen. I was the happiest of men!' (423).

Chaste mysteries? There is little chaste and less mysterious about what went on, but the decorum of the narrative requires that the language lift this event out of the merely sexual and match the sublimity of the union that the story has contrived. The narrative of *Roderick Random*, rough and ready as it is, manages through its manipulation of circumstances to reconcile the impulses of nature and the detail of cultural predicament, and to articulate that reconciliation as no other available genre than the realist novel could do.

What is managed crudely in *Roderick Random* is achieved with infinitely more completeness and subtlety in *Tom Jones*. If the mechanism of Fielding's plot has all the elegance and ingenuity of a Harrison chronometer, Smollett's is a wooden Bavarian wall-clock, and this is an important distinction. Fielding's novel foregrounds its author's excellent artistry, and so makes of his novel a *tour de force* of precise and obvious manipulation, and it is of course so presented that it seems to have been, at its conclusion, a mirror of the Providence that regulates all things, but which only gets a look-in in *Roderick Random* when Roderick describes his bride's bosom as a 'gift of providence'. By contrast with Fielding's hubristic authorial ostentation, Smollett's first-person narration appears virtually undirected: Roderick's life has the seeming randomness of a tennis-ball rebounding from the angled walls of a Real Tennis court (before his birth his mother had dreamed that 'she was delivered of a tennis-ball' – 9)[18] and so seems to reflect the contingency of ordinary human life more persuasively than Tom Jones's, and the unmerited happy ending of his story is in some ways, preposterous though it is, more plausible.

Fielding works with similar ingredients to Smollett. His hero is animated by strong appetites, especially sexuality; the hero is in love with a beautiful, attractive and virtuous woman, but is capable of being distracted; the exigencies of the marriage-market operate against their union; the circumstances of modern life and human venality frustrate and delay it, and at the same time draw the hero particularly into predicaments which reflect ill on him, and at times tend to corrupt him. Where Fielding goes far beyond Smollett, however, is that in so conspicuously shaping these ingredients into a pattern he suggests the other possibility. If there were no supervising and designing Providence of which the authorial plot is the emblem, then the world would indeed be an alarming and vicious chaos. In Fielding much more than in Smollett the reader senses that the retrieval of the story and its participants from catastrophe is a very close shave. In Smollett there is such a storm of events and reversals that the story might as well work out favourably for Roderick and Narcissa as not. Without the existence of an overall design in *Tom Jones* things would be much more likely to go wrong than otherwise, especially as the force of goodness and benevolence in the greater part of humanity as we see it is intermittent and unreliable in comparison with the consistent pressure of self-interest and malice.

The ending of *Tom Jones* has a greater symmetry than that of *Roderick Random*. It brings together two people, two households and two estates, and Tom and Sophia have produced two children, a boy and a girl. The personal relations of the hero and heroine are the perfect epitome of an ideally adjusted cultural structure. This structure is, however, absolutely dependent on this relationship at its heart, because all is not in fact quite as regular as it looks. Tom is not Mr Allworthy's son, but the son of his sister by a clandestine union; Mr Western has no son to inherit his property and most of it has been made over to Tom. But for the love between Tom and Sophia the estates of both Allworthy and Western would have fallen to the proprietorship of the odious Blifil, unsuitable to be the earthly steward of any property (which is why the denouement accords him only an income). The union of Tom and Sophia is thus culturally sanative: it is on its way to restoring a society that was losing its natural health. That Blifil would be incapable of this is indicated in that what sexual interest he has in Sophia is perverse, as the author explains at the point when Sophia is to be coerced into a union with him:

> nor was his desire at all lessened by the aversion which he discovered in her to himself. On the contrary, this served rather to heighten the pleasure he proposed in rifling her charms, as it added triumph to lust; nay, he had some further views, from obtaining the absolute possession of her person, which we detest too much to mention; and revenge itself was not without its share in the gratification which he promised himself. (7.6)

The success of the union of Tom and Sophia does not depend only on the exclusion of Blifil. It also depends on a repudiation of the ideology of love with which Allworthy in his role as a magistrate berates Jenny Jones when he is informed that she is Tom's mother. He tells Jenny of the appalling social consequences of having an illegitimate child, and asks, among other rhetorical questions, 'Can any pleasure compensate these evils? ... Or can any carnal appetite so overpower your reason ... as to prevent your flying with affright and terror from a crime which carries such punishment always with it?' The implied answer to these questions is no, but the actual answer is 'yes, it often does'. 'Love,' he goes onto assert, 'as it is a laudable, is a rational passion . . .' (1.7). Even if he were addressing the right person, the true mother of Tom, and even if there were any point in such an *ex post facto* lecture, this would not be a helpful observation, as 'rational passion' is a verbal construct without any psychological correlative. It is exactly as useful as Friar Lawrence's recommendation to Romeo to 'love moderately' (*Romeo and Juliet*, 2.6). What little we know of Mr Allworthy's own marriage indicates that it was grounded in affection, not reason. It is the force of mutual attraction between Tom and Sophia and their willingness to contest and resist familial and institutional authority that enables the happy and redemptive conclusion.

The way to this conclusion is not, however, simple: if love is something which the magistrate cannot comprehend or control it is by that token lawless. It is liable to be betrayed by Tom's own sexual instincts, and by the sexual allure that attracts Lady Bellaston to him, with the corruption and danger that his affair with her entails. It could be prevented by Sophia's jealousy of Tom's other amours, or ruined by Lord Fellamar's ruthless lust. There is also the risk that when time and opportunity come Tom and Sophia may be unable to speak their love, not because, like Blifil's, it is unspeakable, but because their culture has not supplied them with the language they need, and this is precisely the focus of narrative attention in the critical penultimate chapter of the book, when Western lugs Allworthy out of the room and the pair are left alone together:

> The lovers were now alone, and it will, I question not, appear strange to many readers, that those who had so much to say to one another when danger and difficulty attended their conversation, and who seemed so eager to rush into each other's arms when so many bars lay in their way . . . should both remain for some time silent and motionless.   (18.12)

They sit with their eyes cast down 'for some minutes in perfect silence'. Jones tries to speak, 'but was absolutely incapable, muttering only, or rather sighing out, some broken words'. The moment is not just amorous, but social too, and they do not know how to negotiate it. Eventually Sophia breaks the silence, but by going off in the wrong direction, in politely congratulating Jones on the discovery which has revealed him to be Allworthy's nephew. She is not simply evading the topic of love; in speaking as she does she is pointing out to him that unless he can explain himself (i.e., explain Lady Bellaston) he will not have her. Jones stumbles into an explanation of his letter to Lady Bellaston proposing marriage. This enables Sophia to drive the matter home hard and directly:

> Mr Jones, have I not enough to resent? After what past at Upton, so soon to engage in a new amour with another woman, while I fancied, and you pretended, your heart was bleeding for me? . . . what happiness can I assure myself of with a man capable of so much inconstancy?

This prompts in Tom a flood of elevated rhetoric deriving more from heroic romance and drama than from the real world: 'O! My Sophia do not doubt the sincerity of the purest passion that ever inflamed a human breast. Think, adorable creature, of my situation, of my despair.' If he had thought there was any chance of obtaining Sophia, 'it would not have been in the power of any other woman to have inspired a thought which the severest chastity could have condemned. Inconstancy to you! O Sophia!' There is no bridge between the direct-ness of Sophia's 'How can I trust you?' question and Tom's high-flown asseveration. The narrative impasse is a linguistic impasse. Sophia's resort is not to take Tom's words on trust, but to offer him time, 'A twelvemonth, perhaps', in which to prove himself. In other words the only thing that can bring Sophia and Tom together is more story, but as Fielding pointed out as early as the beginning of Book Eighteen, 'the number of pages' available were scarcely enough to tell the story that had to be told, let alone another year's worth.

What happens is the intervention of another voice and another discourse, attuned not to the careful negotiation of civil relationships but to the urgencies of passion. Squire Western bursts in: 'To her, boy, to her, go to her; – . . . Hath she appointed the day boy, What, shall it be tomorrow . . .?' Tom demurs.

> I thought thou hadst been a lad of higher metal than to give way to a parcel of maidenish tricks; – I tell thee 'tis all flim-flam. Zoodikers! She'd have the wedding to-night with all her heart. Woud'st not, Sophy, . . . What, art dumb? Why dost not speak?

She does not speak because she and Tom are trapped within a discourse that cannot articulate love as an irrational passion. Her way out is temporarily to reconstruct herself in another image, that of the dutiful daughter: 'What would my papa have me do?' Give her hand this moment. The discourse of filial piety is one that she can use: 'Well, sir, I will obey you. – There is my hand, Mr Jones.' And tomorrow will be the day. We do not hear Tom and Sophia speak another word to each other for the rest of the book, but they are left 'to enjoy a few tender moments alone'.

The reward that Tom and Sophia enjoy in a happy life together is not theirs by virtue of their own essential natures. It has had to be mediated through the complex circumstances of modern life, and it is powerless until it is given utterance. Marriage is a social institution and it can only be negotiated in language, the medium of social intercourse, but marriage is also personal and physical and needs other words. Fielding's solution to the lack of a language sufficient to the situation of Tom and Sophia is to bring three discourses together, to create a polyphony out of Tom's elevated heroics, Sophia's directness and Squire Western's earthy vulgarity, and he does so by means of the only literary device available, a piece of narrative. It is 1749 and the representation of the relations of men and women in the new real world has found its genre: the novel can bring the impulses of sex and the constraints of society with their incompatible discourses together through the manipulation of events in time.

5
Writing by Women: the Female Poets and Mrs Manley

In the awareness of most readers it is probably with Jane Austen at the turn of the nineteenth century that authorship becomes recognised as a practice of women as well as men, and certainly by the middle and later nineteenth century, despite the use of male names by some female authors, the question of female authorship is no longer seriously problematic. Many readers could probably identify at least two considerable female authors of fiction before Jane Austen in Fanny Burney and Mrs Radcliffe, and they might well also be aware of Mary Wollstonecraft, feminist and novelist, at the end of the eighteenth century. Students of literary history would be able to identify more female authors, perhaps beginning with Aphra Behn (1640–89), playwright and novelist in the Restoration period. Then perhaps the dramatist Susannah Centlivre (1667?–1723), author of *The Busybody* (1709) among other successful comedies. The scandalous novelist Mrs Manley might be known through references to her notorious *Atalantis* narratives of misdoings in high life, as in *The Rape of the Lock* (3.165), 'As long as *Atalantis* shall be read'. The name of Lady Mary Wortley Montagu (1689–1762) would probably be familiar as that of a woman of letters around the time of Pope and as author of some verse. Eliza Haywood (1693?–1756) might be recognised as a working author (she gets unpleasantly libelled in *The Dunciad*) and for her novel *Betsy Thoughtless* (1751) and it could be that some susurrus of naughtiness would attach to her name which, if known at all, would be more familiar than her work. From the middle of the century the name Sarah Fielding would stand out, as Henry Fielding's sister and as author of *The Adventures of David Simple* (1744), though the suspicion would be that her brother was responsible for what was best in her work. Elizabeth Inchbald (1753–1821) would be known as a dramatist and as author of *A Simple*

Story (1791), and there might be various other names throughout the century such as Mary Davys, Frances Sheridan, Charlotte Lennox, Clara Reeve and Mary Hays which would be dimly recognisable as those of female authors. A few names of women associated with famous authors would also be familiar – Swift's Stella (Esther Johnson), addressee of his *Journal to Stella;* Pope's friend Martha Blount, to whom his second *Moral Essay*, the 'Epistle to a Lady' is dedicated; Richardson's correspondent and adviser, Lady Bradshaigh; Hester Thrale Piozzi, friend and memorialist of Dr Johnson.

Not one of these eighteenth-century names, with the possible exception of Fanny Burney, whose *Evelina* (1778) has attracted widespread recognition and admiration, is connected as author with any of the works commonly thought of as constituting the canon of writing in the period. Why? Why are there no 'great' female authors in the eighteenth century? There is a host of social, cultural and economic reasons, most of them discomfitting to a twentieth-century consciousness. There was a widespread belief that women could not really write; women writers tended to be ghettoised into the treatment of certain 'lesser' – mainly domestic and romantic – topics; the legal status of women, in so far as it existed at all, did not prompt women into the world of public authorship; it was harder for women than for men to receive payment commensurate with the demands of authorship; social custom and prejudice relegated women to the circle of domestic life and activities; contemporary criticism valorised 'masculine' topics and manners in writing; public authorship by women was tainted by an association with loose sexual morality; women's education excluded them from the culture of the classical world which many authors presented as the foundation on which all later Western culture was constructed. There is no real point in pretending that these things did not obtain, although of course attitudes fluctuated with time and from individual to individual, and indeed some of them are sustained into our own period, and still constitute part of an ideological matrix and traditional pattern of power and authority that requires a strong feminist challenge. Undeniably in the eighteenth century literature was overwhelmingly a male practice, even though it often treated the lives of women with greater insight, recognition and sensitivity than had ever been witnessed before in the established corpus of English writing.

Granted all this, the next thing to be noticed about the catalogue of eighteenth-century women writers given here is just how full it is. There were some female authors in the seventeenth century, and before, who commanded considerable respect and even became, like the poet

Katherine Phillips (1631–64), beacons for later women writers, but no comparable list could be drawn up for any period before the eighteenth century. What the list attests is that, inadequate and limited as it may have been, from the first decade of the eighteenth century women had a place, however small, in the world of English letters.

This chapter will not undertake a project of reinstatement. The recuperation of women's writing in the eighteenth century has in any case been under way strongly for two or three decades and is increasingly supported by publishers willing to bring out good editions of works by women authors, such as the Penguin edition of Delarivier Manley's *New Atalantis* edited by Rosalind Ballaster (1992), to give an instance of an author with whom this chapter is going to be concerned.

Two things principally will be attempted here. The first is to look at some of the verse by women collected in Roger Lonsdale's indispensable anthology of eighteenth-century women's poetry[1] and to notice some of the concerns and voices exhibited there. The second is to examine the case of Mrs Manley as an early eighteenth-century working writer, looking particularly at the work which initially made her reputation (for good or ill), *The Secret History of Queen Zarah* (1705) and at her fictionalised autobiography, *The Adventures of Rivella* (1714).

In 1721 Penelope Aubin published a novel whose title-page begins *The Life of Madam de Beaumount, a French Lady; who lived in a Cave in Wales above fourteen years undiscovered, being forced to fly France for her Religion; and of the cruel Usage she had there.* It is a narrative comprising some remarkable settings and incidents which subject female virtue and the protestant consciousness to ordeal by romantic adventure and astonishing event. At appropriate moments it evinces a pietistic morality that became recognised as one of the strains proper to novels by women.[2] What is interesting for present purposes, however, is the tone of the Preface, in which Penelope Aubin talks not as a sympathetic narrator of the adventures but in her role as author; here she writes with a witty sophistication, a fluency in the culture of her time, and an assurance that has nothing to do with gender, and she is not faking a manner that is identifiably masculine. She amusingly compares some of the extraordinary things that have happened in Britain in the years leading up to the publication of *The Life of Madam de Beaumount*, notably the speculative insanity of the South Sea Bubble and the cult success of Madame D'Aulnoy's *History of the Fairies* (1716), with some of the events of her narrative:

A Madness has for some time possest the *English*, and we are turn'd Projectors, exceeded the *French* in extravagant Whimsies, and parted with our Money as easily, as if we had forgot that we were to live a day longer; . . . The Knavish Part of us are employ'd in getting Money; and the Thoughtless, which are the major part, on searching for something new to divert their Spleen: the Tales of Fairies, and Elves, take with them, and the most improbable things please best.

The Story I here present the Publick withal, is very extraordinary, but not quite so incredible as these. This is an Age of Wonders, and certainly we can doubt of nothing after what we have seen in our Days: yet there is one thing in the Story of Madam de *Beaumount* very strange; which is, that she, and her Daughter, are very religious, and very virtuous, and that there were two honest clergymen living at one time. In the Lord de *Beaumount*'s Story, there is yet something more surprising; which is, that he loved an absent Wife so well, that he obstinately refused a pretty Lady a Favour.[3]

In the last sentence here Penelope Aubin touches on a topic, the unreliability and inconstancy of husbands, that is recurrent in eighteenth-century poems by women, but it is more importantly in her tone as an author that she echoes them, and exhibits an ease and assurance that seems altogether natural. She is able to write convincingly about the ambient culture, and to touch lightly on topics of interest both to the polity and to the spirit of the nation, without any touch of deference, or apology for intervention in matters outside a supposed female realm. She comments genially on the morals of the age, and at the same time defends what she is offering to the public. And after this passage she goes on to note, in a voice that is at once that of the urban ironist and of the Horatian cultural critic, that the virtuous endurance of her heroine and hero might be thought a little more plausible if account is taken of the fact that her story is set in Wales, sparsely populated and remote from the corruptions of the metropolis. What all this amounts to is that Penelope Aubin writes with complete assurance of her right to write, and the same conviction is equally characteristic of the women poets.

Because the lives of most women were determined by the characters and manners of the men whose chattels they became on marriage, and who in any case determined the privileged discourses of contemporary culture, the verse by women often positions itself against men. It complains of oppression, by male contempt, by the authority of husbands, by the falseness of lovers, and by the law, but it is seldom querulous: it is more frequently marked by vigour, wit, anger, righteous

indignation, above all by energy and freedom, than it is by the manner
of complaint. Writing becomes a proper women's space, in which they
can say what they will. It might well be that an age which imposed rigid
and exacting codes of conduct, manners, relationship and even of dress,
made the private space of writing a greater field of liberation for
women than it was for men. Because men had far greater opportunities
to profess and succeed in literature as a career their writing was a public
exercise continually subjected or liable to public scrutiny. It thus had to
conform to decorums of manner, form, mode and subject to be proper.
Women's writing was in a sense improper *de facto*, not bound by a
system of decorum that would anyway exclude it.

It is interesting that this is perhaps least true of Lady Mary Wortley
Montagu, who was a society woman, lived the life of the consort of a
man highly placed in public life, and was acquainted with, and corre-
sponded with, some of the most distinguished male writers (notably
Pope before they quarrelled) of her age. She was a very accomplished
poet, and fluent in a range of poetic manners, but her voice, as for example in her 'Six Town Eclogues', can read as exercises in established modes
articulating the values and attitudes of a cultural élite.[4] Even she,
however, can startle with a frankness that is seldom found in the male
poets – and she does this best when her voice comes unmistakably from
the core of female experience. For instance, she leads to the conclusion
of her epitaph on John Hughes and Sarah Drew, two country lovers
who were killed by lightning on the eve of their wedding, like this:

> Who knows if 'twas not kindly done?
> For had they seen the next year's sun,
> A beaten wife and cuckwold swain
> Had jointly cursed the marriage chain.

> (Lonsdale 41)

This poem in fact belongs in the somewhat disagreeable tradition of
cultivated writers exercising themselves in a rather low and jocose style
on the misfortunes of the poor and uncultivated, as seen for instance in
Milton's verses on the holiday-time death of the Cambridge University
carrier, for whom 'Too long vacation hastened on his term.'[5] Even so,
the irruption of realism in the place where decorum might have recommended pathos is striking. In a similar vein, though treating a subject
from a social world nearer her own, she writes 'A Receipt to Cure the
Vapours' for Delia, who is languishing fretfully on the loss of her love.
The cure is simple:

I, like you, was born a woman,
  Well I know what vapours mean:
The disease, alas! is common;
  Single, we have all the spleen.

All the morals that they tell us
  Never cured the sorrow yet:
Choose, among the pretty fellows,
  One of honour, youth and wit.

Prithee hear him every morning,
  And the least an hour or two;
Once again at night returning –
  I believe the dose will do.   (Lonsdale 45)

And better than any male poet Lady Mary writes engagingly of the kind
of person who would attract her, and of what the pleasures and rewards
of a private companionship between the sexes might be. She looks for
a man who 'Would value his pleasure, contribute to mine':

No pedant, yet learnèd; not rake-helly gay,
Or laughing, because he has nothing to say;
To my whole sex obliging and free,
Yet never be fond of any but me;
In public, preserve the decorums are just,
And show in his eyes he is true to his trust;
Then rarely approach, and respectfully bow,
Yet not fulsomely pert, nor yet foppishly low.

But when the long hours of public are past,
And we meet with champagne and a chicken at last,
May every fond pleasure that hour endear;
Be banished afar both discretion and fear.
Forgetting or scorning the airs of the crowd,
He may cease to be formal, and I to be proud,
Till lost in the joy, we confess that we live,
And he may be rude, and yet I may forgive.
                    'The Lover: a Ballad' (Lonsdale 42)

The securing of a space of liberty in the experience of a shared privacy,
free from the decorums of the public world, in this poem echoes the

ability of women's poetry to make for itself a place for its own voice undetermined by public literary convention. One of the attractions of the piece is the simplicity of its rhythm and rhyme. Cast in the form of a ballad, the resilient tetrameters have a buoyancy that transmits the vitality of the poet's engagement in her topic. Largely because of the eminence of Pope and of Dryden before him it has become inevitable that eighteenth-century verse is associated with the heroic couplet. There was, however, a mass of verse written and printed in other forms. In particular there was great inventiveness shown in the popular ballads, narrative poems, satirical squibs and political songs that were published and often sold separately or in higgledy-piggledy anthologies, collections and 'Miscellanies' on the streets. This is a body of verse that has great demotic energy, and a lot of its spirit makes its way into poems by women.

This is apparent even in a rather refined piece like the petition of Anne Finch, Countess of Winchelsea, 'for an Absolute Retreat'. There is a brevity and directness in her appeal for a life of rural simplicity which is lodged in the patterns of the verse, and which is far removed from strainings after a more literary pastoralism. She wishes to be simply dressed, a wish that would have had all the more force in an age when elaborate constraints and conventions of costume concretised many of the other conditions that disciplined the lives of women:

> Clothe me, Fate, though not so gay,
> Clothe me light and fresh as May;
> In the fountains let me view
> All my habit cheap and new,
> Such as, when sweet zephyrs fly,
> With their motions may comply,
> Gently waving to express
> An affected carelessness.
> No perfumes have there a part,
> Borrowed from the chemist's art,
> But such as rise from flowery beds,
> Or the falling jasmine sheds. (Lonsdale 10)

Apart from its strong and clear simplicity, another feature of this poem which characterises much women's verse in this period is, despite its undeniably idealistic feel, its pragmatism. It is about the manners of living, the style and the quality of life. When Pope begins his limpid Horatian poem about the desirability of the retired life, 'On Solitude', the opening verses are preoccupied with the complex social and political principle of proprietorship:

> Happy the man, whose wish and care
> A few paternal acres bound,
> Content to breathe his native air
>   In his own ground.
>
> Whose herds with milk, whose fields with bread,
> Whose flocks supply him with attire,
> Whose trees in summer, yield him shade,
>   In winter fire.[6]

The conditions of happiness and of the style of life which will offer 'health of body, peace of mind' (line 11) are those of hereditary ownership untrammelled by any landlord/tenant relationship or by the complex reciprocities of feudal tenure; and yet the relationship of Pope's happy man to the countryside is that of the proprietor to whom his possessions bring tribute. Pope's conception of happiness is thus not just a state of being, a locality, a way of behaving or a state of mind: it is a condition predicated on freedom established by heredity and on security of possession in fee simple. By contrast, Finch envisages a country life which recovers the lawless simplicities of Eden and in which her relation with the good things of the earth is just a matter of them sharing the same space:

> Courteous Fate! Then give me there
> Only plain and wholesome fare;
> Fruits indeed (would heaven bestow),
> All that did in Eden grow,
> . . . .
> Grapes, with juice so crowded up
> As breaking through the native cup;
> Figs yet growing, candied o'er
> By the sun's attracting power,
> Cherries, with the downy peach,
> All within my easy reach;
> Whilst, creeping near the humble ground,
> Should the strawberry be found,
> . . . .

Women's verse quite naturally covers many of the same topics as are addressed in verse by men: fashion, passion, manners, common philosophy, the natural world, religion and politics. There are many poems from which it would be impossible, and not especially useful, to determine the gender of the author, not because the women write like men but because they write like poets. One example might be the little animal fable by Anne Finch about a philosophical pig and an insensible sheep and goat being taken to the slaughter (Lonsdale 11). Other poems confidently address public topics but do so from a declaredly female point of view: one amusing instance is Susannah Centlivre's energetic warning to Charles XII of Sweden not to lend his arm to a Jacobite invasion of Britain, because British women would not for a moment put up with his rugged northern austerity (Lonsdale 55). Many women, none the less, write about the female condition as they experienced it most intimately and deeply, as wives.

When in 1979 Elaine Showalter categorised writing by women into three phases, feminine, feminist and female, she was drawing on texts from the post-Romantic period, and engaging with debates among feminists about where the focus should lie in approaching women's writing, past and present. Feminine art, in which women authors see no choice but to present themselves in the roles given them by a patriarchal society and imitate writing by men, is, according to Showalter, 'typically oblique, displaced, ironic and subversive; one has to read it between the lines, in the missed possibilities of the text.' The verse I am about to discuss is more robust than this, not subject to an enforced indirectness or tentativeness. Equally it is unlike writing of the feminist phase, deliberately campaigning for a social revolution to remedy the evils of masculine oppression and the structural injustices of society. It is more like Showalter's 'female phase', which she sees as developing from the 1920s and in which 'women reject both imitation and protest – two forms of dependency – and turn instead to female experience as the source of an autonomous art'.[7]

The danger of this taxonomy, as feminist and other writers have noted, is that it may tend to do what male nineteenth-century critics did when reviewing books by (or apparently by) women – ghettoise women's writing into the realms of the home and the heart, thus excluding them from the centres of cultural and political authority and influence. In the nineteenth century such strategic cultural exclusion can be seen not just as a patriarchal prejudice but as a response to a perceived threat to patriarchy itself. In the first half of the eighteenth century, however, literary and political culture was still so overwhelmingly patriarchal that writing by women, if regarded at all, was more novelty than threat. Women could write about anything, but what they could write about better than men (however sympathetic and sensitive) ever could was the experience women alone had and which they had essentially no choice but to endure for good or ill – the experience of living with men.

There are some moving poems of enticement, love fulfilled and bereavement, as in Elizabeth Rowe's touching poem 'Upon the Death of her Husband' (Lonsdale 35), but more common are descriptions of life with husbands who have proved tyrannical, drunken or unfaithful. And it is in some of these that the best qualities of women's verse writing come together, the freedom and confidence to write frankly, the direct use of verse forms that retain prosodic energy, and a pragmatic sensitivity to questions of personal relationship and quality of life. For instance, Mehetabel (Hetty) Wright, the sister of John and Charles Wesley, confronts the coolness of her new husband in simple rhyming couplets that achieve a considerable level of pathos:

. . . what should hinder but that I
Impatient of my wrongs, may try,
By saddest softest strains to move
My wedded, latest, dearest love,
To throw his cold neglect aside,
And cheer once more his injured bride!

O thou, whom sacred rites designed
My guide, and husband ever kind,
My sovereign master, best of friends,
On whom my earthly bliss depends;
If e'er thou didst in Hetty see
Aught fair, or good, or dear to thee,
If gentle speech can ever move
The cold remains of former love,
Turn thee at last – my bosom ease,
Or tell me *why* I cease to please.

'Address to her Husband' (Lonsdale 79)

The voice that informs many of the poems about men is, to repeat, not generally querulous or peevish, but it is often marked by a sense of grievance, a steady anger at injustice (not least about women being deprived of the education their brothers enjoyed, e.g. Lonsdale 1, 23, 28). This is not normally a principled resentment at the fact of the legal and domestic authority vested in men (though that is there), but a resentment at the way that authority is exploited or abused. Mary, Lady Chudleigh begins her address 'To the Ladies', which ends by advising women to shun men altogether, by noting 'Wife and servant are the same'.

This was strictly true in law, except that the servant did have certain rights of redress against an unjust master and a wife had to all intents and purposes none against a husband, no matter how villainous. Lady Chudleigh elaborates the nature of the tyrannical position of the male, but the strength of the poem develops as her account of this is infused with the practical experience of just how awful this tyranny is to live with:

> Wife and servant are the same,
> But only differ in the name:
> For when that fatal knot is tied,
> Which nothing, nothing can divide,
> When she the word *Obey* has said,
> And man by law supreme has made,
> Then all that's kind is laid aside,
> And nothing left but state and pride.
> Fierce as an eastern prince he grows,
> And all his innate rigour shows:
> Then but to look, to laugh, or speak,
> Will the nuptial contract break
> Like mutes, she signs alone must make,
> And never any freedom take,
> But still be governed by a nod,
> And fear her husband as her god.   (Lonsdale 2)

The plea is very often not for the overthrow or even the reform of established social and legal structures, but for decent treatment. Men as they appear in the verses of complaint make themselves disagreeable by plain indifference or insensitivity, not to any especially heightened qualities of female sensibility or romanticised emotional demands, but to the ordinary considerateness and willingness to be kind that is so often evinced in the poems. Sarah Egerton, who made no particular claim to saintliness, and who might well have been stretched to defend one if she did, writes in exasperation about harassment from a suitor who will not take no for an answer, and who interprets even her commonest courtesies as signs of concession. He offends her because he is a pest, and also because he violates the rules of decent conduct that should govern everyone, and he forces her to adopt an uncharitable attitude that is foreign to her instincts:

> I must confess I am not quite so nice
> To damn all little gallantries for vice
> (But I see now my charity's misplaced,
> If none but sullen saints can be thought chaste):
> Yet know, base man, I scorn your lewd amours,
> Hate them from all, not only 'cause they're yours.
> 'The Repulse to Alcander' (Lonsdale 19)

The insensitivity and nuisance lamented and scorned in Sarah Egerton's lover becomes worse in a husband, turning to grossness and mental cruelty, and women frequently notice how husbands exploit the conventional double standard that sanctions all kinds of misconduct in them but not the most trivial delinquency in a wife. As Elizabeth Thomas puts it,

> Equal's the contract, equal are the vows,
> Yet Custom different licences allows:
> The man may range from his unhappy wife,
> But woman's made a property for life.
> 'Epistle to Clemena' (Lonsdale 24)

The poem from which this is taken treats a fictional relationship between Aminta and her brutal libertine husband Nefario, but in its detail it reproduces the texture of actual experience familiar in many of the poems. Nefario spends the afternoon drinking and boasting with his friends, and then,

> Sated at last with fulsome lies and wine,
> Nefario swears aloud, ' 'tis dinner-time;'
> Aminta's called, and calmly down they sit,
> But she not one poor word or look can get.
> 'This meat's too salt, t'other's too fresh,' he cries,
> And from the table in a passion flies:
> Not that his cook is faulty in the least,
> But 'tis the wife that palls his squeamish taste.

He spends the night whoring and gambling, while Aminta lies anxiously awaiting his return:

Fears some mishap, looks out at every noise,
And thinks each breath of wind her dear Nefario's voice.
At last the clock strikes five, and home he comes,
And kicks the spaniel servants through the rooms,
Till he the lovely pensive fair doth spy,
Nor can she scape the sordid tyranny:
A thousand brutish names to her he gives,
Which she poor lady patiently receives;
A thousand imprecations doth bestow,
And scarcely can refrain to give th' impending blow.
Till fired with rage, and overcome with wine,
Dead drunk he falls, and snoring lies supine.

That the tone of this and of other verses like it is satirical rather than peevish is a tribute to the self-confidence and resilience of the writers. Whatever their actual position in relation to men, writing seems to have afforded a space in which women were free to exercise a consciousness of their own superiority to the brutal defectives with whom they had little choice but to make their lives. When Elizabeth Thomas writes in the role of the forsaken wife she anticipates the superbia of the Clarissa who is able to say to Lovelace 'My soul is above thee, man':

    Show me a man that dare be true,
That dares to suffer what I do;
That can for ever sigh unheard,
And ever love without regard:
I then will own your prior claim
To love, to honour, and to fame;
But till that time, my dear, adieu,
I yet superior am to you.   (Lonsdale 32)

More pathetic and more bitter is Arabella Moreton's wish that her mind could be abased to the level at which the female condition forces women to live:

I ask not wit, nor beauty do I crave,
Nor wealth, nor pompous titles wish to have;
But since 'tis doomed, in all degrees of life
(Whether a daughter, sister, or a wife),
That females shall the stronger males obey,
And yield perforce to their tyrannic sway;

Since this, I say, is every woman's fate,
Give me a mind to suit my slavish state.
'The Humble Wish' (Lonsdale 76)

As a measure of how serious and important this body of women's verse in the eighteenth century is, and how heroic is the feat of reasonably cheerful endurance it commemorates, it is worth reflecting that in the Western world in the twentieth century Arabella Moreton's phrase 'my slavish state' could only be used as a metaphor or as rhetorical heightening. In her time, however reasonably some women may have been treated, however content some of them may have been with their lot, whatever gratifications they may have found in love or domesticity, however much more understanding and sympathy they may have met with in literature and society, it was constitutionally exact.

Resistance could, however, be robust and entertaining. Women, a few, and often in private, had found a voice and knew how to use it. One rejoices in the spirit and energy with which an unknown Miss W. throws back at Swift the obscene and voyeuristic imagery of 'The Lady's Dressing Room'. Her opening lines establish a tone that is rough, combative and comic:

Some write of angels, some of goddesses,
But I of dirty human bodies,
And lowly I employ my pen,
To write of naught but odious men;
And men I think, without a jest,
More nasty than the nastiest beast.
'The Gentleman's Study' (Lonsdale 91)

She recounts how a Miss Smith, a milliner, visited Strephon's lodgings in the hope of getting a bill paid, and in his absence had time to look around her at a scene of boundless disorder and squalor. The excellence of Miss W.'s riposte to Swift is in lowering the tone of his poem, making it even more direct and factual, so that the poem is less a work of implication than of record:

For there some stocks lay on the ground,
One side was yellow, t'other brown;
And velvet breeches (on her word),
The inside all bedaubed with t—d,
And just before, I'll not desist,

To let you know they were be-pissed:
Four different stinks lay there together,
Which were sweat, turd, and piss, and leather.

Nothing improves when Strephon returns home almost paralytically
drunk, and is no more than a compound of wildly undisciplined body
functions. Before she leaves he has vomited all over the room and
voided himself, only inaccurately, in the region of the chamber pot. As
she leaves he is unconscious on the bed, farting, hiccuping, groaning
and snoring.

The intertextuality between Swift's poem and Miss W.'s encapsulates
the issue of gender relations that the women's verse bears witness to.
Swift's poem is alive with obscene and prurient implication, working from
a ground of implicit cultural superiority; there, Strephon's is an underhand
investigation of the lady's private world and in his romantic naivety he is
appalled by it; we are partly invited to sneer at his shock, and partly to
share it. It is a poem for other men. Miss W.'s is not really a poem for other
women as much as it is for any reader. 'If that is what you say we are like,'
it argues, 'then this is what you are really like.' Miss Smith lifts no lids,
pries into nothing. The poem is a record of what she sees. She records
things as they are, and that thorough realism is something that poetry by
women offers in a way that is hardly to be found elsewhere in the corpus
of verse writing in the first half of the eighteenth century.

'Do her Eyes love as well as her Pen?'[8] When the Chevalier d'Aumont
puts this question to Sir Charles Lovemore at the beginning of Mrs
Manley's fictionalised autobiography *Rivella* (1714) he is referring to
the most popular author of prose fiction in English between *The
Pilgrim's Progress* (1678) and *Robinson Crusoe* (1719). Her *The Secret
Memoirs and Manners of several Persons of Quality, of both Sexes. From the
New Atalantis, an Island in the Mediterranean* with its disguised narratives of amorous and political intrigue in high society had been
published in 1709, and it was a runaway success, partly *succès d'estime*,
partly *succès de scandale*. When a second volume appeared towards the
end of the year Mrs Manley, her two publishers and the printer were
promptly arrested and imprisoned for some days, not because of the
salacity of parts of the narrative but because of their political charge. As
a convinced lifelong Tory, Mrs Manley's target through the first decade
of the century was the Whig administration, and particularly the machinations and venality of the great Whig general John Churchill, Duke of

Marlborough, and his wife Sarah (née Jennings) who had been the influential favourite of Queen Anne. The year 1710 saw a general election with a landslide victory for the Tories under Robert Harley, soon made Earl of Oxford. Harley's victory owed something to the success of *The New Atalantis*, which Jane Spencer describes as 'probably the most effective attack on the Whigs published at this time'.[9] There were in fact very many other detailed and cogent pieces that came out attacking Whig policy in the volatile years of 1709 and 1710, but Mrs Manley undeniably helped to change the political weather, and in particular she gave a plausible personal focus to her politics: in her writings readers could enjoy the spectacle of ministers behaving badly.

Mrs Manley's great political success was to understand that the secret history or scandalous chronicle could be exploited not merely for the thrills of sexual voyeurism in high life, but to demystify figures in the public world. Seen to be driven by financial and sexual greed, claims that public figures might make to altruistic, patriotic or other elevated motives no longer held water. Mrs Manley goes to the heart of the matter in *The Secret History of Queen Zarah* when she explains how Rollando (Charles II) had been unable fully to possess the affections of his mistress Clelia (the Duchess of Cleveland), who entertained a passion for Hippolito (the young John Churchill). Having shared the king's bed, and seen him without his robes, Clelia can treat him as a man not a monarch:

> Such is the Fortune of Monarchs in Love, when they are with their Mistresses they commonly lay aside that Majesty which dazles the Eyes and affects the Hearts of Mankind; they go undress'd into their Chambers, and make themselves so familiar with their Mistresses, they afterwards use them as other Men.[10]

Secret history did not, however, write itself. It had to be plausible and it had to be attractive, and as the long twenty-one page *Preface* to her first political secret history, *The Secret History of Queen Zarah* – Zarah is Churchill's termagant wife Sarah – reveals, Mrs Manley uses a better and more thoughtfully theorised understanding of how to serve the interests and expectations of the reader of history and imaginative narrative than any author of fiction before Fielding. Its criteria are generally naturalistic, placing particular emphasis on probability, credibility, realistic and consistent characterisation, naturalistic dialogue, the avoidance of moralistic commentary, and all kinds of interpolated material which will frustrate 'the Curiosity of the Reader' and his or her 'Secret Impatience of desiring to see the Discovery of the Action'.[11]

Writing in the vein of literary history in the 1930s, J. C. Major saw narratives like Mrs Manley's as occupying an important place in the evolution of English fiction from romance towards the 'realism' of later eighteenth-century novelists:

> While the distortion of life in the scandal chronicle was not 'realism' in a true sense, the scandal memorialist's rejection of the idealised figure of courtly life helped to prepare middle-class readers for fiction realistically interpreting men and women of their own society. Just as the historical memoirs served as a transition between the conventionalised character of the old Chronicle and the living individual in modern biography, so the disreputable memoirs and histories of fiction served to bridge the gap between the utterly unreal figure of the Heroic Romance and Richardson's *Pamela*.[12]

Apart from whatever role she may take as an unsung heroine of the evolution of imaginative narrative, Mrs Manley is a witty and vivacious writer, capable of venom and indignation, and equally open to sharing the amusement her narratives afford. She takes the reader into the open and hidden motives of her characters, and she discovers them, often quite comically and sometimes quite sexily, *in flagrante delicto*. She often writes in the first person, or about herself, and is in any case distinctively present in the style, manner and manipulation of subjects within her narratives. As author she is a character, a construction of her own fiction, and she repeatedly features in it as a principal subject. It is therefore wholly consonant with her practice that when she turns to a vindication of her career in autobiography she does so in the form of a fiction which is itself a secret history. Her life is an intertext of her own imaginative narratives. The modern editor of *The New Atalantis*, Rosalind Ballaster, describes Mrs Manley as 'an inveterate autobiographer, scattering inset narratives relating to her own intellectual and personal life through much of her writing'.[13] These narratives in a sense relate to a historical Mary Delarivier Manley, but they are more exactly narratives of 'Mrs Manley', author as constructed personality.

The Chevalier d'Aumont's question, 'Do her Eyes love as well as her Pen?', in *Rivella* about the author of *The New Atalantis* prompts the recital by Sir Charles Lovemore which constitutes the narrative of Mrs Manley's life, and it confirms the identity of personality and the works. That an author is a construction of his or her texts is something which we have no difficulty in understanding now, though it has only been fully theorised in recent decades, but it has been implicit in such locutions as 'I am interested in Defoe' from the inception of modern literary studies. In the case of Mrs Manley it has an especial charge as it is heavily loaded with sexual interest: Mrs Manley's narratives were notoriously about sexual intrigue, and d'Aumont's question is an attempt to come closer to the sexual personality implicit in the works. The relationship that exists between author and reader is something like a flirtation preliminary to an affair, with some teasing on one side, some tentative sexual curiosity on the other. There is an extraordinarily brilliant analysis by the Earl of Shaftesbury of the 'coquetry' or 'pretty Amour' in memoir-writing under the heading of 'Advice to an Author' in the revised edition of his *Characteristicks of Men, Manners, Opinions, Times* which appeared in 1713, the year before *Rivella*. It is worth quoting at length as it helps to pinpoint the tone, technique and character of Mrs Manley as an author, despite the fact that its irony deprecates the practice it describes:

> An author who writes in his own person has the advantage of being who or what he pleases. He is no certain Man, nor has any certain or genuine character: but sutes himself on every occasion to the fancy of his reader, whom as the fashion is now-a-days, he constantly caresses and cajoles. All turns upon their two persons. And as in an Amour, or commerce of love-letters; so here the author has the privilege of talking eternally of himself; while he is making diligent court, and working on the humour of the part(y) to whom he addresses. This is the coquetry of a modern author, whose Epistles, Dedicatory Prefaces, and Addresses to the Reader, are so many affected graces, design'd to draw the attention from the subject towards himself . . . [This is notably characteristic of the French, all of whose writing is Memoirs] . . . The whole writing of this Age is indeed a sort of Memoir-Writing. Tho' in the real Memoirs of the Antients, even when they writ at any time concerning themselves, there was neither the *I* nor *Thou* throughout the whole work. So that all this pretty Amour and intercourse of caresses between the author and reader was thus entirely taken away.[14]

The teasing, flirtatious or amorous relationship of Mrs Manley and her reader is mediated in the structure and setting within which she introduces 'The History of Rivella', which is distinguished typographically from the introductory matter and given its own half-title. Each of the devices she uses has an ambivalent modal status: each is comic, and so not to be taken too seriously, and also romantic, so inviting us into the world of Mrs Manley's imagination:

1 The title-page claims that the 'History of the Author of the *Atalantis*' was 'Deliver'd in a Conversation to the Young Chevalier *D'Aumont* in *Somerset-House* Garden, by Sir Charles Lovemore' and that it was 'Done into *English* from the *French*.' French was the language of the romances and *chroniques scandaleuses* which lay at some point behind Mrs Manley's narratives. Sir Charles had delivered his story of Rivella in English, in which language it now appears in print. But the fiction of the title-page is that Mrs Manley's story has, as it were, been in and out of French – it has passed through the filter of romance and taken on its colouring.

2 The setting of Lovemore's recitation in 'Somerset-House Garden' to d'Aumont, who is French ambassador to England, 'On One of those fine Evenings that are so rarely to be found in *England*' (1) while the two gentlemen are taking the air, prepares for the blend of romance, entertainment, gossip, scandal and intimacy the narrative promises.

3 When d'Aumont asks Lovemore to fulfill his promise to tell him Rivella's history he orders the doors to the garden to be closed, thus making the narrative for characters and reader alike a site of especial and privileged secrecy.

4 The name d'Aumont and the role of the French ambassador belong to the world of historical reality. D'Aumont at one point refers to the real Madame Dacier, but Sir Charles Lovemore to whom he mentions her clearly derives from the type-naming of Restoration comedy. Sir Charles mentions that he had a rival for Rivella's affections, 'Young *Lysander*, for so was my rival called' – an unlikely name for one in the young man's occupation, a subaltern in an English regiment. There are frequent references to actual historical events. Real people are mentioned, like the Duchess of Cleveland and the Duke of Marlborough, but they are given fictitious names (Hilaria and Fortunatus). At one stage in Rivella's history the fictitious Sir Charles refers out of the book in which he exists to another, saying 'I must refer you to her own Story, under the name of *Delia*, in the *Atalantis*, for the next Four Miserable Years of her Life' (29). In *The New Atalantis* the story of Mary Delarivier Manley's bigamous marriage to her cousin John Manley is told as the story of Delia. Both Delia and Rivella are names that derive from Mrs

Manley's middle name, but each transmutes into something sounding more romantic or exotic. Rivella thus exists in a kind of ontological Alsace-Lorraine, now in the realm of fiction, now of truth, but of course she is in both simultaneously, the whole point of disguised history. And 'she' is known to us by four different names, not one of which appears as that of author on the title-pages of any of her imaginative narratives. Early in her story Sir Charles says that Rivella did not return the love he felt for her, but that she rejected him 'without any affected Coyness, or personating a Heroine of the many Romances she daily read'. (18)

The effect of these devices and of almost the whole of Mrs Manley's novelistic narratives depends on a collusion of recognition between author and reader, a subtle unspoken understanding that enables a play between fiction and reality to be enjoyed and recognised by each. Mrs Manley is an unmatched virtuoso in manipulating and exploiting this collusion. For instance, in *The Secret History of Queen Zarah* she describes how rapidly at their initial meeting Zarah and Hippolito (Sarah Jennings and John Churchill) move to sexual intimacy. It was a sort of lightning romance which could occur in the realm of fiction, or in more genial climates than England's. (One must remember that this is a story of Zarazians, set in Albigion, and according to the title-page 'Faithfully Translated from the *Italian* Copy now lodg'd in the *Vatican* at Rome'.)

It may be admired perhaps that Two Persons so little acquainted shou'd in so few Minutes become so familiar, but we must know Love in those Countries makes far quicker Progress than in ours, where the Winds, and the Snow, and the Rain, spoil his Wings, and hinder his Flight. (15)

The comedy and the political satire of the passage, which leads into a more detailed account of their union, depends on the reader discounting the fact that this is a story about persons with strange names transacted in a distant (perhaps Italian) state. He reads it as an event of unbridled lasciviousness between the Queen's favourite and the Whig general, neither deterred by the familiar discouragements of the British climate, which help to keep the rest of us normal people within the limits of moderation and decent conduct. Sarah Jennings and John Churchill behave more like overheated foreigners in an erotic Italian romance than like an English lady and gentleman – they are sports in their own land.

Jane Spencer deprecates the fact that 'it is as an erotic writer rather than a political propagandist that Manley has been mostly remembered, and reviled', and she argues that 'Her importance as a Tory writer has been virtually ignored since her death, while the picture she painted of herself as amorous woman and erotic writer has adversely affected her standing in literary history up to the present time.'[15] There may be an element of truth in this, but the fact of the matter is that Mrs Manley has hardly been read at all since her own period, and the reason for this is not that she is an uncomfortably erotic novelist, but that her fiction can *only* be read politically. If, as Dr Johnson could have said, a man were to read Mrs Manley for the sex he would hang himself. To be told that a Mr Smith and a Mrs Jones are having an affair is not very exciting; but to be told that Mr Smith at number 23 in your own street is having an affair with Mrs Jones opposite at number 24 is genuinely titillating. Mrs Manley's narratives depend on political recognition. For all that Jane Spencer makes claims for Mrs Manley's importance as a political writer, and outlines parts of the story of *The New Atalantis* and *Rivella* with the disguise-names explained, she does not really read the narratives politically. She is more interested, as the argument of *The Rise of the Woman Novelist* properly requires, in the implications of Mrs Manley's self-inscription 'as amorous woman and erotic writer'.

There is a difficulty, however: Mr Smith and Mrs Jones are long dead. The political reading of *Queen Zarah* and *The New Atalantis* is essentially irrecoverable except as an exercise of historical scholarship, and even that cannot retrieve the naughty, heady, indignant titillation of scandal among people still in high places. What one can perhaps do, none the less, is grasp something of how complete and apt was Mrs Manley's developed perception that people's sexual stories would open a window on their public lives. The true effect of her books is achieved cumulatively, so that the reader gets the feeling that wherever he looks in high life he finds sexual intrigue, secrecy, corruption and sordid motive. One instance may, even so, indicate something of Mrs Manley's reading of the intimate relation of the sexual and political conditions, and in this episode it is a measure of her accomplishment as a novelist that she does it through a rendering of her principal character's inner thoughts. The secrets of Mrs Manley's secret history are not just of the bed-chamber but of the mind.

In *The Secret History of Queen Zarah* she describes Zarah's behaviour to the Duke of Buckingham (called Mulgarvius). Zarah wants him as a lover sexually, but wishes to oppose him politically. She accordingly takes him as a lover and thereby appears as his intimate friend; but, in furtherance of her political aims, she ingratiates herself with the future queen, whose ear she seeks, by betraying Mulgarvius to her (although she tells him the opposite). This thwarts his hopes for political advancement, and advances her own interest while gratifying her lust. Mrs Manley presents the episode in summary:

> But *Zarah*, whom Fortune had cut out purely for the Service of her own Interest, without any regard to the strict Rules of Honour or Virtue, soon resolv'd within herself how she might make the best Advantage of this every Way, both to the satisfaction of her Ambition, in having the Opportunity of communicating an Affair of this Consequence, both to the King [William III] and *Albania* [the future Queen Anne], and next in gratifying her pleasure with *Mulgarvius*, who was one she greatly admired, and whom she was glad she cou'd appear to be as his most particular Friend, when at the same Time she had taken Measures to frustrate any Success he cou'd pretend to gain by Means of those promising Hopes she design'd to flatter him with about *Albania*.
>
> This was a Treacherous Part as was ever acted by Woman fill'd with *Love* and *Ambition*.   (40–1)

Zarah's exploitation and betrayal of Mulgarvius is inextricably and simultaneously sexual and political; the corruption in one field is image, symbol and consort of corruption in the other. Mrs Manley's narrative through her scandalous histories is not just an account of life in high places but a penetrative vision of its quality.

Rosalind Ballaster writes well of Mrs Manley's

> peculiar adroitness in exploiting popular feeling, turning events in her own biography and rumours of those in others into emblematic or mythic narrative, laying bare the real effects of ideology on the bodies and minds of those denied direct political influence and power such as herself.[16]

Well put as this is, the first part of it is truer than the last because as Ballaster concedes with an almost Swiftean understatement, 'Manley's treatment of women is not unequivocally supportive' (IX). Certainly not if one of those women happens to be Sarah Churchill.

The strength of Mrs Manley's narratives is that she wrote without disguise or pretence as a woman in her time and of her time. Hers was a distinctive voice and in some measure a power in the land. After her release from prison and the Tory electoral victory she was rapidly recruited by the prime minister Harley as a propagandist. She wrote some tracts in her own right, and collaborated with Swift in the Tory political journal *The Examiner*. It is known that she wrote at least six issues in the summer of 1711, and she may well have written more. (Attribution is extremely difficult in this kind of writing, when she was anyway writing, as Swift was, as 'Mr Examiner'.) She only returned to the form of the scandalous narrative with her spirited exercise in self-vindication *Rivella* after the Tory ministry had collapsed during the negotiations that concluded in the Peace of Utrecht in 1713.

In the account which Mrs Manley gives towards the end of *Rivella* of her prosecution following publication of the second volume of the *Atalantis* in 1709, she wittily works with just that equivocation between truth and falsehood which is the basis of the comedy and the satire of her fiction. Pressed in her examination in 'the Secretary's Office' to declare who were the people she was writing about, where she obtained her information, and who else was involved with her in the publication, she recounts that she denied anyone else was concerned and that she intended reflections on particular individuals. But when this was not believed 'and the contrary urg'd very home to her by several Circumstances and Likenesses',

> she said then it must be *Inspiration*, because knowing her own Innocence she could account for it no other Way: The Secretary reply'd upon her, that *Inspiration* us'd to be upon a good Account, and her Writings were stark naught; she told him, with an Air full of Penitence, that might be true, but it was as true, that there were evil Angels as well as good; so that nevertheless what she had wrote might still be by *Inspiration*. (113)

This was certainly inspired cheek, and the comedy attests to Mrs Manley's confidence and sureness in her role as a writer. It would be a long time before the number of women writers could begin to match the number of men, and still longer before some of the wrongs and injustices of which many of them complained were to be even partly redressed, but that *Mrs* Manley could stand up to *Mr* Secretary and outwit him without conceding an inch to his arguments is an indication that women knew, even if all men did not yet, that women really could be authors on level terms with men.

Appendix

The Preface to Mrs Manley's Secret History of Queen Zarah (1705)

Mrs Manley uses terms like 'Romance', 'History' and 'Historian' rather imprecisely. In this summary I have tried to indicate, where necessary, the kind of writing she is referring to. There is some overlapping and repetition of topic. In the extracts I have kept the sequence of her precepts, even though this involves some apparent illogicality.

Although largely translated from a French original and partly derivative (from Aristotle, for example), the preface constitutes a practical *vade mecum* for writing modern imaginative narratives in English.

The typography of the original has been retained, except that the long 's' has been replaced with a short 's' and a few obvious printing errors have been silently corrected.

1   The taste for Romances (stories of heroic and romantic adventure), a kind popular in France and often translated into English, is declining. The English prefer more concise narratives. (England was at war with France in 1705, and so the point is partly a patriotic one.)

> THE *Romances in* France *have for a long Time been the Diversion and Amusement of the whole World; the People both in the City and at Court have given themselves over to this Vice, and all Sorts of People have read these Works with a most surprizing Greediness; but that Fury is very much abated, and they are all fallen off from this Distraction: The Little* Histories *of this Kind have taken Place of* Romances, *whose Prodigious Number of Volumes were sufficient to tire and satiate such whose Heads were most fill'd with those Notions.*
>
> *These little Pieces which have banish'd* Romances *are much more agreeable to the Brisk and Impetuous Humour of the* English, *who have naturally no Taste for long-winded Performances, for they have no sooner begun a Book but they desire to see the End of it.*   (A2–A2ᵛ)

2   Romances are excessively long, have too great a diversity of incidents and characters and are too implausible: The authors of '*Historical Novels*' (imaginative narratives based on contemporary or recent events)

have avoided these faults, but they sometimes '*mix particular Stories*' (interpolated narratives about peripheral characters) '*with the Principal History*' and this can distract the reader.

3 '*For the Reader's better Understanding*' subjects should not be too remote in time or place, and characters should not have barbarous names.

4 The imaginative writer should present attractive characters,

> *but he ought with great Care to observe the Probability of Truth, which consists in saying nothing but what may Morally be believed.*
>
> (A3ᵛ–A4)

5 Unlikely events and improbable behaviour occurs in real life, and so

> *He that writes a True History* [a factual narrative] *ought to place the Accidents as they Naturally happen, without endeavouring to sweeten them for to procure a greater Credit, because he is not obliged to answer for their Probability; but he that composes a History to his Fancy* [writes an imaginative narrative] . . . *is obliged to Write nothing that is improbable.* (A4ᵛ)

6 Characterisation and actions must be plausible. Romances give their heroines impossibly virtuous characters. The virtuous actions of characters should be '*seisable*' (credible) '*to make an Impression in the Brain of Reasonable Persons*'. Modern novels

> *are not fill'd with great Adventures, and extraordinary Accidents, for the most simple Action may engage the Reader by the Circumstances that attend it; it enters into all the Motions and Disquiets of the Actor, when they have well express'd to him the Character. If he be Jealous, the Look of a Person he Loves, a Mouse, a turn of the Head, or the least complaisance to a Rival, throws him into the greatest Agitations, which the Readers perceive by a Counter-blow* [reaction]. (A5ᵛ)

Realistic characterisation and action promotes the vital identification of reader with character:

> *for Fear and Pity in Romance* [fiction] *as well as Tragedies are the Two Instruments which move the Passion; for we in some Manner put our selves*

in the Room of those we see in Danger; the Part we take therein, and the fear of falling into the like Misfortunes, causes us to interest our selves more in their Adventures, because that those sort of Accidents may happen to all the World; and it touches so much the more, because they are the common Effects of Nature.   (A6)

7   The heroes of romantic narrative '*are not Men*': they are impossibly brave and valiant. Readers cannot identify with them:

A Reader who has any Sense does not take part with these Fabulous Adventures, or at least is but slightly touch'd with them, because they are not natural, and therefore cannot be believed.   (A6ᵛ)

By contrast,

The Heroes of Modern Romances [novels with more contemporary settings] *are better Characteriz'd, they give them Passions, Vertues or Vices, which resemble Humanity; thus all the World will find themselves represented in these Descriptions.*   (A6ᵛ)

The ability to become engaged in a narrative is

that which inspires the Reader with Curiosity, and a certain impatient Desire to see the End of the Accidents [outcome], *the reading of which causes an Exquisite Pleasure when they are Nicely handled.*   (a1)

8   Tracing human emotions, '*the Motion of the Heart*', can give even more pleasure,

but the Author ought to have an Extraordinary Penetration to distinguish them well, and not to lose himself in the Labyrinth.
. . . .
the Genius of the Author marvellously appears where he Nicely discovers those Differences, and exposes to the Reader's Sight those almost unperceivable Jealousies which escape the Sight of most Authors, because they have not an exact Notion of the Turnings and Motions of Humane Understanding.   (a1, a1ᵛ)

9   The author should establish time and place briskly, and then in presenting the hero concentrate on '*the Qualities of the Soul which ought to render him acceptable*', and these should not be stressed in minor

characters '*who only serve to bind the Intrigue.*' Heroes should not be recommended '*by Extravagant Expressions, nor Repeated Praises*':

> *their Actions ought to plead for them; 'tis by that they are made known, and describe themselves.*

They should have some failings, '*seeing they are Men*',

> *but their Imperfections ought not to destroy the Character that is attributed to them.* (a2^v)

10 The author should be impartial and non-judgemental in presenting character and action:

> *Every Historian* [author of narrative] *ought to be extremely uninterested* [impartial]; *he ought neither to Praise nor Blame those he speaks of; he ought to be content with Exposing the Actions, leaving an entire Liberty to the Reader to judge as he pleases.* (a3^v)

11 The writer should not show off by commenting constantly on the action:

> *it is . . . not requisite that a Historian shou'd always make use of all his Wit, nor that he should strain himself, in Nice and Lively Reflections.*

Nor should he moralise excessively:

> *Moral Reflexions, Maxims and Sentences are more proper in Discourses for Instructions than in Historical Novels* [narratives of modern life], *whose chief End is to please; and if we find in them some Instructions, it proceeds rather from their Descriptions than their Precepts.*
>
> (a4, a4^v)

12 The writer should bring the narrative briskly to its conclusion because

> *when the End draws nigher, the Curiosity of the Reader is augmented, and he finds in him a Secret Impatience of desiring to see the Discovery of the Action; an Historian that amuses himself by Moralizing or Describing, discourages an Impatient Reader, who is in haste to see the End of the Intrigues.*
>
> (a5)

13   Dialogue should be naturalistic, however finely worked the narrative style. The '*Principal Ornament*' of dialogue

> *consists in the Plainness, Simplicity, Free and Sincere Air . . . we only speak that we may communicate our Thoughts to others.*   (a5–a5ᵛ)

And in any case verbatim reports of long conversations violate the illusion of reality, and tire the reader.

14   Narratives should end in a way readers find gratifying:

> *'Tis an indispensible Necessity to end a Story to satisfie the Disquiets of the Reader who is engag'd to the Fortunes of those People whose Adventures are described to him; 'tis depriving him of a most delectable Pleasure, when he is hind'red from seeing the Event of an Intrigue, which has caused some Emotion in him, whose Discovery he expects, be it either Happy or Unhappy.*   (a6)

15   Although '*the chief End of History is to instruct and inspire into Men the Love of Vertue, and Abhorrence of Vice*' it is not necessary for the most virtuous to end up most happy, but their plight should excite pity, and even if vice is not always punished in the narrative it should be represented in an unattractive light, and so '*known to be worthy of nothing but Chastisements*'.   (a6–a6ᵛ)

6

The Harmony of Things:
An Essay on Man and *Moral Essays*

A passage of somewhat surprising intensity in Thomson's 'Autumn' describes the formation of lakes and rivers. Thomson worked hard on it, elaborating a short passage in the version of 'Autumn' published in 1730, when Pope was working on the poems principally discussed in this chapter, the *Essay on Man* and the four *Moral Essays*, into the long and more scientifically accurate (and heroic) version printed in 1744, the year of Pope's death. Thomson wishes to reveal 'where lurk the vast eternal Springs' of water that he compares with 'CREATING NATURE' and which 'with their lavish Stores / Refresh the Globe, and all its joyous Tribes.'[1] With his poetic eye Thomson penetrates the surface of the earth and discovers among 'the leaning *Strata*, artful rang'd', 'the gaping Fissures' receiving rains and meltwater, layers of gravel, underground channels, 'rocky Siphons' and 'The mighty Reservoirs, of harden'd Chalk, / Or stiff compacted Clay, capacious form'd'. From here 'The crystal Treasures of the liquid World' burst out 'In pure Effusion' (810–28). As Thomson goes on to explain how the exposed waters are then drawn up by the sun in vapours, distilled in rains, and returned in proper proportion all over the earth, it becomes clear that more than hydrology is at stake: the hydraulic cycle is both an instance of a complete and intricate working system, and in being that a confirmation of the governing principle of creation, universal harmony:

> . . . United, thus,
> Th'exhaling Sun, the Vapour-burden'd Air,
> The gelid Mountains, that to Rain condens'd
> These Vapours in continual Current draw,
> And send them, o'er the fair-divided Earth,
> In bounteous Rivers to the Deep again,

> A social Commerce hold, and firm support
> The full-adjusted Harmony of Things.   (828–35)

The closing couplet extends the symbolic value of the hydraulic cycle beyond registering the harmony of the world as a mechanical system into a suggestion that this is how the human world works as well: the rocks and rivers, the sun and the rains, work together in a way that can be called 'social', much as that quintessential social activity 'commerce' (in origin a buying and selling together) operates.

This idealising of the cosmos and of the social world of man is one of the commonplaces of reflective writing in the first half of the eighteenth century. It owes a great deal to the discoveries of Newton and of the other natural scientists,[2] and to the conclusions of Locke and other philosophers, many of whom could be construed as valorising harmony and system because that is exactly what they most wanted to find, and it plays through endless variations. But it was also a social and cultural achievement, constructed in reaction to the volatility and turbulence of British history in the seventeenth century.

In the rhapsodic vision of global peace and harmonious commerce which closes his panegyric poem celebrating the making of the Peace of Utrecht, *Windsor-Forest* (1713), Pope lists all the manifestations of social disturbance which will be excluded by peace from history henceforward:

> Exil'd by Thee from Earth to deepest Hell,
> In Brazen Bonds shall barb'rous *Discord* dwell:
> Gigantick *Pride*, pale *Terror*, gloomy *Care*,
> And mad *Ambition*, shall attend her there.
> There purple *Vengeance* bath'd in Gore retires,
> Her Weapons blunted, and extinct her Fires:
> There hateful *Envy* her own Snakes shall feel,
> And *Persecution* mourn her broken Wheel:
> There *Faction* roar, *Rebellion* bite her Chain,
> And gasping Furies thirst for Blood in vain.[3]

This is a farewell to the horrific and frightening history of the previous century. It is notable that though the poem was published to commemorate the ending of a war, the social evils which it catalogues belong to civil disorder – *Discord, Persecution, Faction, Rebellion* – and not to an international conflict. The overwhelming national dread in the first part of the eighteenth century was not of a resurgence of

French military power but of civil war, the great tragedy of the seventeenth century, that

> . . . dreadful Series of Intestine Wars,
> Inglorious Triumphs, and dishonest Scars

as Pope had described it earlier in the poem (325–6). Even the manner of the list of evils, with its lurid imagery and glaring italicisation of crowding abstract nouns, seems archaic in the age of the new politeness: it is almost as if Pope's *envoi* to history works not just by saying that these things will never be again, but by suggesting that poetry like this will never have to be written again.[4] The new harmonious world was to be articulated in a voice of poised and continuous graceful urbanity – 'Correct with spirit, eloquent with ease' (*Essay on Man* 4.381).

A few years before the publication of *Windsor-Forest*, and a few years after it, Pope wrote two little verses about clocks. The first completes a comparison with the way in which bowls take their direction from the lead weights embedded in them:

> So Clocks to Lead their nimble Motions owe,
> The Springs above urg'd by the Weights below;
> The pond'rous Ballance keeps its Poize the same,
> Actuates, maintains, and rules the moving Frame.[5]

In an earlier poetry this would form part of an allegory about, for instance, the relation of body and soul. This is still available to Pope, but what the poem actually celebrates is the mechanism. The same is true of the other little poem, an exquisite couplet 'on Mr. Hatton's Clocks', although these lines extend commendation of the mechanism into the aesthetic and almost cosmic realms:

> From hour to hour melodiously they chime,
> With silver sounds, and sweetly tune out time.[6]

The light regularity of the rhythm, the emphasis on melody and tune, the touch of luxury in 'silver', and the implication that time itself is regular (as opposed to violent, abrupt, disrupted) combine to generate a sense of ease and assurance, a sense that the elegant ingenuity of man matches the even workings of a harmonious cosmos.

It is no accident, as is pointed out elsewhere, that the endeavour to build an accurate timepiece, for which the Longitude Board in 1714 offered a huge prize, was one of the leading intellectual and scientific quests of the century. A mechanical clock that would enable a mariner to determine his precise longitude would eliminate one more element of uncertainty and danger from the world. The catastrophic wrecking of Sir Cloudsley Shovell's fleet on the Scilly Isles in 1707, with huge loss of life, occurred because the captains did not know their longitude.[7]

The existence of clocks and watches does not, however, mean that in the real world all is harmony – even about the time, as Pope acknowledges at the beginning of *An Essay on Criticism* (1711):

> 'Tis with our *Judgments* as our *Watches*, none
> Go just *alike*, yet each believes his own.   (9–10)

The trouble with elaborate, interlinked systems of mutual dependence is that they are vulnerable. If one thing goes wrong, everything does. This generates its own kind of anxiety, a paranoia about things going wrong that Pope articulates in the first epistle of *An Essay on Man*:

> And if each system in gradation roll,
> Alike essential to th' amazing whole;
> The least confusion but in one, not all
> That system only, but the whole must fall.
> Let Earth unbalanc'd from her orbit fly,
> Planets and Suns run lawless thro' the sky.   (1.247–52)

The first two couplets here are steady, scientific, in poetic terms dull; the third couplet is suddenly electrifying in its vision of instant chaos. The image that controls the last couplet is that of civil disorder, the riot. Planets and suns are in the countless plural; they no longer simply move, but run; the principles that held them in place are lost; they are lawless. Disorder in the heavens is like disorder in the streets.

It is not likely that the earth will lose its orbit, but that things go wrong on earth is common experience. It is significant that when in the first *Moral Essay*, the 'Epistle to Cobham', Pope discovers that the psychological principle of the Ruling Passion will explain the behaviour of even the wildly erratic Duke of Wharton, he draws a simile that will bring something else apparently unregulated in the cosmos – comets – into order:

Nature well known, no prodigies remain,
Comets are regular, and Wharton plain.   (208–9)

What begins to emerge is that the extension of Newton's discovery
(which included calculation of the elliptics of comets and prediction of
their return) that the universe obeys regular and timeless laws into a
reading of social and individual behaviour is something willed, maintained often in the face of contrary evidence. The fear that the human
world was unruly and phenomenal, manageable only by the direct
intervention of a supervising God and vulnerable to the incursions of a
perverse Devil, remained alive, and shows its head again and again –
not perhaps in the lines that have been quoted from Thomson, but
again and again in Pope. Thomson's poem, for all its diversity, looks at
the world through a single window; light keeps breaking in on Pope's
verse from all kinds of unexpected angles.

Nevertheless, through the first part of the eighteenth century, what
scientists now describe as 'the best understanding' was that the universe
was systematic, designed, essentially regular, amenable to mapping and
to understanding. Observation, intelligence, the exercise of right reason
and, for some, the human heart, could demystify the universe, familiarise the unfamiliar, and open the way to the better regulation of the
self and society.

The best understanding that I am describing evolved in the thoughts
and writings of such men as Archbishop John Tillotson, the philosopher Locke, Addison, the Earl of Shaftesbury, and the dedicatee of *An
Essay on Man*, Bolingbroke. They did not all think alike, but they were
all engaged in a kind of collaboration towards an understanding, and to
a degree they took up and worked with each other's perceptions (as
well, of course, as with the revelations of the new science). Pope himself
was not an original thinker, but he was a poet of great intellectual sensitivity and ideas play through his verse (not only, and perhaps not best,
when he is expounding theory) continually and subtly, and his poetry
registers a constant repastination of ideas.

By various ways these thinkers were generally in ageement that there
was at the origin of everything some divine intelligence. One common
route to this conclusion was what was called the argument from design.
It had been a commonplace of seventeenth-century thought that God
expressed himself, and could be read, not only in the Bible but also in
the book of nature. Extended, this can mean that the wonders of the
creation argue the existence and nature of a creator, as the clock attests
the existence of the clockmaker. Tillotson had put it like this:

As any curious Work, or rare Engine doth argue the Wit of the Artificer; so the variety, and order, and regularity, and fitness of the Works of God, argue the infinite wisdom of him who made them.[8]

It is echoed in, among very many other places, Addison's formulation in *The Spectator*: 'The Supream Being has made the best Arguments for his own Existence, in the Formation of the Heavens and the Earth.'[9] It is significant that Addison does not refer to 'Heaven', whose existence would be a matter of faith, but to 'the Heavens', the solar system, planets and stars, ever more visible with better and better telescopes, the universe whose physical operation had been explained apparently comprehensively and conclusively by Newton in terms of physical laws. What is important to note, though, is that to speak of the world in terms of variety, order, regularity and fitness, is not a simple description but a chosen interpretation, an expression of ideological or theological preference. It disregards pain, disease, earthquakes, wasps, chance, madness and all other seemingly irregular and unsought phenomena. In a sense it disregards the Fall. In Milton's century variety, order, regularity and fitness were characteristics of Paradise and were all lost through Adam's error. The seventeenth-century view, to generalise, had required an ever-active and interventionist God to correct the irregularities of the world, to rescue and redeem the good from the miseries and injustices of earthly life and to intercept and punish the evil. The emergent eighteenth-century view tended to render such vigilant supervision and monitoring redundant. A supreme being had designed and set the world working as a perfect self-regulating mechanism, and He could as it were sit back, admire it and enjoy the praise and admiration his works excited in his creatures.

The philosopher who had most influence on the evolution of thought in the early eighteenth century, John Locke (1632–1700), had arrived at a conviction of the existence of a supreme creator largely through reasoning. It was a conviction fed from various channels but essentially, as Locke explains it in *An Essay Concerning Human Understanding* (1690), it was deduced from the ability of the human mind to extend itself from sense-impressions to abstract ideas like dimension and duration, to states of mind and ideas of infinity; from an idea of infinity it was consistent to form an idea of God. This deduction of a supreme being was, as for the Deists and proponents of Natural Religion, much more a matter of human thought and perception than of Revelation. In a culture that expressed itself ever more comprehensively in print, the one book that was declining in significance among the intellectual and cultural élite was the Bible.

In Swift's satire on institutionalised religions, *A Tale of a Tub*, composed in 1696/7 and published 1704, with the three brothers desecrating their inheritance in the course of their virulent rivalry, he is savaging the sectarianism that had grown out of hermeneutic struggle over Biblical authority, and it was of a piece with his impatient vision of humanity always testily wrestling over minutiae and losing sight of what was of central importance. This is why he represents political difference between the Tramecksan and the Slamecksan parties in Lilliput as the difference of 'about the fourteenth Part of an Inch'[10] in the heights of the heels of their shoes. It was not perhaps really the case that the early eighteenth century was less riven by religious and political faction than the seventeenth century, and indeed with the emergence of a sophisticated party-political system it could be argued that faction became part of the permanent structure of British society in a way that it never had before, but a widespread desire to attain consensus rather than simply victory was a new phenomenon. It was what Dryden, as early as 1682, had been reaching for in his theological poem *Religio Laici* when he asserted that whatever ambiguities and problems the Bible presented, the book 'In all things *needful* to be *known*, is *plain*' (369).

Pope as a Roman Catholic with a wide circle of Catholic acquaintance had first-hand experience of the effects of faction. There were constraints on where he could live and what he could do; he endured the civil disabilities which excluded Catholics from the public life of the nation; and he was very much aware of the effect of the discriminatory and punitive death duties which were designed to break the power of Catholic families, and so diminish the threat of the Stuarts to the Protestant Settlement and later to the Hanoverian establishment. For him the appeal of Deism and Natural Religion may well have been partly that it seemed to override faction and make it irrelevant. It gave him access to an alternative social and cultural élite with whom he could find common ground. Howard Erskine-Hill, in an article exploring Pope's relationship with Jacobitism, suggests that his ecumenism may well have been not just a reflection of the deistic spirit of the times but also a reaction against his 'experience of sectarian narrowness and (his) upbringing in a persecuted church'.[11]

Another strand of thought which fed the sympathies of Pope and others was the evolution of ideas of ethics from the instinctive and emotional responses of mankind. Locke and others had elaborated the principles of human association and morality from the play of self-interest. The third Earl of Shaftesbury, whose writings were published as

Characteristicks of Men, Manners, Opinions, Times (1711), looked more to the heart: he believed that man had an instinctive moral sense, and that all things being equal he was inclined towards goodness and benevolently disposed towards fellow humanity. This reading of human nature was particularly flattering and attractive to a culture growing out of a century which had insisted on the original sinfulness of man, his innate wickedness and responsibility for all his sufferings. It seemed to break through into a clearing where ethical conduct would finally be free of the tangles of religion. It certainly opened up the way for the kind of non-doctrinal speculation that was called free-thinking, but perhaps its deepest cultural significance was not so much in its specific philosophical detail as in its general acknowledgement of sentiment and feeling. Fielding's Tom Jones is a hero whose Good Nature is in many ways a realisation of Shaftesburian idealism, though of course Fielding uses the elaboration of Tom's often equivocal story to problematise it.

The 'best understanding' that I have been describing in broad terms here was in its close formulations the property of an élite, even in a period which had as one of its central projects, as Addison expressed it in *The Spectator*, to bring 'Philosophy out of Closets and Libraries, Schools and Colleges, to dwell in Clubs and Assemblies, at Tea-Tables, and in Coffee-Houses.'[12] This may even be construed as more a socialising than a democratising of it (not least as some of the places where he proposes to have philosophy dwelling are places where women would naturally be found). The philosophers, deists, natural religionists and free-thinkers were, as I have suggested, positioning themselves against the prevalent ideologies of the preceding century, but they also increasingly defined themselves against the dominant political culture of the early Hanoverian period, the Whig hegemony, the 'Robinocracy' of Walpole and his fellow grandees and functionaries. The great achievement of the Walpole administrations was that they found a way of making British government work. Britain was prosperous, stable and peaceful (essentially free of challenge from Jacobitism within and from other European powers without). But this was achieved at the cost, it was broadly felt, of a venal collusion between the administration and the selfish opportunism of the money and City interest, of gross and fearless manipulation of the electoral system of the nation, of naked financial corruption and of ceaseless patronage and power-broking. Without entering the complex debate about how far Pope and his friends constituted a conscious and coherent (Tory) opposition to Walpole, it is certain that they constituted a body of resistance to the values and practice of a governmental machine from which they were by choice or history or disposition excluded.

The discovery and celebration of order, regularity and virtue in nature and human nature had class as well as political implications. Celebrants of stability and order were defining themselves against a culture marked by unprecedentedly rapid social change and volatility, with the evolution of a cash economy as against the old economy based on the value of inherited landed property, with a new and disconcerting social mobility, with the gravitation of power to the City of London, and with the development of a correspondingly opportunistic political system. Pope's *Essay on Criticism* (1711) is, like the *Spectator*, in one respect an attempt to make a particular kind of cultural thinking available to a wide audience, but it can also be construed as an attempt to secure enduring values under siege from literary and cultural vulgarity, popularisation and promiscuity. Talking of the discourse of the *Essay*, Nokes asserts that this is what ultimately governs it: 'In the end one is forced to concede that those elliptically expressed axioms to "follow nature" or to put "proper words in their proper places" add up not to a systematic statement of critical principles, but to a code for a patrician sense of decorum.'[13]

What is certainly true is that the most impassioned and moving passage of the *Essay on Criticism*, which is generally marked by wit, poise, perception and control, occurs when Pope laments change in the shape of change in the language in which he is writing. The language of Dryden will become as remote and obscure as the language of the Chaucer whom he had rendered into his own 'modern' English. Pope begins significantly with an image of diminishing patrimony, and then through the image of painting, which often came to him as a register of poignant feeling, traces a trajectory that leads to a death:

Our Sons their Fathers' *failing Language* see,
And such as *Chaucer* is, shall *Dryden* be.
So when the faithful *Pencil* has design'd
Some *bright Idea* of the Master's Mind,
Where a *new World* leaps out at his Command,
And ready Nature waits upon his Hand;
When the ripe Colours *soften* and *unite*,
And sweetly *melt* into just Shade and Light,
When mellowing Years their full Perfection give,
And each Bold Figure just begins to *Live*;
The *treach'rous Colours* the fair Art betray,
And all the bright Creation fades away! (482–93)

It is rather chilling that this image of a 'bright Creation' fading away at the beginning of Pope's public literary career anticipates his vision towards the end of it of universal entropy and cultural death in the conclusion of the second *Dunciad*, when 'Thy hand, great Anarch! Lets the curtain fall; / And Universal Darkness buries All' (4.655–6).

This said, the articulation of enduring values in the face of change, and even the vision of entropic death in Dulness at the end of the *Dunciad*, are not last words. They have the vigour of engagement, of being part of a cultural dialogue, and are infused with the energy of defiance, the daring of opposition, the offensive arrogance of rightness, the fun of impertinence, and the animation of argument. Everything that is said is said in a context, and for all their apparent (or assumed) Olympianism this is as true of what are sometimes called the Augustan Humanists as of anyone else.

Pope's most developed articulations of the network of ideas that can be summed up in Thomson's phrase 'the full-adjusted Harmony of Things' are in *An Essay on Man* (1733–4) and the four pieces published between 1731 and 1735 and collected by Pope's editor Warburton as *Moral Essays*. Each of these, and each book of the *Essay on Man*, was presented by Pope as epistles addressed to various friends. In the eighteenth-century hierarchy of forms, essay and epistle were not interchangeable terms. An essay was less formal than a discourse or a treatise. Copley and Fairer note how eighteenth-century definitions of the essay dwell on its looseness of form and they cite among other things Addison's reference (*Spectator* 249) to his own reflections appearing 'rather in the Looseness and Freedom of an Essay, than in the Regularity of a Set Discourse'.[14] Correspondingly, the epistle has a less formal construction than the essay. Rawson describes how Pope abandoned a notion of modelling *An Essay on Man* on a formal comprehensive work like Lucretius' *De Rerum Natura* in favour of something more in the spirit of Horace's *Epistles*. He says Pope 'retreated behind the less ambitious atmosphere of the Horatian *Epistles*, the more fragmentary and unsystematic causerie in a letter to a friend'.[15] It is none the less significant that in the case of *An Essay on Man* particularly Pope's discourse is open to description as either an essay or an epistle: it exists in a tension between the aspiration towards certainty of the first and the more tentative and exploratory nature of the second, a tension which is registered not only in the intellectual matter of the work but in its style.

The preliminary material to the first Epistle insists rhetorically, and

typographically, that the *Essay* will expound a coherent system: the first
Epistle 'treats of the Nature and State of MAN, with Respect to the
UNIVERSAL SYSTEM; the rest will treat of him with Respect to his OWN
SYSTEM, as an Individual, and as a Member of Society'[16] and Pope
describes his prolegomenary summary or outline of his argument as
'The Design'. The subheading of the Argument of the first Epistle
seems to carry confidence even to the level of hubris: 'Of the Nature
and State of Man, with respect to the UNIVERSE.' It seems to need
scarcely a quizzically lifted eyebrow to suggest this might qualify Pope
for a place in the *Dunciad* – and not as its author.

Such confidence is, however, dispersed when the poem begins with
its opening paragraph addressed to Bolingbroke. This tends to suggest
that comprehensive knowledge of the kind the preliminary material
limns out is impossible. We simply grab what we can in the flux of life:

> Let us (since Life can little more supply
> Than just to look about us and to die)
> Expatiate free o'er all this scene of Man;
> A mighty maze! But not without a plan;
> A Wild, where weeds and flow'rs promiscuous shoot,
> Or Garden, tempting with forbidden fruit.
> Together let us beat this ample field,
> Try what the open, what the covert yield;
> The latent tracts, the giddy heights explore
> Of all who blindly creep, or sightless soar;
> Eye Nature's walks, shoot Folly as it flies,
> And catch the Manners lively as they rise.
> Laugh where we must, be candid where we can;
> But vindicate the ways of God to Man.   (3–16)

It seems as though rather than tracing a design, Pope and his friend are
going simply to take what offers, and respond to it as best they can. The
exercise is to have about it the ease of recreation rather than the discipline of work, and the whole is to be more miscellany than programme.
The three images which introduce the 'scene of Man', the maze, the
wild(erness) and the garden are also problematic in context. A maze is
a place where you are bewildered and lose sense of direction. (Pope's
original phrasing of line 4 was 'A mighty maze of walks without a plan',
which would seem very much to contradict the spirit not just of the
preliminary material but of the whole project of the *Essay*.) Wild places,
wildernesses, were a much more powerful image in past centuries than

in ours. The wilderness was what surrounded the Paradise garden, undisciplined and dangerous, nature beyond control. An indication of the symbolic force of the wilderness could be taken from *The Duchess of Malfi* when the Duchess, about to embark on her secret, forbidden and socially transgressive marriage to Antonio, soliloquises,

> . . . wish me good speed
> For I am going into a wilderness,
> Where I shall find nor path, nor friendly clew
> To be my guide.[17]

The third image, the garden, might seem reassuring, if it were not so evidently governed by the idea of the Garden where man tasted the 'forbidden fruit' and fell from Grace.

However much the poetic force of the passage might seem to disrupt the philosophical project the damage is not fatal. Mazes, wild(ernesse)s and gardens were features commonly built into eighteenth-century estates, even into Pope's pastiche of a country estate on his five acres at Twickenham. Thus they could exist within a realm that was ultimately controlled, adding diversity without true risk. And indeed the imagery that runs through the whole passage figures Pope and his friend walking around a 'scene' as around a known landscape, like a pair of gentlemen on a relaxed morning shoot. Apart from maze, wild and garden, the scene incorporates the field, open and wooded ('covert') areas, low land ('latent tracts'), elevations and walks. It is a familiar and unalarming diversity, and is in effect a revisiting of the edenic landscape which Pope described some twenty years earlier at the beginning of *Windsor-Forest*, where the whole point of its diversity was that its different elements illustrated the existence of a presiding harmony:

> Here Hills and Vales, the Woodland and the Plain,
> Here Earth and Water seem to strive again,
> Not *Chaos*-like together crush'd and bruis'd,
> But as the World, harmoniously confus'd:
> Where Order in Variety we see,
> And where, tho' all things differ, all agree.   (11–16)

A difference remains, none the less. The Windsor landscape is seen through the eye of an eulogist, or an idealising painter prepossessed with composition. The scene of man is by contrast to be visited by satirists, a pair of sportsmen, or wildfowlers, looking not at the landscape but for game. What we have with *An Essay on Man* is a much more restless project than the panegyric, idealistic *Windsor-Forest*. The central conviction of a presiding harmony remains in place, but it is contested from without by alternative ideologies and the wilfulness of man, and from within by doubt, tetchiness, impatience, anxiety and wit.

Modern readings of *An Essay on Man* tend to respond to and confront its polyphonic character. There is no single controlling expository voice, but a play of contradictions. White and Tierney read it in a tradition of satires on mankind, designed rather to expose fallacy than to construct a coherent philosophical system.[18] Rawson, very sensitive to the poetic qualities of the *Essay*, finds it unconvincing in philosophical terms, 'a *tour de force* of poetic summation rather than an expression of urgent philosophical convictions'. Pope evinces in the poem 'his own high imaginative delight in ideas of order', and though his ideas about life subsisting in a conflict of opposing elements and passions are not new, 'he differs from some older poets, and from his own blander contemporaries, in the particular charge of tension, and the special vibrancies of resolution, with which he renders them'.[19]

Something of what goes on in *An Essay on Man* can be epitomised in two consecutive paragraphs in the third *Moral Essay*, the 'Epistle to Bathurst' on the topic of the 'Use of Riches'. They form part of a developing consideration of how some hoard riches and some are prodigal. Pope directs his reader to find such diversity reconciled in universal principle:

> Hear then the Truth: 'Tis Heav'n each Passion sends,
> And diff'rent men directs to diff'rent ends.
> Extremes in Nature equal good produce,
> Extremes in Man concur to gen'ral use;
> Ask we what makes one keep, and one bestow?
> That POW'R who bids the Ocean ebb and flow,
> Bids seed-time, harvest, equal course maintain,
> Thro' reconcil'd extremes of drought and rain,
> Builds Life on Death, on Change Duration founds,
> And gives th' eternal wheels to know their rounds. (161–70)

This locates man's behaviour in a general principle governed by a supreme power, celebrates that power as it is expressed in the regularity of the grand movements in time and space, and in its final couplet marries metaphysics (in the first line) with mechanism (in the image of a reliable clock). The overall effect is genuinely grand and reassuring: refractory and awkward as it may seem, man's behaviour is part of the grand design elaborated in the mind of God. The principle is then spelled out in terms of riches in the next paragraph:

> Riches, like insects, when conceal'd they lie,
> Wait but for wings, and in their season fly.
> Who sees pale Mammon pine amidst his store,
> Sees but a backward steward for the Poor;
> This year a Reservoir, to keep and spare,
> The next a Fountain, spouting thro' his Heir,
> In lavish streams to quench a Country's thirst,
> And men and dogs shall drink him 'till they burst.   (171–8)

As a confirming instance of the principle of balance and compensation just elaborated this is disconcerting. All the seductive mellifluity and harmony of the 'ebb and flow' of the natural world is gone. This is a different kind of vision, a different poetry, governed not by a beautiful reconciliation but by ugliness, illness, indiscipline and greed. Riches have only disagreeable manifestations: hoarded, they are maggots, spent, flies. The frugal Mammon seems sick – pale – and he pines amid plenty. That he could be construed as a backward steward for the poor seems untrue, as his frugality is meanness rather than any kind of trusteeship. As a reservoir he has no human value, but his spendthrift heir is not preferable: he is simply a waterspout through which everything held back rushes out in a flood. There is no restraint, no proportion, no discrimination. Men and dogs are alike in their gluttonous desire to guzzle him up until they destroy themselves. The image conforms with Ruth Perry's psychological reading of Pope in which she identifies an obsession with toilet-training in his satirical verse: 'His most savage satire, written towards the end of his life, was also his most excremental.' She has principally in mind the scatalogical extravagances and images of all kinds of voiding in Pope's overwhelming heroic satire the *Dunciad*. She generalises, 'Pope believed that what threatened the social order was unrestrained private impulse, and so moral training for him consisted in the discipline of instinctive response.'[20] The passage under discussion here may be an instance of the principle of balance and compensation, but it is extremely hard to see how it could be accommodated in the image of a well-regulated clock.

What needs to be said, however, is that neither paragraph is out of place in the poem. The two different poetic voices (and there are of course others throughout the 'Epistle to Bathurst') exist in tension with one another, refining, checking and contesting, and cumulatively amassing a poesy very much more intricate and interesting than that of the landscape passage from *Windsor-Forest* or of Thomson in the hydrology passage in 'Autumn'.

In *An Essay on Man* there are very many passages which evince what Rawson describes as Pope's 'delight in the creation or staging of harmonious and orderly systems' and his 'high imaginative delight in ideas of order'.[21] This is seen, for instance, in his celebration of the chain of being at the beginning of Epistle Three:

> Nothing is foreign: Parts relate to whole;
> One all-extending all preserving Soul
> Connects each being, greatest with the least;
> Made Beast in aid of Man, and Man of Beast;
> All serv'd, all serving! Nothing stands alone;
> The chain holds on, and where it ends, unknown. (3.21–6)

The poetic effect of this is not vitiated by the likelihood that Pope did not have a literal belief in the chain of being, and that it may have been for him what Rawson, appropriating Wallace Stevens's phrase for the world of the imagination, calls a 'supreme fiction'.[22] It is problematised much more by the following passage, a sequence of rhetorical questions which ask why man ('thou fool!', 27) supposes all things in the natural world were made for his use, and conclude in the injunction,

> Know, Nature's children all divide her care;
> The fur that warms a monarch, warm'd a bear;
> While Man exclaims, 'See all things for my use!'
> 'See man for mine!' replies a pamper'd goose. (3.43–6)

There is a shift of mode from the didactic, and almost panegyric, to the comic or satirical. This is apparent in the first couplet, and made sharper in the second, which is by far the more disruptive to the assumed tenor of the poem. The hubris of the pampered goose is shot out of the water by our knowing what it does not, that it is only being fattened to be eaten. So is man right, or is he just like the goose, smugly eating his way to his own destruction? It is not really the question, or the answer, that matters: what matters is that a universal collaboration and harmony seems to have been displaced by a rough image of exploitation and violence. In *An Essay on Man* irenic formulations of harmony are never true resting places, never uncontested by their poetic context.

A poem that should be deliberative and steady again and again turns spontaneously acerbic, and always about man, his attitudes and his habits. He may be the glory of the world, but Pope expends very litle effort in persuading him of this. Jest and riddle he certainly is, and that is by no means the worst of it. If he is 'wond'rous creature!' (2.19) he is only so in ironic comment on his presumption. Rather than speculating, and imagining himself supreme, man had better, Pope tells him, 'drop into thyself, and be a fool!' (2.30). What favourable images there are of human life are, like the presentation of the naive 'poor Indian' content with his limited hope for an afterlife where 'His faithful dog shall bear him company' (1.112), not images of our sophisticated modern life. The Indian exists in the poem only to illustrate our arrogance and presumption:

> Go, wiser thou! And in thy scale of sense
> Weigh thy Opinion against Providence;
> Call Imperfection what thou fancy'st such,
> Say, here he gives too little, there too much;
> Destroy all creatures for thy sport or gust,
> Yet cry, If Man's unhappy, God's unjust;
> If Man alone ingross not Heav'n's high care,
> Alone made perfect here, immortal there:
> Snatch from his hand the balance and the rod,
> Re-judge his justice, be the GOD of GOD!   (1.113–22)

Throughout the poem Pope seems to be engaged less in what 'The Design' proposes as a consideration of man than in a quarrel with him, answering human objections, claims, resistances. The mode is dialogic and the manner tetchy. Dialogue and refutation, explicit or implied, govern the rhetorical structure of the poem:

> Why has not Man a microscopic eye?
> For this plain reason, Man is not a Fly   (1.193–4)

> This light and darkness in our chaos join'd,
> What shall divide? The God within the mind.   (2.203–4)

> See! And confess, one comfort still must rise,
> 'Tis this, Tho' Man's a fool, yet GOD IS WISE.   (2.293–4)

Has God, thou fool! Work'd solely for thy good,
Thy joy, thy pastime, thy attire, thy food?
Who for thy table feeds the wanton fawn,
For him as kindly spread the flow'ry lawn.   (3.27–30)

    Look next on Greatness; say where Greatness lies?
'Where, but among the Heroes and the Wise?'
Heroes are much the same, the point's agreed,
From Macedonia's madman , to the Swede;
The whole strange purpose of their lives, to find
Or make, an enemy of all mankind!   (4.217–22)

If one supposes that the aim of philosophical discourse is to establish a sequence of consensuses, like so many stepping stones leading towards an agreed truth, then Pope's is an extraordinary methodology, as it is predicated on endlessly recurring disagreements. Of course there is someone exempt from this antagonism, the other second person of the poem, Bolingbroke. He is not the 'you' or 'thou', the generalised second person who is rebuked, insulted and corrected through the length of the poem: that is mankind in general, who is apostrophised in such lines as,

Presumptuous Man! The reason woudst thou find,
Why form'd so weak, so little, and so blind!   (1.35–6)

Bolingbroke is by contrast the addressee of the closing lines of the poem, 'my Friend, my Genius . . . master of the poet and the song' (4.373–4). It is on Bolingbroke's own style that Pope wishes to model his own discourse. He wishes,

Form'd by thy converse, happily to steer
From grave to gay, from lively to severe;
Correct with spirit, eloquent with ease,
Intent to reason, or polite to please.   (4.379–82)

As the inspiring spirit of the poem Bolingbroke is the 'guide, philosopher, and friend' (4.390), a being vastly superior to the crass 'you' of the bulk of the poem. But there is also a third second person who is not addressed directly but on whose existence and participation the entire *Essay* is predicated, and who is identified in the preliminary material as 'THE READER'. The reader enjoys much more of Pope's respect than

'Man'. This is apparent as Pope explains why he is publishing the Epistles separately. One reason is so that he need not 'impose upon the Publick too much at once of what he thought was incorrect'. The other is that he hopes to profit from the public's 'Judgment on the Parts' with a view to making 'the Whole less unworthy'.[23]

Pope, then, is able to suppose a 'Publick' deserving of consideration and capable of judgement, not to be identified with the superiority of Bolingbroke but equally not to be relegated to inclusion in the foolish mass of mankind. The reader, the public, is positioned between two fictions: one is that 'Man' is immensely perverse, proud and wayward, and the other is that only the epistolary second person, Bolingbroke, and his acolyte the poet are exempt from this universal folly. 'The Reader' is positioned between the two ideologies whose contention vexes and animates the whole essay.

This reader, this public, is also the unacknowledged addressee of the four poems that constitute the *Moral Essays* or 'Epistles to Several Persons', and is perhaps best conceived of as a suitable, understanding witness of a rhetorical act. In *An Essay on Man* he or she is perhaps more subject to the turbulence generated as Pope's irritation or disturbance breaks the smooth surface of the poetic celebration of system than in the *Moral Essays*; in *An Essay on Man* the rhetoric is earnest and urgent and inevitably elicits a degree of response. The mood in the 'Epistles' is somewhat more relaxed. If the drift of *An Essay on Man* is towards a rehearsal of human life as tragedy, in the 'Epistles' the reader seems more to be witnessing the parade of the human comedy, as Pope canvasses for his distinguished correspondents the problematics of human character and social behaviour.

This is apparent, for instance, in a part of the 'Epistle to Cobham' where Pope clinches his argument that the diversity of human conduct is made comprehensible once it is understood that all individuals are driven by a Ruling Passion, by offering a pageant of people exhibiting their ruling passions just as they die. This sequence of vignettes, from line 228 to the end, owes debts to the parade of the seven deadly sins and to the dance of death, but its effects are comic and poignant rather than harrowing. Narcissa dies true to the vanity that has governed her existence; she wishes to be buried in expensive imported lace rather than in the homespun woollen death-cloths the law required:

Odious! In woollen! 'twoud a Saint provoke,
(Were the last words that poor Narcissa spoke)
No, let a charming Chintz, and Brussels lace

Wrap my cold limbs, and shade my lifeless face:
One would not, sure, be frightful when one's dead –
And – Betty – give this Cheek a little Red.   (1.242–7)

Narcissa as she dies is engagingly alive in her language, with the modish 'Odious!', 'charming', 'one', and 'frightful'; Pope's epithet for her – 'poor Narcissa' – redirects criticism into a measure of compassion; she has a sort of integrity in remaining comically true to her own small values; and surviving in a joke, she attains immortality in a small social heaven. Who breaks a butterfly upon a wheel? Pope does when Sporus deserves it in the 'Epistle to Arbuthnot', but not here.

What is required of the reader in the *Moral Essays* is a sensitivity to tone that will allow him or her to accompany Pope into the appropriate moral and stylistic registers for the topics of his discourse as it plays through a sequence of subjects, and so attain with him a kind of collaborative understanding. It is significant that where *An Essay on Man* is characterised by the pugnacious second-person address, the *Moral Essays* frequently approach their topics through the first person plural – 'we', 'our' – or through a 'you' that functions like the 'one' of common experience. Both usages are seen in the fine passage in 'to Cobham' which describes the difficulty of knowing even our own minds, when they keep their form no longer than flowing water:

> Our depths who fathoms, or our shallows finds,
> Quick whirls and shifting eddies, of our minds?
> Life's stream for observation will not stay,
> It hurries all too fast to mark their way.
> In vain sedate reflections we would make,
> When half our knowledge we must snatch, not take.
> On human actions reason though you can,
> It may be reason, but it is not man:
> His Principle of action once explore,
> That instant 'tis his Principle no more.
> Like following life thro' creatures you dissect,
> You lose it in the moment you detect.   (29–40)

One effect of this assumed sympathy is that at times when Pope wishes to establish the constant application of a theory or operation of a system he is doing so within a context that supposes consent. In comparison the procedure of *An Essay on Man* is essentially eristic and at its high moments it triumphs in proving man wrong:

All Nature is but Art, unknown to thee;
All Chance, Direction, which thou canst not see;
All Discord, Harmony not understood;
All partial Evil, universal Good:
And spite of Pride, in erring Reason's spite,
One truth is clear, 'Whatever IS, is RIGHT.'   (1.289–94)

The 'Epistle to a Lady' begins with Pope endorsing a proposition
that is flagged up by its position in the poem as highly contentious:
'"Most Women have no Characters at all"' (2.2). His endorsement,
'Nothing so true', would seem like the introduction to a rather clubbish
essay in the long and unadmirable tradition of satires on women, but
this impression is modified as it registers on one that the 'you' with
whom the observation originated is the addressee of the poem, a
woman: 'Nothing', says Pope to her, 'so true as what you once let fall
. . .' (2.1) And it needs to be remembered that through the length of
the poem Pope is engaged in a discussion of the nature of women with
a woman. However apparently provocative the proposition is, the
poem is starting on a note of consensus.
    The paragraph that follows amplifies the meaning of the proposition
by drawing attention to a social fact, that society women like to have
themselves represented in portraiture in a kaleidoscopic variety of pose,
costume and character:

How many pictures of one Nymph we view,
All how unlike each other, all how true!
Arcadia's Countess, here, in ermin'd pride,
Is there, Pastora by a fountain side:
Here Fannia, leering on her own good man,
Is there, a naked Leda with a Swan.   (2.5–10)

These representations may be diverse and contradictory, but they are all
in some respects 'true': the proud countess is in another mood a shep-
herdess. What emerges is that women in society adopt the characters in
which they seek to present themselves or have themselves seen. Pope
calls this Folly grown 'Romantic' (16) – imaginative or fanciful – and
says, drawing on the imagery of the art which next to poetry meant
most to him, it is what he wishes to paint:

Come then, the colours and the ground prepare!
Dip in the Rainbow, trick her off in Air,

Chuse a firm Cloud, before it fall, and in it
Catch, ere she change, the Cynthia of this minute.   (2.17–20)

To represent women requires the most refined skills of art; the imagery
may be all to do with change, but it is delicate and alluring: to be
painted with a brush dipped in the rainbow, to be sketched in air, to be
seen like the moon momentarily posed on the edge of a cloud, is rather
to be flattered than to be abused.

To claim that Pope's is an engaging art is not to deny in the least that
he is patronising, looking at women *de haut en bas*, or that there is a structural sexism in his writing about women. But it must also be remembered
that Pope knew women in society better than any other male author had
ever done, and wrote about women with a depth of sympathy greater
than any male poet before him, and few since. Pope in this poem works
by developing an understanding and a deep reading of women's self-
representation: affected, inconsistent, emotionally exposed and vulnerable, condemned to lives meaningless in terms of all the values of the
masculine world, forced to create lives out of nothingness, desired as
brides and scorned as wives, they constitute a population that is by no
means treated dismissively in the sequence of portraits Pope offers. When
he reaches his major proposition about what animates women it is one
that invites the same kind of real consideration that the reader is invited
to give to the larger theory of the Ruling Passion in 'to Cobham':

In Men, we various Ruling Passions find,
In Women, two almost divide the kind;
Those, only fix'd, they first or last obey,
The Love of Pleasure, and the Love of Sway.   (2.207–10)

Traditional anti-female satiric discourse would stop at this point, resting in a dismissive summation of female character. Pope, however, goes
on to explain, that it is partly the fault of 'Man's oppression' that
women are as they are:

That [*love of pleasure*], Nature gives: and where the lesson taught
Is but to please, can Pleasure seem a fault?
Experience, this [*love of sway*]; by Man's oppression curst,
They seek the second not to lose the first.   (2.211–14)

This is a very long way from fully-developed feminism, but it is recognition that women's condition is by no means entirely a matter of

choice, and Pope's very strong language, 'by Man's oppression curst',
acknowledges the reality of the civil, legal and domestic disabilities
women had to endure. The rhetorical question in the first couplet
implies agreement, and so Pope, the lady he is addressing and the reader
concur in a far more sympathetic account of women's lives than any
other male writer of Pope's time would proffer.

Some of the thematic material of the third Epistle 'to Bathurst' is
treated elsewhere in this study (Chapter 3). The Epistle's main ideological aim is, as the 'Argument' expresses it, to demonstrate 'That the
conduct of men, with Respect to Riches, can only be accounted for by
the ORDER OF PROVIDENCE, which works the general Good out of
Extremes, and brings all to its great End by perpetual Revolutions.'[24] In
this chapter mention has already been made of how what Barrell and
Guest call 'the discourse of economic theodicy'[25] is problematised in
Pope's poetic illustration of it in this poem.

The workings of a balanced economic system are attributed in the
beginning of the poem to 'careful Heav'n' in supplying 'two sorts of
Men, / To squander these, and those to hide agen' (3.13–14). The
'careful' working of heaven might be supposed to imply a construction of some delicacy, designed to operate smoothly, like a well-
regulated clock, but the experience of the poem reflects something
much more reckless and haphazard. The vision of a society intoxi-
cated with acquiring and spending 'commodious Gold' (3.21) seems
Hogarthian in its wildness and indiscipline rather than a model of
'The full-adjusted harmony of things'. Even the word 'commodious'
embodies the two contending visions of the poem: gold can be
constructed as 'commodious' as it facilitates smooth transactions in
an orderly system, but it is also 'commodious' as it is a commodity
which ushers in the unruly mass of other commodities that seem to
run riot through the poem. This is the key to Pope's chaotic fantasy
of a society in which gold is replaced by the things it can buy or be-
token:

His Grace will game: to White's a Bull be led,
With spurning heels and with a butting head.
To White's be carried, as to ancient games,
Fair Coursers, Vases, and alluring Dames.
Shall then Uxorio, if the stakes he sweep,
Bear home six Whores, and make his Lady weep?
Or soft Adonis, so perfum'd and fine,
Drive to St. James's a whole herd of swine?   (3.55–62)

Gold it appears is 'commodious' – useful – in a social sense too. For a society that valorises politeness, it disguises what is really going on. Riches may not be ministering to a genuine refinement of society, just supplying in a dazzling variety of new forms those old true commodities, 'Meat, Fire and Cloaths. What more? Meat, Cloaths, and Fire' (3.82).

The 'Epistle to Bathurst' is the most various and animated of the four *Moral Essays*. It demonstrates an economy in action, but it is one that does not seem to run with the measured sweetness of Mr Hatton's clocks. If it calls to mind any clock it is the wonderful, vulgar, painted timepiece Huckleberry Finn so much admires in the Grangerford house:

> It was beautiful to hear that clock tick; and sometimes when one of these peddlars had been along and scoured her up and got her in good shape, she would start in and strike a hundred and fifty before she got tuckered out.
>
> (*The Adventures of Huckleberry Finn*, Chapter 17)

There is nothing in the poem that calls the supervision of 'the ORDER OF PROVIDENCE' into question, but it does seem to offer a bumpy ride, and it is interesting that the two most salient exemplary figures it presents do not seem to fit very well into the presiding schema. The first is the Man of Ross. There is no doubt that he is a figure who must be piously admired, but his quiet virtue generates little poetic excitement, and his remoteness and provinciality indicate that he is out of the game. His is not exactly a Horatian retirement: in his borderland marginality he is just irrelevant. He only really becomes interesting in a poem of this kind when his cash income is mentioned, thus providing something to measure him with:

> Of Debts and Taxes, Wife and Children clear,
> This man possest – five hundred pounds a year. (3.279–80)

Yet the moralistic apostrophising of the rich in Pope's next line seems forced and emotionally factitious: 'Blush, Grandeur, blush! Proud Courts, withdraw your blaze!'

The other case is also that of a provincial, the Cornish Sir Balaam, an extreme instance of the social mobility the new economics afforded, who rises from modest competence by way of luck and opportunism to great affluence; he buys a seat in the House of Commons, takes a foreign bribe, is impeached and hanged. His life follows the trajectory familiar in traditional tragedy, a rise to greatness followed by a sudden fall. At the beginning he was rather like the Man of Ross, 'Religious, punctual, frugal', and uninteresting, as the dismissive conclusion of the full line makes clear: 'Religious, punctual, frugal, and so forth' (3.343). What, however, makes him a really curious apparition in this poem is that his rise and fall are not attributed to the workings of a system but to the devil, who is mentioned five times in the story, and whose intervention is responsible for each stage of his career.[26]

As has been said earlier, a deistic belief in the presiding harmony of things was essentially the property of an intellectual and philosophical élite of which Pope was, in a manner of speaking, the laureate; Sambrook is probably right to assert that despite the importance and distinction of the Augustan humanists, 'the intellectual, moral, and social life of Britain was overwhelmingly Christian'[27] – or at least nominally so. Sir Balaam's story is clearly a story of the times, but its course seems to be determined by a construction of human life that ought to have little place in the Popeian schema. Its presence perhaps registers a lingering sense in Pope that the new economy was so spectacular in its turbulence that it called for cruder metaphors to illustrate it than those of balance and harmony.

Pope recovers his poise (to use a clock metaphor – the poise is the pivot on which the balance mechanism turns) in the most sublime of the four *Moral Essays*, the 'Epistle to Burlington'. There is a lot that is abrasive and entertaining in this poem in both sharp couplets and set pieces like the description of Timon's villa, but overall is the sense that Pope, Burlington and the reader are unanimous in how they position themselves. In their ideological composure are drawn together all the positives of Augustan humanism – sense, taste, nature, balance, time, progress and peace.

Two important recognitions are transacted in the poem. The first is that the aberrant and uncomfortable ostentation of Timon's villa will in the course of time and through the operation of nature be obliterated and transformed into a productive estate. The second is that the intelligent and sensitive aesthetic principles that are recommended in the poem's theory and concretised in Burlington's practice will have civic value and contribute to the growth and glory of the nation. Timon's ostentation, which inadvertently clothes the poor and feeds the hungry (4.169) is smoothed away in the little verse paragraph that constitutes the poetic bridge between his house and Burlington's:

> Another age shall see the golden Ear
> Imbrown the slope and nod on the Parterre,
> Deep Harvests bury all his pride has plann'd,
> And laughing Ceres re-assume the land.   (4.173–6)

The gold is to be manifested in the ripe ears of corn, and a fruitful field will displace the barren terrace. Time and Nature, the agents of 'the ORDER OF PROVIDENCE', will in enacting the designs of the supreme being annihilate the short-sighted planning of human pride.

Burlington will be the type of the wise builder. He will create an estate that has the traditional virtues of the old world of land, but it will generate and foster a prosperity that will spread outwards and enable a transformation of Britain from a traditional to an urban society that follows the pattern of natural growth rather than the crazy iconoclasm of the new economy. He will be one,

> Whose chearful Tenants bless their yearly toil,
> Yet to their Lord owe more than to the soil;
> Whose ample Lawns are not asham'd to feed
> The milky heifer and deserving steed;
> Whose rising Forests, not for pride or show,
> But future Buildings, future Navies grow:
> Let his plantations stretch from down to down,
> First shade a Country, and then raise a Town.   (4.183–90)

The concluding lines of the poem urge Burlington to continue his work of reviving the landscaping vision of Inigo Jones and the architectural purity of Palladio, and also to be an example to monarchs who will imitate him in sponsoring public infrastructural works (harbours, temples, bridges, sea defences) that will secure honour and peace for 'happy Britain' (4.203).

In 'To Burlington' Pope achieves a poetic discourse that articulates the social ideology of an élite culture and, marrying it with the traditional and enduring forms of the natural world, that seems to confirm the strength and supervision of an orderly providence over a harmonious world, Burlington's Palladian villa at Chiswick could be read as an embodiment of this imaginative construction. This exquisite building was probably built in 1727–9, the years immediately preceding the composition of *An Essay on Man* and the *Moral Essays*. It is set in a beautifully modelled landscape, is exceptionally elegantly proportioned; it lacks all unnecessary ornament, relying only on its own beauty. Inside it has a pattern of rooms, on the first floor, laid out symmetrically to accommodate the kind of social function that the beau monde generated at which to perform its easy superiority. The only shortcoming of the house is that it is useless for living in: it has no bedrooms, no offices, no kitchens. It was built as the annexe to an older country house that performed all the ordinary functions of existence, and it was joined to that house, sometime in the years of the composition and publication of Pope's poems, by a convenient two-storey link building. The old country house was eventually demolished, but the link building, which saw all the traffic between the mundanities of life and its sublimities, still remains. As an emblem of the stylistic and thematic reconciliation between the world as it may be constructed and life as it must be lived, which was Pope's project in *An Essay on Man* and the *Moral Essays*, it is articulate and poignant.

7

Science and Nature:
The Spectator, Gulliver's Travels and *The Seasons*

In *Spectator* 565 (9 July 1714) Addison describes himself taking a delightful walk at sunset. As the stars come out he is, however, prompted to a sobering speculation:

> when I considered that infinite Hoste of Stars, or, to speak more Philosophically, of Suns, which were there shining upon me, with the innumerable Sets of Planets or Worlds, which were moving round their respective Suns; When I still enlarged the Idea, and supposed another Heaven of Suns and Worlds rising still above this which we discovered, and there still enlightened by a superior Firmament of Luminaries, which are planted at so great a Distance that they may appear to the Inhabitants of the former as the Stars do to us; In short, whilst I pursued this Thought I could not but reflect on that little insignificant Figure which I myself bore amidst the Immensity of God's Works.[1]

In *Paradise Lost* which appeared in 1667, just five years before Addison's birth, the human pair were the focus of universal attention, divine and satanic, angelic and diabolic. By the time Addison at thirty-six was writing, the discoveries of the new science had so far penetrated the national consciousness that they seemed to call for an entire new understanding of the cosmos, and a radically revised theology to explain it. It was not so much that all the discoveries were new as that the habits and technologies of investigative science, with the telescope and the microscope particularly, had confirmed them with an unimaginable comprehensiveness: it seemed not only that a new universe extending from atomic minuteness to multi-galactic vastness had come into view, but that a new way of knowing it had emerged. Science was displacing

Revelation, investigation and demonstration shouldering aside faith and intuition. This chapter looks at some of the intellectual and cultural implications of the new science and at how these surfaced in the work of Addison, Swift and Thomson.

An awareness is now emerging that science and the discoveries that it excited have hitherto been inadequately contextualised in commentary on early eighteenth-century culture. Roy Porter argues,

> Historians [of science] are too little sensitive to the architectonic images used to render the earth intelligible. They have charted the growth of positive knowledge and concepts about the earth, but they have been deaf to the *meanings* with which these resonated.[2]

The fact that with Newton and his popularisers mathematics supplied the privileged discourse for the description of natural phenomena needs to be understood not simply in itself but in terms of the descriptive discourses it supplanted. Porter hints at some of the questions consideration of the cultural impact of the new science might prompt. For instance, 'Was anti-anthropocentric naturalism a strategy for securing the independence of man from kings and priestcraft?' (314). It may have been, but the question in turn raises others about royal or aristocratic patronage of the investigative sciences, and so forth. Science does not exist in a vacuum but in a limitless universe of meanings.

There is also a common implication that once discoveries were made they became common knowledge, but the extent of the percolation of scientific knowledge among even the literate, educated, male population is very hard to gauge. What did people know, how genuinely scientific was their knowledge, and how had they come by it? M. H. Nicolson, writing of Dr John Arbuthnot, later Queen Anne's physician and a close friend of Pope, says that his 'Essay on the Usefulness of Mathematical Learning' in 1700 'indicated a general acquaintance with new theories of light and color'.[3] This is quite impressive as Newton's theories and speculations on light, although they had been aired and adumbrated in various learned places earlier, did not get brought together in book form until the publication of the *Opticks* in 1704. Pope's poetry from the *Essay on Criticism* (1711, but composed around 1709) onwards makes frequent use of the new theories of light and colour, and his great philosophical poem *An Essay on Man* (1733–4) is permeated with Newtonian science, but he does not seem to have collected any scientific works. Maynard Mack's account of the 750 or so books Pope appears to have had at Twickenham contains no true works of science or natural philosophy, nor do any appear among the 150 or so books extant known to have been owned by Pope. There is a 1674 edition of Bacon's *Of the Advancement of Proficiency of Learning* and a home-doctorish book by Boyle, but nothing by or about Newton. Locke, Hume and other philosophical writers feature, but not scientists.[4]

What happened to a degree was that scientific ideas attained a currency among what are nowadays rather contemptuously called the chattering classes – not dilettantes, but people of lively intellectual interests, more interested perhaps in the implications than in the detail of discoveries. This is certainly apparent in Henry Pemberton's introduction to his *A View of Sir Isaac Newton's Philosophy* (1728):

> Every Gentleman, who has a moderate Degree of Literature and Politeness, may by this [his book's] Assistance form a comprehensive View of the stupendous Frame of Nature, and the Structure of the Universe, with the same Ease he now acquires a Taste of the Magnificence of a Plan of Architecture, or the Elegance of a beautiful Plantation; without engaging in the minute and tedious Calculations necessary to their Production.[5]

The apparent languor of this does not, however, indicate the extent to which the new discoveries were profoundly exciting to the imagination, especially as it sought to extrapolate from science to theology. This is evident in the language used by Denham in an influential work of physico-theology:

> if in the sun and its planets, altho' viewed only here upon the earth at a great distance, we find enough to entertain our eye, to captivate our understanding, to excite our admiration and praises of the infinite CREATOR and Contriver of them; what an augmentation of these glories shall we find in great multitudes of them! In all those systems of fixt stars throughout the universe . . . [6]

This excitement or sense of captivation, even of entertainment, is interestingly witnessed in a different field of discovery in a publication of 1681, Captain Robert Knox's *An Historical Relation of the Island Ceylon*. This records Knox's geographical, social and scientific observations of Ceylon which he made while held there for a number of years. It is produced by the Royal Society printer Robert Chiswell and carries two testimonials to its veracity, one of which is by Sir Christopher

Wren, who was a founder-member of the Royal Society. It also has a Preface by Robert Hooke, Secretary to the Royal Society and a keen proponent of the accurate and detailed recording of voyages with a scientific content. He commends Knox's account as an ideal example. The book thus has impeccable scientific credentials; but, intriguingly, as Hooke approaches the end of his Preface he departs from his somewhat arid official manner and launches into a rhapsody which suggests that as the reader proceeds he will be captivated and imaginingly transported into a rich and almost paradisal world:

> Read therefore the Book itself, and you will find yourself taken Captive indeed, but used more kindly by the Author, than he himself was used by the natives.
>
> After a general view of the Sea Coasts, he will lead you into the Countrey by the Watches, through the Thorney Gates, then Conduct you round upon the Mountains that Encompass and Fortifie the whole Kingdom, and by the way carry you to the top of *Hommalet* or *Adam's Park*; from those he will descend with you, and show you their Chief Cities and Towns, and pass through them into the Countrey, and there acquaint you with their Husbandry, then entertain you with the Fruits, Flowers, Herbs, Roots, Plants and Trees, and by the way shelter you from the Sun and Rain, with a Fan made of the *Talipat-Leaf*.[7]

By way of the imagination science becomes a property of the culture as knowledge is translated into experience, and this is what made the new science so exciting or, as it was irresistible, captivating.

In the nineteenth and twentieth centuries advances in science have led to transformations in the world we live in, making actual lived experience excitingly – or for some deplorably – different. Although the point is to some extent disputable, the excitement of the new science in the first half of the eighteenth century was essentially internal. Great changes were taking place in the culture: the financial revolution had permanently altered the national polity; changes in political structures and the rapid evolution of parliamentary party-politics added new dimensions to the national life; power was shifting from landed to city interests; the culture was becoming urbanised, and the countryside was being redesigned; print technology and the extension of literacy brought hundreds and thousands of men and women into a community of discourse that had never existed before. But none of these things was due to the staggering enlargement of the natural, global and cosmic universes being effected in science.

Although in 1700 Britain was pre-eminent (though not unrivalled, especially by France) in the field of science, it was not otherwise pre-eminent. As D. S. L. Carswell states, 'It is generally agreed that up to the beginning of the eighteenth century Britain was technologically and industrially backward.' He notes, though, that the British were good at learning practical things from others, and at importing skilled technicians. Carswell adds,

> As late as the beginning of the eighteenth century Daniel Defoe could admit, complacently, that the English were no good at making original inventions, although they were competent enough at copying other people's ideas and turning them to profitable account.[8]

It had in fact been part of the original project of the Royal Society 'to improve the knowledge of natural things, and all useful arts, Manufactures, Mechanic practices, Engynes and Inventions by experiment'[9] and this is reflected in the practical emphasis of reports of experiments in the *Philosophical Transactions* of the Royal Society, but it is hard to argue a link between experimental science and any technological advance in the period. Bernard Mandeville is of course characteristically sceptical about the matter:

> They are very seldom the same Sort of People, those that invent Arts, and Improvements in them, and those that enquire into the Reason of Things: this latter is most commonly practis'd by such, as are idle and indolent, that are fond of Retirement, hate Business, and take delight in Speculation: whereas none succeed oftener in the first, than active, stirring, and laborious Men, such as will put their Hand to the Plough, try Experiments, and give all their Attention to what they are about.
> . . . Soap-boyling, Grain-dying, and other Trades and Mysteries, are from mean Beginnings brought to great Perfection; but the many Improvements, that can be remembered to have been made in them, have for the Generality been owing to Persons, who either were brought up to, or had long practis'd and been conversant in those Trades, and not to great Proficients in Chymistry or other Parts of Philosophy, whom one would naturally expect those Things from.[10]

It is probable, in fact, that as Peter Mathias argues, the development and popularisation of mathematics had more bearing on the practicality of existence, especially in navigation, surveying, accounting and architecture, than many of the apparently more serviceable investigations of the era.[11]

Although the Royal Society with its many distinguished members and carefully established procedures for experiment and record was the leading scientific society of Europe in the late seventeenth century, it nevertheless encountered, as will be seen, both hostility and ridicule. What gave science its amazing prestige and intellectual glamour was the cerebrally charismatic figure of Isaac Newton. It would be a mistake to see Newton as a solitary genius who single-handedly revolutionised global science: exceptional as he was, he was also fostered by the intellectual and cultural ambiance in which he worked. But he became the focal point of Britain's intellectual enterprise. He was identified with his achievements in gravitational theory, in the mathematics that articulated it, and spectacularly in optics. His theory systematised the phenomena of the world and provided an intellectual model for an intelligible cosmos. Where Francis Bacon's knowledge had been endlessly compendious and extensive, Newton brought extent and limitlessness into order and was able expound what scientists now sometimes call a Theory of Everything. His explanation of the movements of the heavenly bodies offered an image of the cosmos as reassuringly regular and orderly, and repudiated Descartes' rather wild and alarming hypotheses about the universe consisting of whirling vortices of matter; but if there was one achievement that seemed to symbolise Newton's intellectual mastery, it was his calculation of the orbits and cyclicity of comets. Hitherto unpredictable, inexplicable and portentous, comets now became part of the clockwork of the universe:

> He, first of men, with awful wing pursu'd
> . The COMET thro' the long Elliptic curve,
> As round innumerous worlds he wound his way;
> Till to the forehead of our evening sky
> Return'd the blazing wonder glares anew,
> And o'er the trembling nations shakes dismay.[12]

The poem from which this is taken, 'A Poem Sacred to the Memory of Sir Isaac Newton' by James Thomson, who had studied Newtonian science in London in Watt's Academy, formed part of an outpouring of eulogy that followed Newton's death in 1727. The late 1720s and the 1730s saw the period when his reputation most nearly approached apotheosis before it was gradually occluded by the strains of sentiment, gloomy sublimity and melancholia that became a feature of British cultural life from the mid-century. There is a view that Newton's achievements in optics were those which most caught the public, or more strictly the poetic, imagination, not least because of Pope's exquisite use of light and colour imagery in poem after poem, but it was really the totality or the totalising nature of his theory that was so overwhelming in the range of its application. One single paragraph of Thomson's poem celebrates Newton's explication of gravitation as the force sustaining the solar system, his work on the moons of other planets, his explanation of the apparently aberrant movements of our moon, and his account of tidal movements (lines 39–56). Even so, it is Newton's work on light that raises Thomson to his highest pitch, and to which he devotes most lines in his poem:

> Nor could the darting BEAM, of speed immense,
> Escape his swift pursuit, and measuring eye.
> Even LIGHT ITSELF, which every thing displays,
> Shone undiscover'd, till his brighter mind
> Untwisted all the shining robe of day;
> And, from the whitening undistinguish'd blaze,
> Collecting every ray into his kind,
> To the charm'd eye educ'd the gorgeous train
> Of PARENT COLOURS.   (91–92)

Newton's resolution of white light by way of the prism into its constituent rainbow colours seemed to bring his mind very close to that of the God for whom light was a conventional metaphor, and facilitated the reconciliation of physical discovery and faith which as 'Natural Religion' (as in George Cheyne's *Philosophical Principles of Natural Religion*, 1705), or as 'Physico-Theology' (the title which Denham gave to his Boyle lectures of 1711–12 when he collected them for publication) became one of the orthodoxies of the first part of the century. It argued essentially from the wonderful immensity and diversity of the natural world to the necessity of a Creator or Contriver of it all, and so it became in essence a work of piety, or a form of worship, to study the creation.

    Scientific method as it had evolved in Britain through the seventeenth century worked from observed data to theory, the inductive method, rather than beginning with a theory or hypothesis and then testing it or assembling the data that would support it. Newton himself was famously hostile to working from hypotheses: 'hypotheses ... have no place in experimental philosophy' (*Principia*

Mathematica). Physico-theology seemed to bring religious belief very close to scientific method: the microscope and the telescope had revealed such an infinity of forms, such a continuity from the least to the greatest of living creatures appeared from the work of the naturalists, and mathematics demonstrated such a coherence and uniformity of organisation in the cosmos, that to infer a designer from the design seemed altogether congruous with orthodox scientific procedure.

For the most part one has to assume that the progress of the new science and religious belief went hand in hand. The Royal Society attracted some stigma of atheism from an association with Hobbes, but the scientists and Newton himself were all religious men, as were in varying degrees such writers who engaged with the new epistemology as Addison, Pope and Thomson. Swift's antagonism to science will be discussed later but it is worth recording now that his hostility did form part of a reactionary tradition that arose not so much in response to the totalising theories of Newton as to the practice of the scientists: the accumulation of a mass of data without any predetermined purpose and the conduct of seemingly bizarre experiments of no evident practical value exposed them to the ridicule of an age that often articulated its resistances in satire. In 1699 Dr Samuel Garth had ridiculed the quack science of physicians and apothecaries in his mock epic poem *The Dispensary*. William King's 'Useful Transactions in Philosophy' (1709) is, like Swift's *Mechanical Operation of the Spirit* in part, a skit on the *Philosophical Transactions* of the Royal Society. Most dissenting, or qualified, responses to the new science dwelt not so much on its achievements as its limitations: scientists seemed able to explain what the universe was like and how it worked, but not why, and there were other phenomena, such as the existence of instinct in animals (a topic we will see Addison taking up), on which they could say nothing. Poems like Prior's *Solomon on the Vanity of the World* (1718) and Pope's *An Essay on Man* both accept the descriptive capabilities of the new science, and underline the areas of knowledge where it cannot go.

There is another tradition of reservation which can be construed as originating in anxiety about what happens if a perfectly regulated interlocking system goes wrong. In Pope's vision,

> Let Earth unbalanc'd from her orbit fly,
> Planets and Suns run lawless thro' the sky.
>
> (*Essay on Man*, 1.251–2)

Poetic accounts of the Last Judgement or of the world-ending Conflagration, such as Elizabeth Rowe's dating from about 1708, reveal the Newtonian universe in deconstruction:

> And now begins the universal wreck;
> The wheels of nature stand, or change their course,
> And backward hurrying with disorder'd force,
> The long establish'd laws of motion break . . .
> No mightier pangs the whole creation feels;
> Each planet from its shatter'd axis reels
> And orbs immense on orbs immense drop down,
> Like scatt'ring leaves from off their branches blown.[13]

The existence of this apocalyptic tradition is an important context for Pope's great anti-Newtonian vision in the second *Dunciad* of 1742–3, which envisages at the end of the fourth book the extinction of the great principle of light which had illuminated the decades of Pope's adult life:

> She comes! She comes! The sable Throne behold
> Of *Night* Primaeval, and of *Chaos* old!
> . . . .
> Thus at her felt approach, and secret might,
> *Art after Art* goes out, and all is Night.
> . . . .
> Lo! Thy dread Empire, CHAOS! Is restor'd;
> Light dies before thy uncreating word;
> Thy hand, great Anarch! Lets the curtain fall;
> And Universal Darkness buries All.

> (4.629–56)

By far the most popular long philosophical poetic work of the eighteenth century, Young's *Night Thoughts* (1742–5), does not contest the principles of Newtonian science but equally it does not draw from them the inference that Pope was able to do in *An Essay on Man*, that all apparent discord is harmony misunderstood, that partial evil is in fact a component of a larger universal good, and that 'Whatever IS, is RIGHT' (1.291–4). Young's world is one of disaster, discomfort, pain and sorrow. For him, most of 'this terraqueous Globe' is

... a *Waste*,
Rocks, Deserts, frozen Seas, and burning Sands;
Wild haunts of Monsters, Poison, Stings, and Death.[14]

One of the achievements of the new science had been to extend in scope
and accuracy the measurement and mapping of the globe, but for
Young the precise documentation of the earth's dimensions simply
affords a metaphor for human distress:

Such is Earth's melancholy Map! But far
More sad! This Earth is a true Map of *man*.   (Night 1.288–9)

When he takes up the age's favourite image for a well-regulated mechanism, he finds that in the human realm it is a clock going wrong, at
variance with itself:

Though grey our Heads, our Thoughts and Arms are Green;
Like damag'd Clocks, whose Hand and Bell dissent
Folly sings six, while *Nature* points at Twelve.   (Night 5.633–5)

While Young accepts the discoveries made by the telescope and the
microscope in particular he sees that the limited information they can
offer may lead to scepticism and free-thinking. For him all knowledge
must always be placed in a divine perspective, and information should
never supplant faith. Addressing the sceptical free-thinker he advises
him not to read just a few pages in the book of nature but to consider
the whole of God's text:

... Who most Examine, most Believe.
Parts, like Half-Sentences, confound; the *Whole*
Conveys the Sense, and GOD is understood;
Who not in *Fragments* writes to Human Race;
Read his *whole* Volume, Sceptic! ...   (Night 7.1237–41)

Young's modern editor believes *Night Thoughts* to be evidence of a
continuing vital Christian orthodoxy through the earlier eighteenth
century and that it should help to repudiate 'exaggerated claims of
widespread indifference to religion' in the period:

It gauges the theological temper of the age more accurately than
Pope's *Essay on Man* or Thomson's *The Seasons*. Its exceptional

popularity points to a vital orthodox religious life in the years previous to the later famous revivals.[15]

It is probably true that an orthodox religious life, or various versions of
it, continued from the previous century untroubled by the facts or
implications of the new science, but there was no single 'temper of the
age' and writers did seek to address those facts and implications, and
not only in a literature focused on a cultural élite.

It was famously one of the objectives of *The Spectator*, the periodical
produced daily by Steele and Addison from March 1711 to December
1712, and thereafter by Addison and others until 1714, to bring
'Philosophy out of Closets and Libraries, Schools and Colleges, to
dwell in Clubs and Assemblies, at Tea-Tables, and in Coffee-Houses.'[16]
Although the context of the expression of this aim is much more jocu-
lar than is normally recognised, it is nonetheless the case that it was a
function of *The Spectator* to make knowledge and thought less the
private preserve of a few and more of a public and social property, to
make it part of a common and not a privileged discourse.

The Spectator takes up a huge range of topics in its trawl, in a tone
varying between the flippant and comic and the deadly earnest, and naturally its topics included the phenomena revealed by the new science and
the implications of those revelations. Two points need to be made about
The Spectator to begin with: firstly, most of the papers consist of essays.
The essay was a discursive form less casual than that of the epistle, but
more relaxed than the discourse or treatise, and in the hands of Steele and
Addison it is a highly personal form. The authorial voice is that of a well-
disposed, sociable, thoughtful individual man, as it were an idealised
companion of a reader much like himself. What goes through Mr
Spectator's head might go through that of any reasonably well-informed
person. Mr Spectator is not, like Newton, an extraordinary genius but an
ordinary man. The second point is that the journal was very successful,
and from shortly after its inception the publishing project was extended
to make *The Spectator* available in sets, and later in collected volumes.
This meant that from about April 1711 the authors were writing with
some kind of permanence in view. Whether in its purely entertaining or
in its more serious modes it was not going to be simply disposable. In so
far as it addressed important topics, then, it did not represent what
should be taken for passing observations but for solid reflection.

This is particularly true of the sequence of eleven papers produced by Addison on the single topic of 'the pleasures of the imagination' (*Spectators* 411–21, 21 June – 3 July 1712). These were a revision of an earlier essay by Addison and it is a reflection of the degree to which they constitute an intellectual whole that despite the normal practice of having the *Spectator* papers printed by an alternating pair of printers, these papers were – exceptionally – all printed by one, who had received the copy *en bloc* and in advance.[17] The 'pleasures of the imagination' papers treat the phenomenon of sight, nature, cultivated landscape, art, sculpture, architecture, literature and music, but they are dominated by the first of these subjects, and they could not have been composed except in the light of Newton's work on optics and of discoveries made with the microscope and telescope. They are not expositions of theory or discovery, but reflections on topics related to them.

Spectator 411 begins,

> Our Sight is the most perfect and most delightful of all our Senses. It fills the Mind with the largest Variety of Ideas . . . Our Sight . . . spreads itself over an infinite Multitude of Bodies, comprehends the largest Figures, and brings into our reach some of the most remote Parts of the Universe.

Inscribed in this are the implications that sight is the indispensable faculty of the investigative scientist (looking through a telescope, for instance) and that it is 'Our' sight, common to all. Knowledge and experience are as it were democratised in this discourse. (There was a minor preoccupation in the period with 'the man born blind' which is discussed by M. H. Nicolson, *Newton Demands the Muse*, pp. 83–4.) Sight furnishes the imagination with images that can be summoned up at will, and Addison conceives of this in terms of liberation, even for one seemingly deprived of freedom:

> by this Faculty a Man in a Dungeon is capable of entertaining himself with Scenes and Landskips more beautiful than any that can be found in the whole Compass of Nature.

Unlike the sense of feeling, sight 'is not streightened and confined in its Operations' to what is at hand. The identification of sight with freedom continues into the next paper:

> The Mind of Man naturally hates every thing that looks like a Restraint upon it, and is apt to fancy itself under a sort of

Confinement, when the Sight is pent up in a narrow Compass, and shortned on every side by the Neighbourhood of Walls or Mountains. On the contrary, a spacious Horison is an Image of Liberty . . .   (No. 412, 23 June 1712)

Sight not only confers, or constitutes liberty; it can also convey a kind of ownership. 'A Man of Polite Imagination'

often feels a greater Satisfaction in the Prospect of Fields and Meadows, than another does in the Possession. It gives him, indeed, a kind of Property in every thing he sees, and makes the most rude uncultivated Parts of Nature administer to his Pleasures.

(No. 411)

A man of active imagination endowed with the faculty of sight is thus not only free but lord of all he surveys both in the sense of proprietorship and of mastery. That Addison should generate a constitutional construction of sight could lend support to Porter's speculation that science might encode 'a strategy for securing the independence of man'. Squirearchical status and squirearchical pleasures cease in Addison's reflections on optics to be the exclusive preserve of the squirearchy.

This covert and of course not extreme politicising of science had some point in 1712, when the Whigs (and *The Spectator*, though disavowing party allegiance, is a broadly Whiggish paper) argued that the Tory administration was ending the long war with France by capitulating , and so surrendering English constitutional liberty to the absolutist Louis XIV. The Whigs championed the 1689 Bill of Rights as enshrining in the British constitution fundamental parliamentary and civic freedoms and rights, and had construed the war with Louis partly as a defence of these in the face of the dangers of monarchical tyranny. The freedoms revealed by an understanding of natural phenomena and the freedom which the Glorious Revolution sought to secure thus seem to consort naturally together.

Addison finds sight to discover particular pleasure in what is '*Great, Uncommon*, or *Beautiful*' (No. 412), three characteristics of what was being uncovered in the natural world and the cosmos by the new science. The identification of pleasure in the uncommon here is particularly significant as Addison argues that 'The Supreme Author of our Being' has deliberately associated novelty with pleasure in the human brain in order to promote discovery:

He has annexed a secret Pleasure to the Idea of any thing that is *new* or *uncommon*, that he might encourage us in the Pursuit after Knowledge, and engage us to search into the Wonders of his Creation; for every new Idea brings such a Pleasure along with it, as rewards any Pains we have taken in its acquisition, and consequently serves as a Motive to put us upon fresh Discoveries.

(No. 413, 24 June 1712)

Here Addison sees no need to give scientific enquiry any justification outside itself, in utility for instance. He does not even here advance the common argument that discovery of the wonders of the Creation prompts love and admiration of the Creator.

As part of an argument that sight is most gratified when what it sees resembles art, and that art is most gratifying when it resembles nature, Addison describes as 'The prettiest Landskip I ever saw' the image projected on the walls of what is evidently a camera obscura, of which there was in his time a well-known example at Greenwich. Describing the scene he notes, 'The Experiment is very common in Opticks.' The image includes movement, of 'the Waves and Fluctuations of the Water', moving ships, the shadows of trees waving, and deer leaping. Newton's experiments had thus extended the range of available aesthetic experience and pleasure (No. 414, 25 June 1712).

In an extraordinary passage in *Spectator* 413 Addison ponders the phenomenon of colour, which had been so salient in the new optical science. He sees light and colour as given by God 'to add Supernumerary Ornaments to the Universe, and make it more agreeable to the Imagination'. He imagines how bleak life would be without them: 'what a rough unsightly Sketch of Nature should we be entertained with, did all her Colouring disappear, and the several Distinctions of Light and Shade vanish.' At present we go through the world 'like the Enchanted Hero of a Romance' but without colour we would be like 'the disconsolate Knight' when the vision breaks up and he is left 'on a barren Heath, or in a solitary Desert'. Addison goes on to wonder if the state of the soul immediately after death may not be like this 'in respect of the Images it will receive from Matter', but then speculates that 'the Ideas of Colours are so pleasing and beautiful' that they will not disappear in the after-life but be supplied by some other 'Occasional Cause' than through 'the Organ of Sight'. The new science had so heightened sensitivity to the wonderful phenomena of life that Addison now imagines a heaven which must offer compensations for the loss of the world in death, and it is also interesting that in his vision of the condition of life immediately after death he thinks of the disconsolate Knight being deprived not only of sensation but of society.

Particularly striking through all these reflections and speculations is Addison's readiness to take the new science on board, and then to build not just on but with it in order to investigate areas of experience, aesthetic or religious, that would normally have been thought inaccessible to such procedures. Science has in effect created a new way of thinking about everything.

In the penultimate 'pleasures of the imagination' paper Addison talks about writers who stimulate the imagination by writing of factual matters, 'Historians, natural Philosophers [i.e. scientists], Travellers, Geographers', and develops his theme to argue that,

> among this Sett of Writers, there are none who more gratifie and enlarge the Imagination, than the Authors of the new Philosophy, whether we consider their Theories of the Earth or Heavens, the Discoveries they have made by Glasses, or any of their Contemplations on Nature.   (No. 420, 2 July 1712)

He expatiates on the wonder of finding 'every green Leaf swarm with Millions of Animals, that at their largest Growth are not visible to the naked Eye' and of contemplating 'those wide Fields of *Ether*, that reach in height as far as from *Saturn* to the fixt Stars, and run abroad almost to an infinitude.' He discusses how pleasant it is for the fancy 'to enlarge it self' by pondering the relative size of things from the most minute to the most vast; and how even the smallest particle of matter might contain within itself 'a Heaven and Earth, Stars and Planets, and every different Species of living Creatures'.

> such a Speculation . . . appears ridiculous to those who have not turned their Thoughts that way, tho', at the same time, it is founded on no less than the Evidence of a Demonstration.

The point Addison wishes to deal with, however, is that while we can conceptualise infinite range of scale, we cannot imagine it:

> the Understanding, indeed, opens an infinite Space on every side of us, but the Imagination, after a few faint Efforts, is immediately at a stand, and finds her self swallowed up in the Immensity of the Void that surrounds it.

Wondering why this should be, Addison conceives that 'this Defect of Imagination may not be in the Soul itself' but may in fact be a function of human physiology: 'Perhaps there may not be room in the Brain for such a variety of Impressions, or the Animal Spirits may be incapable of figuring them in such a manner, as is necessary to excite so very large or minute Ideas.' His hope is, however, that 'hereafter' we may all be more perfect in this faculty, and 'the Imagination will be able to keep Pace with the Understanding, and to form in itself distinct Ideas of all the different Modes and Quantities of Space.' It is a measure of how comprehensively Addison has assimilated the facts and implications of the new science that he imagines a heaven where the human imagination will be as free to make the Newtonian universe his property as is 'the Man of Polite Imagination' to acquire a kind of proprietorship in the fields and meadows that now gratify his sight.

It is an attractive little reciprocity that the name of Sir Isaac Newton appears in the list of those who subscribed to the 1712–13 collected octavo edition of *The Spectator*.[18] Apart from the ways in which his thought features in the 'pleasures of the imagination' papers, Newton would have found explicit references to himself in numbers 23, 101, 543, and 554, and, had he subscribed the following year, in 565 and 635. And he would not have dissented from the conclusion which Addison comes to when in number 120, 18 July 1711, he ponders the inexplicable mystery of instinctual behaviour in animals:

> I look upon it as upon the Principle of Gravitation in Bodies, which is not to be explained by any known Qualities inherent in the Bodies themselves, nor from any Laws of Mechanism, but, according to the best Notions of the greatest Philosophers, is an immediate Impression from the first Mover, and the Divine energy acting in the Creatures.

The easy commerce evinced in *The Spectator* between science and letters (and even the unsuitability of making so absolute a distinction) is famously not a feature of Swift's writing. In *The Rhetoric of Science* (see note 13) Jones sees Swift's satire on science as originating in a classicist's disdain for the intellectual promiscuity and vulgarity of experimenters and collectors of natural curiosities:

> ... the enthusiasm of Swift's account of the experiments in the Grand Academy of Lagado is not accidental. The fervor of detail in

the dozens of impractical projects shows that Swift was familiar with actual experiments described by members of the scientific societies of London and Paris and that he deplored the unclassical mind that mixed Newton's laws of motion with accounts of monstrosities, and accounts of strange discoveries from all parts of the world.   (73)

Swift was clearly ridiculing the scientists whose zeal for experimentation and speculation led them to excess and away from the decorum of a classical gentlemen. To Swift the Royal Society encouraged corrupt taste, and so he satirized its members playfully but also unmercifully.   (74)

Although there may be an element of truth in this (granting that 'playfully but . . . unmercifully' is an intelligible formulation) but it does not go to the heart of the matter or get the tone right. Swift writes of science and its procedures with a blistering sarcasm that reflects not elegant disdain but intellectual and spiritual anger. It is less important that he had a classical education than that he was a high-church clergyman with a caustic temper.

The very thing that so excites Addison's wonder and makes his imagination yearn 'to enlarge it self', the endless relativity of scale in the universe, becomes the satiric mechanism on which the first two books of *Gulliver's Travels* are based. In fashioning the Lilliputians and the Brobdingnagians Swift aligns himself with those to whom 'such a Speculation . . . appears ridiculous', and demonstrates that they are right. His narrator Gulliver is not so minded; his is essentially, though not always in *Gulliver's Travels*, a modern intelligence of the kind Swift gives very short shrift. When he has been picked up and almost squeezed to death in the fingers of the Brobdingnagian farmer he comments,

> Undoubtedly Philosophers are in the Right when they tell us that nothing is great or little otherwise than by Comparison: It might have pleased Fortune to let the *Lilliputians* find some Nation, where the People were as diminutive with respect to them, as they were to me. And who knows but that even this prodigious Race of Mortals might be equally overmatched in some distant Part of the World, whereof we have yet no Discovery?[19]

The brilliance and remorselessness of Swift's satire here can only be gauged by taking note of how easily a reader might respond to this passage by saying, 'Now that *is* absurd', the same reader who has entered into the spirit of the narrative by imagining just how big a Brobdingnagian must be and what it would be like to be picked up by one. Isn't Gulliver lucky not to get trodden on as he lies in the field?

The Brobdingnagians receive a fairly good press from Swift commentators for their comparative moderation and relatively sensible political and social attitudes, but they are nonetheless a function of Swift's satirical intention. The king, who is taken to epitomise good Brobdingnagian qualities, is not exempt:

> The King, although he be as learned a Person as any in his Dominions and has been educated in the Study of Philosophy, and particularly Mathematicks; yet when he observed my Shape exactly, and saw me walk erect, before I began to speak, conceived I might be a piece of Clock-work, (which is in that Country arrived to a very high Perfection) contrived by some ingenious Artist.   (2.3.103)

To conclude that a man is a piece of clockwork makes the king a version of the scientist who would explain the world in terms of mechanism. The aptitude of the Brobdingnagians for clockwork is a reminder that the race to make a clock accurate enough to navigate with was well under way by 1726. When the king hears Gulliver speak in his language he goes off-target and starts wondering whether Glumdalclitch and her father had somehow contrived this 'to make me sell at a higher price'.

The king, who appears to be something of a patron of science, orders 'three great Scholars' to examine Gulliver, but they are no more able than he is to see what is obvious, that Gulliver is a – to them – minute human being. In presenting their conclusions Swift's sarcasm overwhelms the fictional voice of Gulliver:

> After much Debate, they concluded unanimously that I was only Relplum Scalcath, which is interpreted literally *Lusus Naturae* [trick of nature]; a Determination exactly agreeable to the Modern Philosophy of Europe: whose Professors, disdaining the old Evasion of *occult Causes*, whereby the Followers of *Aristotle* endeavour in vain to disguise their Ignorance; have invented this wonderful Solution of all Difficulties, to the unspeakable Advancement of human Knowledge.   (2.3.104)

The Voyage to Brobdingnag is prefaced with an absurd map consisting largely of white paper, but which marks Brobdingnag as

'Discovered AD 1703'. Swift was not more friendly to the enterprise of geographers and cartographers than to the scientists. Only three years before 1703 William Dampier, the former pirate, had been in command of a ship which was engaged on a hydrographic survey of the coasts of New Guinea and Australia.[20] Gulliver refers to him in the 'Letter from Capt. Gulliver to his Cousin Sympson' as 'my Cousin *Dampier*'. The text of Book Two begins with a navigational record of the voyage and then proceeds to a preposterously detailed account of the seamanship needed to weather the 'Southern *Monsoon*'. This is in keeping with Royal Society commendations to mariners engaged on scientific or para-scientific voyages to keep detailed journals, later to be digested into narrative accounts, for the sake of record. Swift's sense of their irrelevance to what really matters is confirmed when at the conclusion of all this information, Gulliver informs the reader that in the storm, 'we were carried by my Computation about five hundred Leagues to the East, so that the oldest Sailor on Board could not tell in what part of the World we were' (2.1.84). This ironic procedure is reversed in the ending of the voyage. Gulliver is carried some way out to sea by a Brobdingnagian eagle and then dropped. He appears to be picked up at latitude 44 degrees (North) and longitude 143. This might be helpful in pinpointing Brobdingnag if the flight habits of the local eagles were known, but as it is it is useless. The reference places Captain Wilcocks's ship some thousand miles west-south-west of Vancouver Island, but it is in any case dubious in the light of the lack of any accurate way of computing longitude. Gulliver supplies details of the navigation back from this point, but as in the case of the information at the beginning of the book, it is a worthless record.

What above all distinguishes *Gulliver's Travels* from the mass of imaginary voyages, oriental tales, voyages to the moon, and so on produced in the first three decades of the eighteenth century is that Swift establishes his traveller in a dynamic relationship with his hosts and represents the conditions of life in the places he visits. In the third voyage Swift does not simply ridicule the eccentricities and excesses of scientific endeavour: he conceives of the inconveniences, discomforts and the spiritual blight of living in a world conditioned by the practice and ideology of science:

> Their Houses are very ill built, the Walls bevil, without one right Angle in any Apartment; and this Defect ariseth from the Contempt they bear for practical Geometry; which they despise as vulgar and mechanick . . . in the common Actions and Behaviour of Life, I have

not seen a more clumsy, awkward, and unhandy People, nor so slow
and perplexed in their Conceptions upon all other Subjects, except
those of Mathematicks and Music.   (3.2.163)

The Laputans do not only lead uncomfortable lives; they are touchy
and quarrelsome, especially over political matters. When Gulliver
records, 'I have indeed observed the same Disposition among most of
the Mathematicians I have known in *Europe*' (3.2.164), Swift is allud-
ing to Newton's querulous and unbecoming dispute with Leibniz
about who had first developed the calculus, or 'fluxions' as Newton
called it.
    Further to this, the Laputans' speculations and discoveries lead to
perpetual 'Disquietudes' and anxiety – about the inevitability of the
earth crashing into the sun, about the sun's losing its heat, and especially about the return of a comet 'which they have calculated for One
and Thirty Years hence' (3.2.164). Swift parodies the rhetoric of science
both in its lexicon and in its aspirations to precision:

if in its Perihelion it should approach within a certain Degree of the
Sun . . . it will conceive a Degree of Heat ten Thousand Times more
intense than that of red hot glowing Iron; and in its Absence from
the Sun, carry a blazing Tail Ten Hundred Thousand and Fourteen
Miles long; through which if the Earth should pass . . . it must in its
Passage be set on Fire, and reduced to Ashes.   (3.2.164–5)

Newton's famous calculations of the elliptics and surface temperatures
of comets are here reduced to absurdity.
    The intellectual preoccupations of the Laputan men render them
useless as husbands, and their wives and daughters fly for ordinary
comforts to the land below. The brutal and tyrannical manner in which
this land is treated, as described in chapter 3, is an allegory of Britain's
relations with Ireland, but it is also a measure of the dehumanising
effects of living in a world of theory.
    Chapters 5 and 6, which describe Gulliver's visit to the Grand
Academy of Lagado, are a satirical *tour de force*. They do, of course,
especially in Chapter 5, mock many of the experimental activities and
intellectual projects of the Royal Society and the other scientific societies that sprang up in the early eighteenth century in London and the
provinces. In their high-spirited vulgarity they reflect, as Jones indicated, a snobbish disdain for the gracelessness and degradation of practical science, an attitude which had been fostered in the Scriblerus Club

of 1713–14 centring on Swift, Pope, Arbuthnot and Gay: it existed to mock 'false tastes in learning' through the writings of one Martinus Scriblerus. Scriblerus's *Memoirs* were eventually published in Pope's *Prose Works* in 1741, but the satire on science in Book Three of *Gulliver's Travels* began its life then.[21]

The full effect of this satire as presented in the narrative does not inhere in the preposterousness of individual experiments, corresponding though some of them do with experiments recorded in the *Philosophical Transactions* and elsewhere, but in the cumulative impression of claustrophobia and melancholia. The Academy is made up of several decaying houses, but the effect is of being in a single ramshackle building of passageways and rooms giving off one another with the sounds and smells of the various projectors' activities seeping from one to another. It is a vision of a disordered, insane and airless community in which any door leads only to new lunacy and squalor, and as such it is proleptic of that kind of representation of an irrational and alarming space which is both product and image of the mind that has become familiar in the miserable dilapidation of Dostoevsky's St Petersburg or Kafka's Prague. If Addison was able to conceive of a heaven in which his imagination would extend itself to encompass Newton's universe, Swift's conception of a life in science is more like hell. It is significant that the account of the visit to the Academy is concluded with one dispirited little paragraph:

> I saw nothing in this Country that could invite me to a longer Continuance; and began to think of returning home to *England*.

Swift's distaste for science may originate partly in 'classical' disdain for intellectual disorder, but it has other sources which can be largely identified by inference and speculation. By temperament Swift was repelled by all kinds of modishness, and the translation of science in his own century into fashion and cult clearly grated on him. Gulliver's susceptibility to the manners and perspectives of Lilliput and Brobdingnag is a reflection of that, as is his complicity in the complacent and narrow ideology of the rational horses. He is unable to keep his personality, his social identity and the true values of his own culture or species (however manifold its defects) about him. He never prays. He loses a sense of proportion.

In a striking episode in Book Two Gulliver watches a Brobdingnagian nurse give suck to a baby, and he is revolted by the sight of her breast with its nipple 'about half the Bigness of my Head, and the Hue both of

that and the Dug so varified with Spots, Pimples and Freckles, that nothing could appear more nauseous.' Gulliver is led to 'reflect upon the fair
Skins of our *English* ladies' which only seem beautiful

> because they are of our own Size, and their Defects not to be seen
> but through a magnifying Glass, where we find by Experiment that
> the smallest and whitest Skins look rough and coarse, and ill
> coloured.   (2.1.91)

The 'experiment' of looking at human skin under the microscope is not
a futile or disgusting project like trying 'to reduce human Excrement to
its original Food' or calcinating ice into gunpowder (3.5.180) but
simple and practicable. What it does not determine is what human skin
is like. It might be possible to argue that Swift suggests that a lady's
skin is beautiful if we look at it through our God-given optics and only
rebarbative when seen through an unnaturally magnifying glass (out of
proportion), and that his attitude concurs with Pope's answer to the
question 'Why has not Man a microscopic eye?' –

> For this plain reason, Man is not a Fly.
>
> (*Essay on Man*, 1.193–4)

But things are never so simple with Swift. Strephon looks where he
should not in Celia's dressing-room, and what he sees disgusts him, but
it is none the less there. The 'author' of *A Tale of a Tub* records a couple
of 'late Experiments'. Among them, 'Last Week I saw a Woman *flay'd*,
and you will hardly believe, how much it altered her Person for the
worse' ('Digression on Madness'). Swift's response to the new science,
its cult and its implications is deeply unsettled. It amounts to what
Marlow in *Heart of Darkness* calls 'the fascination of the abomination',
a monstrous but compelling vision of what things might really be like
if all faith and belief were to crumble.

The composition of Thomson's *The Seasons* began with 'Winter' in the
spring of 1726, the year in which *Gulliver's Travels* was published and
the year before Newton's death, and it continued through the writing of
the three other poems and the preparation of many editions and versions
over the next twenty years, until the revised edition of the complete
Seasons was published two years before Thomson's death in 1748.
     The Seasons is a poem of extremely fine and detailed observation of

the natural world through the year; it incorporates the language and perceptions of natural science; and it is a work of sustained physico-theology. It is a reverential scientific pastoral, and it is work of pervasive appropriation: it brings into itself a multitude of the literary, cultural and social preoccupations and suppositions of its time, or more precisely of the first three decades of Thomson's life, which were also the first three decades of the century.

At the core of *The Seasons* is a belief in an invisible God who as 'Th'informing Author' presides over and inspires a Newtonian universe, 'this complex stupendous Scheme of Things', and who manifests himself in his works:

> Inspiring GOD! Who boundless Spirit all
> And unremitting Energy, pervades,
> Adjusts, sustains, and agitates the Whole.
> He ceaseless works *alone*, and yet *alone*
> Seems not to work; with such Perfection framed
> Is this complex stupendous Scheme of Things.
> But, tho' conceal'd, to every purer Eye
> Th'informing Author in his Works appears.[22]

The new science removed from the modern consciousness the idea of a directly intervening deity, and this is why God '*alone*' in the imaginable cosmos 'Seems not to work'. He operates through the systems he has contrived. In 'Summer' Thomson addresses the sun, which as the source of light and energy for our solar system is described as 'Soul of surrounding Worlds!' but the sun is also a striking manifestation of God's creative power, and also the one 'in whom best seen / Shines out thy Maker!' The gravitational forces that hold the solar system together are attributed to the sun and not to God, because their actual operation is through the objects of the creation:

> 'Tis by thy secret, strong, attractive Force,
> As with a Chain indissoluble bound,
> Thy system rolls entire: from the far Bourne
> Of utmost *Saturn*, wheeling wide his Round
> Of thirty Years; to *Mercury* . . .   ('Summer' 97–101)

Just as God is 'Th'informing Author' of all his works, so the sun is addressed as

> INFORMER of the planetary Train!   (104)

As his apostrophe to the sun continues Thomson takes for granted one of the more startling suppositions of the new science, that the universe comprises other worlds like ours. The planets are assumed to sustain life:

> INFORMER of the planetary Train!
> Without whose quickning Glance their cumbrous Orbs
> Were brute unlovely Mass, inert and dead,
> And not as now the green Abodes of Life.   (104–7)

The theological implications of this are considerable, as the idea of what was called 'the plurality of worlds'[23] contradicts the biblically based doctrine of the uniqueness of creation. The matter does not trouble Thomson: his poetic mode is hospitable to many different discourses, mirroring in a sense the multiplicity of natural forms that it celebrates. It at no point strains after the intellectual and theological coherence and consistency that had been one of the triumphs of *Paradise Lost* some seventy years earlier. For instance, despite its grasp of the universe as a mechanism, *The Seasons* is infused, whenever it treats of the animal kingdoms, with a totally unembarrassed anthropomorphism. This is evident throughout the long passage in 'Spring' on '*the Passion of the Groves*', the mating practices of birds (581ff.), or in such small details as his observation of a window

> where, gloomily retir'd,
> The villain Spider lives, cunning, and fierce,
> Mixture abhorr'd! Amid a mangled Heap
> Of Carcasses, in eager Watch he sits
> . . . .
> The Prey at last ensnar'd he dreadful darts,
> With rapid Glide, along the leaning Line;
> And, fixing in the Wretch his cruel Fangs,
> Strikes backward grimly pleas'd.   ('Summer' 268–78)

There is of course a touch of mock-heroic comedy about this, but it none the less reflects a persistent rhetorical habit, a habit that is grounded in sympathetic and careful naturalistic observation. When, for instance, he describes the darkening sky and first stirrings of the air as a winter storm approaches Thomson notices how,

> With broaden'd Nostrils to the Sky upturn'd,
> The conscious Heifer snuffs the stormy Gale.   ('Winter' 132–3)

'Conscious Heifer' would be a pretty difficult phrase to get away with in another context, but it has a part that is not ridiculous in Thomson's highly diversified discourse of nature.

Frequently Thomson draws on the language of science, or on the scientific meanings of language, to give technical accuracy and completeness to his accounts of the natural world. Elementary life-forms are 'Atoms organized' ('Summer' 290); a rainbow is 'refracted from yon eastern Cloud' ('Spring' 203); rain is 'genial' ('Spring' 186) because it gives life; lightning is generated from vapours of 'Niter, Sulphur, and the fiery Spume / Of fat Bitumen' ('Summer' 1108–9); snow comes from 'precipitated Air' ('Winter' 154); among 'the leaning *Strata*' ('Autumn' 810) of the mountains are 'rocky Siphons' (820) and 'mighty Reservoirs, of harden'd Chalk' (821) from which waters will eventually flow 'in pure Effusion' (828); the all-pervading power of frost is able to open the earth by virtue of 'Myriads of little Salts, or hook'd, or shap'd / Like double Wedges' ('Winter' 718–19).

It is extremely unusual, however, for Thomson to describe the world in exclusively scientific terms. Scientific language or technical description is usually blended with modes of expression that are heavily loaded with wonder or panegyric, so that a characteristic effect is a kind of natural/cultural rhapsody, as in the lines in 'Spring' describing the rainbow:

> Meantime refracted from yon eastern Cloud,
> Bestriding Earth, the grand etherial Bow
> Shoots up immense; and every Hue unfolds,
> In fair Proportion, running from the Red,
> To where the Violet fades into the Sky.
> Here, awful NEWTON, the dissolving Clouds
> Form, fronting on the Sun, thy showery Prism;
> And to the sage-instructed Eye unfold
> The various Twine of Light, by thee disclos'd
> From the white mingling Maze.   ('Spring' 203–12)

There are many other topics in *The Seasons* than have been mentioned here – the growth of cities, the evils of hunting, the wonders of remote parts of the globe, Britannia's magnificent commerce, love, marriage, meteors, and the migration of birds among them. It is its inclusiveness that makes the poem such an important cultural witness. From the decades of *The Seasons* onwards all kinds of writing, literary and non-literary, would become increasingly specialised. It is even difficult to make that distinction before this period. Thomson was one of the last writers to be able to take so much for his province, as Britain's first great empirical scientist Bacon, claimed in his letter to Lord Burleigh in 1592 to 'have taken all knowledge to be my province'. *The Seasons* is not a scientific poem: it is a poetic and imaginative vision of the natural world and its place in the cosmos that could never have come into being without the discoveries of the new science, and without a willingness to take them fully and at face value. It is also the fullest witness of the extent to which the new science had changed not just how the world was described but how it was imagined.

8

Country and City, the Choice of Life: Dr Johnson

Cambridge, London, Goslar, Paris, Orleans. Wordsworth knew about cities. His 'Lines Composed a Few Miles above Tintern Abbey' (1798) are not just a celebration of the 'beauteous forms' of the natural landscape; they are a resumption of a long negotiation, one of the major preoccupations of the eighteenth century, between constructions of urban and rural life. In the 'Lines' the site of this negotiation is not so much the viewpoint above Tintern as the mind harassed and weary in the city:

> . . . oh! How oft –
> In darkness and amid the many shapes
> Of joyless daylight; when the fretful stir
> Unprofitable, and the fever of the world,
> Have hung upon the beatings of my heart –
> How oft, in spirit, have I turned to thee,
> O sylvan Wye! Thou wanderer thro' the woods,
> How often has my spirit turned to thee!   (50–7)

Contemplation of the landscape and natural forms can bring to the mind trapped 'in lonely rooms, and 'mid the din / Of towns and cities' those 'sensations sweet' which will offer the 'tranquil restoration' which can quiet the eye 'by the power / Of harmony, and the deep power of joy' (25–49). Thus, at the end of the century Wordsworth is able to bring within the compass of a single consciousness the realms of 'the world' and of nature, the city and the country, whose differentnesses had seemed frequently over the preceding hundred years to present what Johnson's Abyssinian prince calls 'the choice of life'.[1]

This chapter will examine some of the ways in which rural and urban life were imagined and represented in the first half of the eighteenth century and will then focus on the issues involved in the writings of

197

one, Dr Johnson, who is seen conventionally as the urbanite *par excellence*, but each of whose major writings problematises and at least partly, rejects city life.

The dominant literary culture of the period between the Restoration in 1660 and the beginning of the eighteenth century valorises the accomplishments of urban living – wit, sophistication, money, sociability, promiscuity, entertainment. Plays of the period – the established theatre was of course pre-eminently an urban phenomenon – recreate the vitality, for good or ill, of the city and make it exciting and central. And this was not a passing thing: the city was here to stay. There were many reasons for this, to do with changes in the national polity, with the extension of literacy, with the financial revolution, with changes in the pattern of manufacture and of agriculture, with improved communications, with the increasing cultural significance of the bourgeoisie, and so forth. What matters is that during the Restoration period and into the eighteenth century the conception of metropolitan existence entered into public awareness and became an issue as it never had before. But the city was not autonomous either in fact or in the imagination. It existed in relation with the countryside, and that relationship was negotiated as a play of differentnesses. Conceptions, or constructions, of both the city and the country define themselves in distinction from the other. In the Restoration period the city/country distinction was fairly easily represented in binary opposition – urbane versus bucolic, citizens versus bumpkins, sophisticated ladies and gentlemen versus naive country wives and coarse squires. As the century turned, however, the cultural ground shifts and such simple binarism starts to give way to a much more mature and in many ways troubled interpretation of the urban/rural opposition: world and nature start to interpenetrate, and some significant lives, Pope's for instance at Twickenham, are positioned exactly in the site of cultural confluence, where town and country met and each took on something of the flavour of the other.

Of the dramatists practising in the first decade of the eighteenth century, after Congreve's *The Way of the World* (1700) had more or less brought the curtain down on the habits that had prevailed in stage comedy over the previous four decades, Farquhar was the one who most nearly preserved the daring and energy of the Restoration stage. Even so, it is significant that his two most popular comedies, *The Recruiting Officer* (1706) and *The Beaux Stratagem* (1707) are both set out of the metropolis, in Shrewsbury and in Johnson's birthplace Lichfield. In *The Beaux Stratagem* Mrs Sullen, who would have been easily at home in a typical Restoration comedy, is stuck in the country, married to an intractable and insensitive country squire. Her sister-in-law Dorinda tries to console her by saying, 'You share in all the Pleasures the Country affords', only to excite a scathing response from Mrs Sullen:

> Country Pleasures! Racks and Torments! dost think, Child, that my Limbs were made for leaping of Ditches, and clambring over Stiles; or that my Parents wisely forseeing my future Happiness in Country-Pleasures, had early instructed me in the rural Accomplishments of drinking fat Ale, playing at Whisk, and smoking Tobacco with my Husband; or of spreading of Plaisters, brewing of Diet-drinks, and, stilling Rosemary-Water, with the good old Gentlewoman, my Mother-in-Law?[2]

Taken slightly aback by the fierceness of this reply Dorinda asks, 'pray, Madam, how came the Poets and Philosophers, that labour'd so much in hunting after Pleasure, to place it at last in a Country Life?' 'Because they wanted Money, Child,' replies Mrs Sullen, 'to find out the Pleasures of the Town: Did you ever see a Poet or a Philosopher worth Ten Thousand Pound?'

There are no sides to be taken in this discussion. It is a comic enactment of a play of attitudes, but it is not absurd. Mrs Sullen's energetic extremism marks her at this point as a caricature of urban intolerance and so invites the suggestion that her attitude to the country is insensitive and bigoted. But her complaint also rings true: real country living could be comfortless, dull and socially barren. Dorinda's point about poets and philosophers preferring rural retirement to urban mayhem is of a piece with an age becoming increasingly interested in rendering Horace's 'Beatus ille' formula for rustic retirement into its own cultural language. When Mrs Sullen cynically derides any facile idealisation of rural life as the product of poverty she identifies philosophical retirement as the fall-back position of the loser in the game of modern existence, and as we shall see there was more than a grain of truth in this; on the other hand, her naming of so huge a sum as ten thousand pounds also confirms a reading of the city as a site of expense and luxury. She does go on to note that there is one aspect of rurality that she *can* relish:

> Not that I disapprove rural Pleasures, as the Poets have painted them; in their Landschape every *Phillis* has her *Coridon*, every

murmuring Stream, and every flowry Mead gives fresh Alarms to Love. – Besides, you'll find that their Couples were never marry'd.

That pastoralism could be a venture into a world of erotic pleasure was not a major component of the discourse of rurality in eighteenth-century constructions of country life (though it is present in a robust form in Fielding, for instance), but it is there, if often translated into a celebration of the innocent loves of the creatures, as in Thomson's account of '*the Passion of the Groves*' in 'Spring' (581ff.). If the country might be thought of as a site of amorous liberty, the city which Mrs Sullen represents was associated with licence, as she indicates a little later when after an exchange with her brutish husband she apostrophises the town:

> *London*, dear *London* is the place for managing and breaking a Husband . . . a fine Woman may do any thing in *London*: O' my Conscience, she may raise an Army of Forty thousand Men.

Mrs Sullen's extravagance is, as the play's evolution reveals, the flailing around of a woman in a melancholy predicament. Her country life is unbearable, but she draws back from the city licence she praises. In the end of the play she joins in a 'Country-dance' with the man who has been courting her and who has engineered for her a divorce from her gross squire of a husband.

Pope covers some of the same ground in his elegantly comic 'Epistle to Miss Blount, on her leaving the Town, after the Coronation'(1714).[3] Zephalinda is taken back to the country by her mother just as she is mastering the arts of flirtation and the manners of love in the town:

> Just when she learns to roll a melting eye,
> And hear a spark, yet think no danger nigh;
> From the dear man unwilling she must sever,
> Yet takes one kiss before she parts for ever:
> Thus from the world fair *Zephalinda* flew,
> Saw others happy, and with sighs withdrew.   (3–8)

She withdraws to a life of silence, solitude, dullness and slowness, brilliantly enacted in the tempo of Pope's verse:

> She went, to plain-work, and to purling brooks,
> Old-fashion'd halls, dull aunts, and croaking rooks,
> She went from Op'ra, park, assembly, play,

To morning walks, and pray'rs three hours a day;
To pass her time 'twixt reading and Bohea,
To muse, and spill her solitary Tea,
Or o'er cold coffee trifle with the spoon,
Count the slow clock, and dine exact at noon;
Divert her eyes with pictures in the fire,
Hum half a tune, tell stories to the squire;
Up to her godly garret after sev'n,
There starve and pray, for that's the way to heav'n.   (11–22)

The contrast between actual and imagined pastoral is captured in the rhyming of literary 'purling brooks' with mundane 'croaking rooks'. That the real pastoral is no release into the careless love of 'Phillis' and 'Coridon' is underlined in the only figure the country offers for amorous dalliance:

Some Squire, perhaps, you take delight to rack;
Whose game is Whisk, whose treat a toast in sack,
Who visits with a gun, presents you birds,
Then gives a smacking buss, and cries – No words!
Or with his hound comes hollowing from the stable,
Makes love with nods, and knees beneath a table;
Whose laughs are hearty, tho' his jests are coarse,
And loves you best of all things – but his horse.   (23–30)

The cases of both Mrs Sullen and Zephalinda are in a sense rehearsals of an old theme, or an old joke, albeit one that would retain a lot of vitality even into the twentieth century. The contemporary discourse of city and country in the first half of the eighteenth century found itself in many other terms as well, and it had an urgency because both town and country were constructions in a sense more literal than that which has been used so far in this chapter.

In the first place London itself was under reconstruction following the Great Fire – the fifty new churches were still being built in Anne's reign – and to accommodate a steadily expanding population. Other cities, too, were expanding, but London was the metonym of urban life in the period. It was starting to become a city that would be recognisable as the London of, if not the 1990s, of the period before modern building techniques facilitated the construction of very tall buildings with non-structural walls. The City and Westminster were approaching one another. The famous squares of large houses were being built in open country that would gradually be filled in with humbler streets and structures. Brick and stucco and Portland stone displaced timber frames. Paving stones suited to carriage traffic began to replace cobbles. There were new sites of public resort, pleasure gardens and their associated buildings. Suburban residential areas were being developed, not least along the banks of the Thames from Chelsea to Twickenham. At the same time the countryside, called by one commentator 'England's greatest work of art',[4] was changing – not all of it, but those parts most accessible from the cities. Open land and common land was being enclosed, sometimes for sheep, sometimes for agriculture. Old forests were being felled for clearance, construction and ship-building. A new aesthetics of country life was inventing a park-landscape for the wealthy. Old, low Elizabethan and seventeenth-century country and farm houses were being replaced or made over in the modern versions of Palladian style. The land was made increasingly productive to feed the new large urban populations, and more congenial for those who wanted retreat without wilderness.

These things, together with manifold shifts in the focuses of power in the nation, with successful merchants and financiers buying themselves into land, and the traditional aristocracy reinvigorating their wealth by financial investment, made the relation of city and country culturally salient and problematic as it had never been before. For instance, in the middle of the preceding century when Marvell in 'An Horatian Ode'(1650) describes Cromwell making his move into public life, he moves

> . . . from his private gardens, where
> He lived reserv'd and austere
>   (As if his highest plot
>   To plant the bergamot)   (29–32)

The point about the pun on 'plot' is that the two meanings are quite distinct. Cromwell moves from his innocent rustic 'plot' to the world of political machination. The paradise garden and the political plot belong to different conceptual realms. Even when Marvell introduces the idea of the garden as the place of the Fall, it is a fall that does no harm:

> Stumbling on melons as I pass,
> Insnared with flowers, I fall on grass.   ('The Garden' 39–40)

By the eighteenth century no simple oppositional construction such as this was sufficient to articulate the complex relation of city and country. If one takes an instance from the latter end of the period this study treats, Fielding's account of Squire Allworthy's residence – Paradise Hall – in the fourth chapter of *Tom Jones* (1749) appears to embody all the qualities a rural existence might offer. The house is set on a hillside, sheltered from north-east winds by woods, but still affording a 'charming prospect'. It epitomises 'order in variety': there is a lawn, and by contrast 'a rock covered with firs'; there is a tumbling waterfall that eventually settles into a lake by the house; there is pasture grazed by sheep; there is meadowland and woodland, populated villages and a ruined abbey in view; there are pleasure grounds exhibiting a diversity of 'hills, lawns, wood, and water' tastefully laid out, 'but owing less to art than to nature'. In the distance is the sea, behind are mountains. The only thing that can outdo this prospect of natural perfection is the image of pious and sociable man, Mr Allworthy, appearing on his terrace, 'a human being replete with benevolence, meditating in what manner he might render himself most acceptable to his Creator, by doing most good to his creatures.' There is nothing wrong with this, just too much that is right. Fielding has, as he says, led us up to the top of a high hill, from which we shall all have to 'slide down together'. We are accordingly invited to move from the Gainsborough-like representation of Mr Allworthy presiding over his landscape to join Bridget, Mr Allworthy and the author at breakfast.[5] Idealism has to yield at times to appetite; even Allworthy eats. In the evolution of Fielding's story the country house will have to be the site in which idealism and appetite become reconciled if it is not to call into question the harmonious and equitable dispensation of Providence. Fielding's plot must incorporate both Cromwell's public and private plots.

Before returning to this theme it is worth examining a temperament, and a text, which takes as its axiom that the country and country life embodies all that is of the deepest and most enduring human value – Thomson in *The Seasons*. The seasons are the seasons of the rural year, and the country and the natural world are the constant points of reference throughout, and the starting and finishing point of all scientific, philosophical and religious speculation in the work.

The first city to be mentioned in *The Seasons* is no city at all, but the tree-top dwellings of the rook,

> . . . who high amid the Boughs
> In early Spring, his airy City builds.[6]   ('Spring' 768–9)

The rookery is built near a farmstead, 'a rural Seat', where Thomson can study an instance of social organisation, a polity:

> . . . there, well-pleas'd,
> I might the various Polity survey
> Of the mixt Household-Kind.   (770–2)

What Thomson discovers in the rookery and the farmstead are not the city and the polity of London and government, but reinscriptions of them in rural terms; in a context where they are stripped of vice and corruption. Repeatedly by instinct and conviction Thomson represents the country as the site of the good life, epitomised in 'Spring' as,

> An elegant Sufficiency, Content,
> Retirement, rural Quiet, Friendship, Books,
> Ease and alternate Labour, useful Life,
> Progressive Virtue, and approving HEAVEN.   (1161–4)

Thomson is, however, too honest and intelligent not to acknowledge that such a cultural achievement, such a poise, is on the one hand not the whole story of British life in the eighteenth century, and on the other that it is not a primitive condition, but one that has been made possible only by the gradual emergence of man from elemental savagery.

One of his resorts is simply to celebrate the city as an idealised construction, as a centre of productive energy and creative gratification. In his panegyric on Britain in 'Summer' he eulogises the new urban vitality:

> FULL are thy Cities with the Sons of Art;
> And Trade and Joy, in every busy Street,
> Mingling are heard: even Drudgery himself,
> As at the Car he sweats, or dusty hews
> The Palace-Stone, looks gay.   (1457–61)

Preposterous though it may seem, it is important to realise that the city *could* be constructed in these terms, that Hogarth could engrave a persuasively jolly Beer Street as well as an apocalyptic Gin Lane.

The complex culture of modern social existence, whether rural or urban, was the achievement of a process of which Thomson sees industry (creative work) as the engine. In a long passage celebrating industry he represents it as

> . . . the kind Source of every gentle Art,
> And all the soft Civility of Life.   ('Autumn' 45–6)

Industry alone enabled the emergence of the social concept of 'home' out of primitive savagery. It is a high achievement, a focus of comfort, solidarity and affection:

> ... Home is the Resort
> Of Love, of Joy, of Peace and Plenty, where,
> Supporting and supported, polish'd Friends,
> And dear Relations mingle into Bliss.   (65–8)

The same energy that creates home also fosters all social relations and all the cultural pleasure associated with urban life, the development of government and law, art, construction and commerce, and migration from the countryside:

> HENCE every Form of cultivated Life
> In Order set, protected, and inspired,
> Into Perfection wrought. Uniting All,
> Society grew numerous, high, polite,
> And happy. Nurse of Art! The City rear'd
> In beauteous Pride her Tower-encircled Head;
> And, stretching Street on Street, by Thousands drew,
> From twining woody Haunts, or the tough Yew
> To Bows strong-straining, her aspiring Sons.
> THEN Commerce brought into the public Walk
> The Busy Merchant; the big Ware-house built;
> Rais'd the strong Crane; choak'd up the loaded Street
> With foreign Plenty ...   ('Autumn' 109–21)

What Thomson is confronting and acknowledging is the fact that without the processes that lead to modern urban life, and perhaps without that life at all, mankind will not be able to enjoy 'Civility', 'polished Friends', 'Cultivation' in its cultural sense, or 'Art'. Even so, this acknowledgement made, the choice of life of the philosophical and sensitive will be to turn from all this populous activity to the quiet isolation of the countryside. Later in 'Autumn' Thomson is again celebrating the life of

> ... the Man, who, from the World escap'd,
> In still Retreats, and flowery Solitudes,
> To Nature's Voice attends ...   (1304–6)

And 'Nature' here really does mean the world of natural history, not the diffused quasi-metaphysical principle that is Pope's cultural touchstone.

It is also the case that despite all he has said, the city remains for
Thomson a Bad Place. 'This', he says of a country existence, 'is the Life
which those who fret in Guilt, / And guilty Cities, never knew'
(1348–9).

In 'Winter' contrasting pictures are drawn of an evening spent in the
country and one in the city. In the country we have 'the Goblin-Story',
'the rural Gambol', 'Rustic Mirth', 'The simple Joke', 'the long loud
Laugh, sincere', 'The Kiss, snatch'd hasty', and 'Notes / Of native
Music' (619–28). In the city these bucolic revels are supplanted by a
febrile decadence, and only gradually is something like comfortable
luxury allowed in:

> THE City swarms intense. The public Haunt,
> Full of each Theme, and warm with mixt Discourse,
> Hums indistinct. The Sons of Riot flow[7]
> Down the loose Stream of false inchanted Joy,
> To swift Destruction. On the rankled Soul
> The gaming Fury falls; and in one Gulph
> Of total Ruin, Honour, Virtue, Peace,
> Friends, Families, and Fortune, headlong Sink.
> Up-springs the Dance along the lighted Dome,
> Mix'd, and evolv'd, a thousand sprightly Ways.
> The glittering Court effuses every Pomp;
> The Circle deepens: beam'd from gaudy Robes,
> Tapers, and sparkling Gems, and radiant Eyes,
> A soft Effulgence o'er the Palace waves:
> While, a gay Insect in *his* Summer-shine,
> The Fop, light-fluttering, spreads his mealy Wings.
>
> ('Winter' 630–45)

It is interesting that as we come down from the fury of the urban
gamblers to the harmless fop, the image that conveys him is drawn
from natural history.

The Seasons is overwhelmingly about the natural world, which
Thomson represents as huge, dynamic and violent as well as tranquil,
but what is important is that writing about the natural world is a choice
of one subject as against others possible. It is in itself an escape into
rurality, and one that can only be effected by an author himself the
product of the civility, cultivation and polish made possible by the social
and technological evolution that also generates the energy and corruption of the city. David Nokes observes that 'The culture of Augustan

writers such as Pope and Addison, Fielding and Johnson draws its sustenance from the social life which it describes. It is a celebration of the values of good fellowship, conversation, civilization and humanity which society, at its best, exists to foster.'[8] The rehearsing of the contrast between urban and rural life or between 'the world' and retirement, in much writing of the first part of the eighteenth century, is an endeavour to discover where those values might best be nurtured and sustained.

There are two problems with Thomson's version of rural life. The first is, as the picture of the rustic evening indicates, that it was archaic. One key to this is the inclusion of the 'Goblin-Story' as part of the entertainment, because fairy stories belonged to a lost past. J. Paul Hunter spends some time elucidating what he calls 'the mystery' of 'what happened to fairy tales during the seventeenth century, for they disappeared from the English consciousness, their household familiarity in Shakespeare's day having dwindled to nothing by the time of Henry and Sarah Fielding'.[9] They had been part of 'the old oral culture of the English countryside', but there is nothing outside Thomson that suggests they were a vital part of village life in his own century. The second problem is that the gratifications of a retired life focused on the observation of the natural world are, despite 'polished Friends/ And dear Relations', essentially the pleasures of solitary reflection, and so they cannot be the model for an alternative sociability to that of the city.[10]

Thomson's bucolics were inaccessible because they had disappeared; 'country Pleasures' were as coarse and limited as Mrs Sullen knew them to be, and as Zephalinda might dread them; hermetic retirement was unsociable; none of these could gratify temperaments attuned to the cultural and productive dynamics of city life. But city life itself was made intolerable by greed, guilt and corruption. The tensions these contradictions involved became themselves a source of creative energy in the period, and at times could generate unprecedented images of social existence, or at least glimpses of new possibilities.

As I have intimated in speaking of Mr Allworthy's Paradise Hall, one salient construction – in both senses – in the period's negotiation of the city/country antinomy is the country house. Virginia Kenny in *The Country-House Ethos in English Literature, 1688–1750* argues that eighteenth-century writers appropriated the values expressed in the panegyric country-house poems of the seventeenth century, such as Jonson's 'To Penshurst' and Marvell's 'Upon Appleton House', as a basis for 'a theory of the right use of wealth and power applicable by all to the problems of a new age'.[11] It is her argument that,

Wherever in early eighteenth-century literature one finds in the same work reference to both the rural and urban mores (or to the customary and civil social structures), there are likely to be present some of the constellation of images associated with the ethos celebrated in the country-house panegyric.   (3)

That ethos embodied a triad of lordly virtues – hospitality, independence and stewardship (5–6). The idea of the country house 'led to its being pervasively used in the early eighteenth century as the model for the good society' (9). That there is a lot in this is confirmed in the frequency of the use of the word 'seat' in the sense of established rural residence in favourable contexts throughout the period, as in Thomson's 'rural seat' and in the way the forests and the 'green Retreats' around Windsor are commended in the opening couplet of Pope's poem as

At once the Monarch's and the Muse's Seats.   (*Windsor-Forest*, 2)

Even so, the idea does need to be treated with a little care. It may well be that the well-managed country estate of the Lord Munodi whom Gulliver visits in *Gulliver's Travels* (3.4) is a 'pattern of the good society' (*The Country-House Ethos*, 108), but it is less than axiomatic that in Book Four 'the horses are to be admired for their way of life . . . they are a simple agrarian society, self-sufficient, non-speculative and decorously gregarious' (108). Furthermore, however attractively the country house may be constructed in some eighteenth-century discourse, it is not so everywhere. Not only is Paradise Hall visited with Fielding's irony, but Allworthy's neighbour's estate, Squire Western's, is characterised by indiscipline, coarseness, passion, autocracy, violence and persecution. And Richardson's heroines Pamela and Clarissa, and Harriet Byron in *Sir Charles Grandison*, undergo very dreadful experiences of social, sexual, familial and criminal oppression and persecution in country houses. They may have been places where freedom could be found, but they were also places where it could be abused.

Pope is intimately associated with the idea of rural retirement and with the concept of good stewardship through his little early recension of Horace *Epodes* 2.1, the 'Ode to Solitude'; through his preoccupation with the notions of nature and the natural; through his interest in the landscape; through his construction of a miniature or pastiche country estate at Twickenham, and through his celebration of good practice, as in the ending of the fourth *Moral Essay*. But even so it is notable that his most famous rural residence, Timon's villa, is a country house abused. It is built in defiance of human scale and at variance with nature, and it ministers to nothing but vanity and discomfort ('Epistle to Burlington', 99–126). Equally to the point is the fact that the contrasting example of good practice at the end of the poem does not simply celebrate good management for its own sake, but because it will contribute to the extension of national growth and prosperity. The good landlord's plantations will 'First shade a Country, and then raise a Town' (190). Natural growth properly cultivated will promote a growing civility.

Maynard Mack aphoristically begins his study of Pope's use of rural and urban topoi with the assertion that 'Pope's poetry . . . begins with a garden and ends with a city'.[12] The garden is the Horatian 'few paternal acres' of the juvenile 'Ode on Solitude' and the city is the urban nightmare of the four-book *Dunciad*. A few pages later Mack refines this by saying, of the 'Epistle to Arbuthnot', 'like all Pope's works, it is ultimately about the City'.[13] It might be as true to say that all Pope's works are about the country, for throughout city and country as conceptual entities exist only by implicit or explicit comparison with the other.

One instance of Pope's negotiation of the city/country relation is seen, as W. B. Carnochan points out,[14] in the successive revisions of the 'Ode on Solitude', which more or less cover the span of Pope's creative life. The first version, appearing in a letter of 1709, though Pope claims to have composed it 'at around twelve years old', reads in its first verse,

> Happy the man, who free from care,
> The business and the noise of towns,
> Contented breathes his native air,
>   In his own grounds.

Here there is a simple opposition between the calm of rurality and the loud activity of the city. By the time of the first printed version in 1717, revision indicates that, in Carnochan's words, 'Hostilities between city and country have deepened.'[15]

> How happy he, who free from care,
> The rage of courts, the noise of towns,
> Contented breathes his native air,
>   In his own grounds.

The final (1736) version simply writes out the city altogether:

> Happy the man, whose wish and care
> A few paternal acres bound,
> Content to breathe his native air,
>   In his own ground.

The absence of the city from the wording of this verse does not mean it is absent from its implications. The man is happy who has chosen to reject or disregard the vexations of city life. It was there for many readers anyway, who would have known Horace's familiar original in which the happy man is in the opening line placed 'procul negotiis' – far from all business.

For Pope and writers like him rejection, criticism or in this case obliteration, of the city was not just a lifestyle preference. It was in part at least politically oppositional. It was a disdainful repudiation of the manifold corruptions and venal machinations which sustained Walpole's Whig administrations. Rurality was the site of the alternative society, of those who were excluded from the practices of power but who felt themselves to be, in their adherence to more enduring values than political manipulation and financial opportunism, the guardians of a true patriotism. In this context Mack cites the last couplet of the short poem which Pope composed about the grotto which was a distinctive feature of his villa at Twickenham, and where he enjoyed meeting like-minded acquaintances. Pope names a number of his friends, including the philosopher and former statesman Viscount Bolingbroke, and concludes,

> Let such, such only, tread this sacred Floor,
> Who dare to love their Country, and be poor.[16]

In his later poetry Pope constructed, in Mack's words, 'an imagined ideal community of patriarchal virtues and heroic friends: a community of the garden and the "grot".'[17]

Pope's villa at Twickenham was an articulate compromise between the ideal of absolute retirement which the 'Ode on Solitude' commends, and the city whose life, vices and follies supplied the material of the bulk of his most characteristic writing. It was indeed situated on 'A few . . . acres' (five, in fact) but they were certainly not 'paternal', and not 'his own ground'. Pope was free to shape, improve, and landscape them as he wanted, but they were leased. Furthermore, although

Twickenham was in the 1720s and 1730s certainly sufficiently far from 'The rage of courts, the noise of towns' to be considered country, it was by no means remote. Although it is somewhat misleading to use the term, Twickenham was suburban. It was indeed separated from the more or less continuous development of villas, and homes with gardens, and villages that extended from Chelsea up to Richmond, but it was much more than a hamlet or small village. As the relevant section of John Roque's map of *c.*1746 of the environs of London makes clear, Pope's little estate, though right on the edge of Twickenham, had very similarly sized houses with laid-out gardens on either side of it; all these are, however, surrounded by hedged pastures, ploughed land and common land.[18]

If we judge by Pope's later poems, the city was for him a place of discontinuities, interruptions, fragmentation. By contrast his home in the country was where his mind could resume pattern and steadiness:

> Soon as I enter at my Country door,
> My mind resumes the thread it dropt before;
> Thoughts, which at Hyde-Park-Corner I forgot,
> Meet and rejoin me, in the pensive Grott.
>
> ('Imitations of Horace' 2.2.206–9)

It is significant, however, that he represents the resumption of his former thoughts as a kind of social occasion in which old acquaintances meet and rejoin, so that even alone at Twickenham Pope is once again among friends; he has avoided the kind of vacancy that invests Thomson's images of retreat. Nokes's list of social values – 'good fellowship, conversation, civilization and humanity' – can thus be preserved and reconciled with solitude in Pope's construction of retirement.

As the century moved on this social construction of retirement was more and more displaced by a sense of the country as being the place where mankind and his doings could be avoided completely. As John Sitter argues, 'increasingly towards the mid-century, the Fall into society and history is seen not as a fortunate fall but as a catastrophe' and he takes Thomson as an instance of a writer for whom nature had come to exclude human nature: with *The Seasons* 'We have entered the world of modern usage, where "nature" typically means a place without people (or without any people but me) and where "society" is seen as radically "unnatural".'[19] For Pope and his like-minded contemporaries so absolute a position would have been not only undesirable, but in the truest sense unimaginable.

Samuel Johnson's life span (1709–84) stretched right across the eighteenth century from the last breaths of the Restoration (Congreve still had twenty years to live when Johnson was born) into the early years of the Romantic period (Wordsworth was fourteen when Johnson died). He did not inherit the values of a traditional society and he did not belong to that other world of financial manipulation and power-broking. He had, more than any other man of letters of the era, to make a career out of the eighteenth century, and that in effect meant making a career in London. His working life was a constant engagement with the life of the city. But even for Johnson, whom we have come to associate almost exclusively with London, regarding expeditions such as that to the Western Islands in 1774 as a kind of aberration, the city existed in the context of other possible existences and so became one among the choices of life available to those who might have the privilege of choosing. Each of his three major works of 'imaginative' writing addresses the issue of the city and alternatives to it.

It supplies the theme of the work which first brought Johnson wide acclaim. Boswell records how when *London*, Johnson's imitation of Juvenal's third Satire attacking Rome and the corruptions it fostered, appeared in 1738, 'Every body was delighted with it; and there being no name to it, the first buzz of literary circles was "here is an unknown poet, greater even than Pope".'[20] This admittedly was the reaction in the Tory city of Oxford, but that it was shared in London is confirmed by the poem's appearing in three editions in two months. Its anti-Walpole politics probably contributed to its success, but it is above all else a diatribe against the city, and this clearly did not grate on contemporary readers.

The greater part of the poem is spoken by a friend of the poet, Thales, who is leaving the city, exercising his choice of life at the last moment. There are still some 'small remains' of his 'dissipated wealth', although no more admittedly than can be accommodated in a 'wherry' or small rowing boat.[21] Thales and the poet are saying goodbye at Greenwich as Thales waits to embark on his journey to 'Cambria's distant shore' (7). Greenwich is, like Twickenham, a point outside London from which the city can be viewed with a degree of detachment, but not so far that it can be out of sight or out of mind. Thales' diatribe against London life is animated, wide-ranging, fiercely expressed, at times virtually paranoid, and relentless. John Hardy, in his 1968 study of 'The Country versus the City' in the poem, cited the surprise earlier commentators had felt that such a piece should have been written by 'one who found the metropolis such a congenial home'.[22]

Thales is going to Wales, and in the introductory lines the poet commends this kind of choice, asking,

> . . . who would leave, unbrib'd, Hibernia's land,
> Or change the rocks of Scotland for the Strand? (9–10)

(Significant here is the word 'unbrib'd'. Thales is fortunate that he has just enough independence left to set up elsewhere; the poet has no choice: he is condemned at the end of the poem to turn back to the squalid city where he must make a living.) Remote places like Wales, Scotland or Ireland did not have for Johnson any of the picturesque or romantic associations that were to become frequent in literary and social culture by the end of the century, but their appeal was not merely negative, that is not merely in being as far as it was possible to get from London. They proffered a resort in which the 'true Briton' (8), 'the harrass'd Briton' (47), might find repose, a 'happier place, / Where honesty and sense are no disgrace' (43–4). Throughout the poem it is implied that the true patriot, and anyone attuned to the historical glories and virtues of traditional British culture, will find a home on the periphery of a society whose centre has been eaten away by urban disorder, by political and financial corruption, by servility to foreign powers, and by capitulation to the corrosive and invasive acts of exploitative immigrants.

There is in the poem little serious celebration of country or natural pleasures: Thales' yearning for

> Some pleasing bank where verdant osiers play,
> Some peaceful vale with nature's painting gay; (45–6)

may be real but in poetic terms it is perfunctory. More interesting is the passage (210–23) in which Thales expresses a wish that the poet likewise could establish himself in a country residence 'on the fair banks of Severn or of Trent' (211). Either place could be distant rather than peripheral, like Thales' own retreat. He imagines the poet not simply finding content there, but actually bringing back into order an estate, a 'deserted seat', which has been neglected because of some venal MP's absence in London. Country activities are realised more convincingly here because they exist in explicit and implied contrast with the wretchedness, expense and dangers of city life:

> Couldst thou resign the park and play content,
> For the fair banks of Severn or of Trent;

There might'st thou find some elegant retreat,
Some hireling senator's deserted seat;
And stretch thy prospects o'er the smiling land,
For less than rent the dungeons of the Strand;
There prune thy walks, support thy drooping flow'rs,
Direct thy rivulets, and twine thy bow'rs;
And, while thy grounds a cheap repast afford,
Despise the dainties of a venal lord:
There ev'ry bush with nature's musick rings,
There ev'ry breeze bears health upon its wings;
On all thy hours security shall smile,
And bless thine evening walk and morning toil.   (210–23)

The purely pastoral elements in this are completely undistinguished but the lines, lodged as they are in the context of a ferocious indictment of London, and situated in the tension between rural and urban existences, acquire a poignancy mere ruralism cannot attain. (And for readers who have come to know the author through the full narrative of his life, there is something engaging and novel in the image of the unhandy, short-sighted and testy Johnson trying to direct a rivulet or twine a bower.)

Johnson, it hardly needs saying, is not a writer of landscape or scenery. It is probably not true that his weak eyesight robbed him of all capacity to appreciate it: as Donald Greene says, 'His accounts of his Scottish and Welsh tours are full of descriptions of natural scenery',[23] but they are very often offered in the context of the contemplative moods or reflections they prompted. Pat Rogers cites Johnson's mocking of travellers who have nothing more to offer than accounts of landscape in *Idler* 97.[24] He notes that in the *Journey to the Western Islands* 'a steady pull is felt to the wild and remote'[25] but it is the cultural remoteness of the population not the romantic wildness of the scenery that pulls him, and in recollecting his journey Johnson emphasises the ideas not the images he has retained: 'I got an acquisition of more ideas by it than I can remember; I saw quite a different system of life.'[26] It does not seem to be the case either that Johnson was drawn to representations of the country in art. Folkenflik comments about the pictures Johnson owned, 'Johnson's own modest collection would seem to have consisted entirely of portraits.'[27] As there were one hundred and forty-six items this seems a fairly distinctive preference;

In Johnson's second poetic masterpiece, *The Vanity of Human Wishes* (1749), the ills of human existence are generalised but they are overwhelmingly focused on urban, public, civic and social life. One way in which this is conveyed is through the poem's discourse of plurality: although delusive images of happiness (and subsequent misery) are repeatedly crystallised in individual cases (Wolsey, Charles XII of Sweden, Swift) the sense is always that they represent a multitude of others, and in outlining the thematic programme of the poem Johnson uses images of crowding and frequency to achieve rhetorical emphasis:

> Remark each anxious toil, each eager strife,
> And watch the busy scenes of crowded life.   (3–4)

> . . . the knowing and the bold
> Fall in the general massacre of gold;
> Wide-wasting pest! That rages unconfined,
> And crowds with crimes the record of mankind.   (21–4)

In the universal devastation of desire and ambition only the impoverished countryman seems comparatively exempt, austere and precarious as his life may be, from the anxieties that vex more prominent lives:

> How much more safe the vassal than the lord,
> Low skulks the hind beneath the rage of power,
> And leaves the wealthy traitor in the Tower,
> Untouched his cottage, and his slumbers sound,
> Though Confiscation's vultures hover round.   (32–6)

The conclusion of the poem does propose an alternative to the hectic tragedies of modern life, an alternative to be found in stoical resignation of the individual will to the choice and power of God. Johnson chooses for the place that faith may find after death, where 'celestial wisdom calms the mind', the image of the country house that has been recurrent in the city/country discourse through the half-century before the publication of *The Vanity of Human Wishes*, 'a happier seat' (363).

The image recurs ten years later in *The History of Rasselas, Prince of Abyssinia* (1759). The philosopher Imlac warns Rasselas against all the perils and disturbances he will encounter in the world which he yearns to leave the Happy Valley in order to see, and advises him, 'Amidst wrongs, and frauds, competitions and anxieties, you will wish a thousand times for these seats of quiet, and willingly quit hope to be free from fear.'[28] Although the country/city negotiation is by no means the exclusive theme of *Rasselas*, it is recurrent and is one of the channels through which consideration of the choice of life is frequently manipulated.

The Happy Valley which is the first setting of the narrative is a pastoral paradise:

> The sides of the mountains were covered with trees, the banks of the brooks were diversified with flowers; ... All animals that bite the grass, or brouse the shrubs, whether wild or tame, wandered in this extensive circuit, secured ... All the diversities of the world were brought together, the blessings of nature were collected, and its evils extracted and excluded.   (2)

Rogers notes about the oriental setting of *Rasselas*, and the topography of the Happy Valley in particular, that it is

> a conventional framework in which [Johnson] could explore large issues without the distraction of the familiar and the distractingly particular. The Happy Valley is generalized, if not quite mythic, whereas the Thames Valley would have been uncomfortably precise and referential.[29]

The point, however, is that the representation of the Happy Valley, admittedly not a realistic or detailed account of a natural landscape, is true to one of the ways in which the natural world could be represented; indeed, if one compares it with Pope's opening description of the Thames-side landscape in *Windsor-Forest* the difference is much less than Rogers suggests. There is similar generalisation and idealisation in each. What is proffered in Johnson's narrative is one of the common constructions of the natural world.

In order to persuade 'the sons and daughters of Abyssinia' to remain 'pleased with their own condition' in the Happy Valley despite the tedium and vacuity of life there, their teachers brainwash them, or represent 'the world' to them in travesty:

> The sages who instructed them, told them of nothing but the miseries of publick life, and described all beyond the mountains as regions of calamity, where discord was always raging, and where man preyed upon man.   (4)

One of the functions of Rasselas's quest for the choice of life is thus to put to the test received constructions of rural and urban life. It is, not surprisingly, inconclusive as regards ultimate choice, but *Rasselas* none the less takes its hero and his companions through a wide-ranging course of demystification.

In Chapter 12 Imlac, as well as warning Rasselas about the perils of the world outside the valley, gives his protégé an account of urban life which differs from that which the sages commonly deliver:

> I found in Cairo a mixture of all nations; some brought thither by love of knowledge, some by the hope of gain, and many by the desire of living after their own manner without observation, and of lying hid in the obscurity of multitudes: for, in a city, populous as Cairo, it is possible to attain at the same time the gratifications of society, and the secrecy of solitude. (32)

This is a striking formulation: visitors to the city in eighteenth-century literature – and nineteenth for that matter – frequently comment on the ability of city-dwellers to live cheek by jowl and yet to have absolutely no knowledge of their neighbours, and this usually carries unfavourable implications about the dehumanising effect of urban life. It is thus a remarkable perception of Johnson's that what the city above all offers is privacy. That the city can 'at the same time' extend the advantages of both retirement and society makes it another version of Pope's grotto, where he had both retirement and the company of his friends. The question which is none the less raised by Imlac's commendation is, what do they need this 'secrecy' for? What have they got to hide? It seems a rather desperate choice in view of the further account Imlac gives of life in 'the world': 'you will find a sea foaming with tempests, and boiling with whirlpools: you will be sometimes overwhelmed by the waves of violence, and sometimes dashed against the rocks of treachery' (35). Quite a high price to pay for the anonymity of urban existence.

Rasselas and his sister are unable to live in the city when they first reach Cairo. They do not know the language, but more significantly they do not know how to live in a society of reciprocal relationships and mutual accommodations. They have to learn that they 'were to expect only such regard as liberality and courtesy could produce' (40). Urban life is an art which takes, in their case, two years to master before they are able to mingle in society. Once in society Rasselas is disappointed to discover that he does not feel as happy as those around him appear to be. Imlac explains to him that they are not as happy as they seem:

In the assembly, where you passed last night, there appeared such sprightliness of air, and volatility of fancy, as might have suited beings of a higher order, formed to inhabit serener regions inaccessible to care or sorrow: yet, believe me, prince, there was not one who did not dread the moment when solitude should deliver him to the tyranny of reflection.   (43)

It is apparent that one thing one can hide in the city is one's own unhappiness. If in Pope's constructions country solitude was a place of retreat from the vexations of the city, in Johnson's revisions society is a place of retreat from the vexations of solitude. This is not just an inversion of a contemporary trope, but a deepening of it, and a profound commentary (informed as it may be by Johnson's own depressive disposition) on the emergent cult of melancholic reflection evinced in the huge popularity of Young's *Night Thoughts* (1742–5) and epitomised in Gray's *Elegy Written in a Country Churchyard* (1751).

Johnson was famously antagonistic to the cult of pastoralism. In the *Life of Milton* he is scathing about the fabrications implicit in *Lycidas* – 'Where there is leisure for fiction there is little grief' – and he anatomises pastoral poetry sardonically in successive *Ramblers*. In the narrative of his own life in *Rasselas* Imlac mentions that he had visited Arabia,

> where I saw a nation at once pastoral and warlike; who live without any settled habitation; whose only wealth is their flocks and herds; and who have yet carried on, through all ages, an hereditary war with all mankind, though they neither covet nor envy their possessions.   (24)

This takes the critique of pastoralism a stage further than Johnson's distaste for the literary mode: in the case of not an imagined but an actual pastoral society, what is discovered is not an improved model of human relations, but a more wilfully destructive model.

In the course of their own explorations Rasselas and Nekayah encounter shepherds and speculate as to 'whether all our searches are not to terminate in pastoral simplicity' (49). These shepherds are, however, also discouraging as models. They are 'so rude and ignorant . . . that very little could be learned from them.' And 'it was evident that their hearts were cankered with discontent; that they considered themselves as condemned to labour for the luxury of the rich, and looked up with stupid malevolence towards those that were placed above them' (49).

Johnson's interest in the pastoral idea does not, however, stop at this point. With the subtlety and delicacy that is characteristic of *Rasselas* at very many points he represents Nekayah as reluctant to surrender the notion that a country life is the best of all available. She 'could not believe that all the accounts of primeval pleasures were fabulous, and yet was in doubt whether life had anything that could be justly preferred to the placid gratification of fields and woods' (50). And there is nothing in the narrative or in its tone to deride her for this persistence.

It is true that shortly afterwards they meet the hermit who, having exhausted the interest and pleasures of natural history, finds that his 'fancy riots in scenes of folly', and who, deciding that 'The life of a solitary man will certainly be miserable, but not certainly devout', has resolved 'to return to the world tomorrow' (54). He is not, however, a very good example to follow: his retreat into the country was prompted by an extreme extrapolation from his own frustrated military ambitions, and his return to the city seems precipitate, and determined not by philosophical choice but by mental imbalance. The image of his fancy 'rioting' is hardly inspiring.

The experience of Pekuah is more refined. Her abduction into the harem is a kind of enforced pastoral retreat. Although she is prepared to make the best of it she finds the limitations of the secluded female society intolerable. Their occupations are unfulfilling, merely physical, and she longs for the intellectual stimulation of the city: 'I could do all which they delighted in doing by powers merely sensitive, while my intellectual faculties were flown to Cairo' (95). And besides this, her companions had no worthwhile talk: 'Nor was much satisfaction to be hoped for from their conversation: for of what could they be expected to talk? They had seen nothing; for they had lived from early youth in that narrow spot' (95).

The account of the city in *Rasselas* would seem to confirm Wain's summary of Johnson's feelings about London: 'Johnson always saw London as a heartless city, where those who fell were trampled without mercy. At the same time he always accepted it at the level of intellect and art.'[30] The conclusion of the narrative does not, however, entirely reinforce this. After the rather sober reflections prompted by their visit to the catacombs the company returns to Cairo. Here they are for a time confined by the rising waters of the Nile and they ponder 'the different forms of life which they have observed' (122) and contemplate which they might choose. None of them, even in fancy, opts for life in the city. Each of the young people is attracted by the idea of a limited community: Pekuah is drawn to the notion of being the prioress of a small convent; Nekayah would like to 'found a college of learned women'; Rasselas's ambition is for 'a little kingdom' in which he could oversee all aspects of government. Their elders 'were contented to be driven along the stream of life' with no particular destination. Each realising that none of these ambitions is to be attained, they collectively resolve, when the flood is over, to return to Abyssinia, though not necessarily (one assumes) to the Happy Valley.

Johnson's interventions in the eighteenth-century debate about the relative virtues of country and city life do not bring it to any conclusion, but do advance it by problematising the idea of choice itself. Through most of the first part of the eighteenth century the country/city issue had been essentially a matter of alternative styles of living or of negotiating an accommodation between the two that would minister best to individual and social comfort. What Johnson does is to turn the matter inward, and to understand that city and country exist as they are perceived and represented. It is not strictly accurate to say of London that

> Here falling houses thunder on your head,
> And here a female atheist talks you dead.   (*London* 17–18)

but it may be that, if you want to castigate the instability and immorality of Walpole's metropolis, it is an effective thing to claim it. For Johnson, neither society nor the individual can do very much to deflect the torrents of man's fate. Choice of life, in other words, is not really the issue. Johnson himself had in effect no choice but to live in the city. Thales could leave it. Rasselas and his friends could drift back to Abyssinia. The author of *The Vanity of Human Wishes* knew that his best choice, in whatever circumstance, was to pray for 'a healthful mind', 'a will resigned', 'love', 'faith' in 'a happier seat' hereafter, in the conviction that with these things 'celestial wisdom' would calm the agitated mind and bring the happiness which neither an urban, nor a rural, nor any other life could guarantee him.

Notes

Chapter 1 Other Worlds – Narratives of Travel

1 James Thomson, *The Seasons*, ed. James Sambrook (Oxford: Clarendon Press, 1981), 'Summer', ll. 685–9.
2 The place of botanical classification in the evolution of British attitudes to the natural world is interestingly discussed in Douglas Chambers, *The Reinvention of the World: English Writing, 1650–1750* (London and New York: Arnold, 1996) pp. 64–71.
3 Jonathan Swift, *Gulliver's Travels* (1726), ed. Herbert Davis (Oxford: Basil Blackwell, 1965) 2.3.104. All references are to this edition and give book, chapter and page numbers.
4 Daniel Defoe, *Robinson Crusoe* (1719) (Harmondsworth: Penguin, 1965) p. 61.
5 Ian Watt, *The Rise of the Novel* (1957) (Harmondsworth: Penguin, 1963) p. 16.
6 (Peter Whalley), *An Essay on the Manner of Writing History* (1746), ed. K. Stewart, Augustan Reprint Society Publication number 80 (Los Angeles, 1960) p. 11.
7 Marcus Rediker, *Between the Devil and the Deep Blue Sea: Merchant Seamen, Pirates, and the Anglo-American Maritime World, 1700–1750* (Cambridge: Cambridge University Press, 1987) p. 21.
8 See J. Paul Hunter, *Before Novels: The Cultural Contexts of Eighteenth-Century English Fiction* (New York and London: Norton, 1990) *passim*, but especially Chapter 8.
9 Chambers, *Reinvention of the World*, p. 5.
10 Michael McKeon, *Origins of the English Novel, 1600–1740* (Baltimore and London: Johns Hopkins University Press,1987) p. 101.
11 Frances Bacon, *The Essayes or Counsels, Civill and Moral* (1625) pp. 101–2.
12 McKeon, *Origins of the English Novel, 1600–1740*, p. 103.
13 Paula R. Backscheider, *Daniel Defoe: His Life* (Baltimore and London: Johns Hopkins University Press, 1989) p. 48.
14 Hunter, *Before Novels*, p. 353.
15 François Petis de la Croix, fils, *Turkish Tales* (trans.)(1708) sig. A2–A2^v.
16 (F. H. Misson), *A New Voyage to the East-Indies by Francis Leguat and his Companions* (1708) p. iii.
17 David Blewett, *The Illustrations of Robinson Crusoe, 1719–1920* (Gerrard's Cross: Colin Smythe, 1995).
18 See G. A. Starr, *Defoe and Spiritual Autobiography* (Princeton: Princeton University Press, 1965).
19 Daniel Defoe, *The Life, Adventures, and Pyracies, of the Famous Captain Singleton . . .* (London, 1720) p. 170.
20 Hunter, *Before Novels*, p. 353.

222　　　　　　　　　　　　　*Notes*

21 Chambers, *The Reinvention of the World*, p. 61.
22 Ian Bell, *Defoe's Fiction* (London and Sydney: Croom Helm, 1985) p. 106.
23 McKeon, *Origins of the English Novel, 1600–1740*, p. 335.
24 David Nokes, *Raillery and Rage: A Study of Eighteenth-Century Satire* (Brighton: Harvester Press, 1987) p. 188.
25 Claude Rawson, *Gulliver and the Gentle Reader: Studies in Swift and Our Time* (London: Routledge and Kegan Paul, 1973) pp. 1, 9, 17.
26 'It all comes back to that, to my and your "fun" – if we but allow the term its full extension', *The Art of the Novel* (New York: Charles Scribner's Sons, 1934): *Golden Bowl*, Preface, p. 345.
27 See Mikhail Bakhtin, *The Dialogic Imagination: Four Essays*, ed. M. Holqvist, trans C. Emerson and M. Holqvist (Austin: University of Texas Press, 1981).
28 John Traugott, 'A Tale of a Tub' (1983), repr. in *Modern Essays on Eighteenth-Century Literature,* ed. Leopold Damrosch (New York and Oxford: Oxford University Press, 1988) p. 40.
29 Terry Castle, *Masquerade and Civilization: The Carnivalesque in Eighteenth-Century English Culture and Fiction* (London: Methuen, 1986) p. 6.
30 Isaiah Berlin, 'Two Concepts of Liberty', in *Four Essays on Liberty* (London: Oxford University Press, 1969), pp. 118–72.
31 See also Chapter 7 below, 'Science and Nature'.
32 Jonathan Swift, *Some Remarks on the Barrier Treaty* (1711) and *The Conduct of the Allies* (1712).

Chapter 2 Wit and Virtue

1 Alexander Pope, *The Poems of Alexander Pope*, ed. John Butt (Bungay: Methuen, 1968) p. 153.
2 Henry Fielding, *Tom Jones* (1749)(London: Dent, 1962) Book 1, Chapter 1.
3 Samuel Richardson, *Selected Letters*, ed. John Carroll (Oxford: Clarendon Press, 1964) p. 168.
4 Martin C. Battestin, *The Providence of Wit: Aspects of Form in Augustan Literature and the Arts* (Oxford: Clarendon Press, 1974) p. 1 and n.
5 David Nokes, *Raillery and Rage: A Study of Eighteenth-Century Satire* (Brighton: Harvester Press, 1987) p. 94.
6 William Congreve, *The Way of the World*, in *Four English Comedies of the Seventeeth and Eighteenth Centuries*, ed. J. M. Morrell (Harmondsworth: Penguin, 1950) p. 133.
7 Notably Collier's *A Short View of the Immorality and Profaneness of the English Stage* (1698).
8 Pat Gill, *Interpreting Ladies: Women, Wit, and Morality in the Restoration Comedy of Manners* (Athens and London: University of Georgia Press, 1994) p. 119.
9 Ibid., p. 119.

10 Samuel Richardson, *Clarissa* (1747–8), 4 vols (London: Dent, 1932), Letter 7 (1.32). Volume and page numbers in the text are to this Everyman edition.
11 Daniel Defoe, *Moll Flanders*, ed. G. A. Starr (Oxford: Oxford University Press, 1971) p. 20.
12 For the fullest account of the status of women in respect of property law see Beth Swan, *Fictions of Law: An Investigation of the Law in Eighteenth-Century English Fiction* (Frankfurt: Peter Lang, 1997), Chapters 2 and 3.
13 Richardson, *Selected Letters*, ed. Carroll, p. 101.
14 Battestin, *The Providence of Wit*, pp. 164, 165.
15 Richardson, *Selected Letters*, ed. Carroll, p. 233.
16 Gill, *Interpreting Ladies*, p. 13.
17 Richardson, *Selected Letters,* ed. Carroll, pp. 203–4.
18 Gillian Beer, ' "Our Unnatural No-voice": The Heroic Epistle, Pope, and Women's Gothic' (1981), repr. in Leopold Damrosch, *Modern Essays on Eighteenth-Century Literature* (New York and Oxford: Oxford University Press, 1988) p. 383.
19 'Epistle Dedicatory' to *The Plain-Dealer* in *The Plays of William Wycherley*, ed. Peter Holland (Cambridge: Cambridge University Press, 1981), ll. 34–42.
20 Gill, *Interpreting Ladies*, Introduction.
21 Richardson, *Selected Letters*, ed. Carroll, p. 298.

Chapter 3   Money and Government

1 Alexander Pope, *The Poems of Alexander* Pope, ed. John Butt (Bungay: Methuen, 1968), 'Epistle to Burlington', ll. 173–6.
2 Raymond Williams, *The Country and the City* (St Albans: Paladin, 1975) p. 59.
3 Cedric Watts, *Literature and Money: Financial Myth and Literary Truth* (London and New York: Harvester Wheatsheaf, 1990) p. 105.
4 Arthur Young, *Annals of Agriculture*, vol. 2 (1784) p. 381.
5 James Sambrook, *The Eighteenth Century: The Intellectual and Cultural Context of English Literature, 1700–1789* (London and New York: Longman,1986) p. 69.
6 The details of some contemporary writers' engagement with, and in some cases (Pope, Gay) investment in, the South Sea scheme are traced in Colin Nicholson, *Writing and the Rise of Finance: Capital Satires of the Early Eighteenth Century* (Cambridge: Cambridge University Press, 1994) Chapter 2.
7 There is a print of the first state in the British Museum (see British Museum Catalogue of Satiric Prints).
8 Douglas Chambers, *The Reinvention of the World: English Writing, 1650–1750* (London and New York: Arnold, 1996) p. 34.
9 David Nokes, *Raillery and Rage: A Study of Eighteenth-Century Satire* (Brighton: Harvester Press, 1987), p. 42.

10 *The Spectator*, ed. Donald F. Bond, 5 vols (Oxford: Clarendon Press, 1965) 2.187.

11 Sambrook, *The Eighteenth Century*, p. 91.

12 John Dyer, *Poems* (1761) (Menston, Yorkshire: Scolar Press, 1971) 'The Fleece', Book 3, p. 138.

13 Daniel Defoe, *The Review*, 6 March 1705 (repr. New York, 1938) 2.9.

14 Nicholson, *Writing and the Rise of Finance*, p. 4.

15 Ibid., p. 3.

16 Paul Langford, *A Polite and Commercial People: England, 1727–1783* (London and New York: Guild Publishing with Oxford University Press, 1989) p. 4.

17 Pope, *Poems*, ed. Butt, 'Epistle to Bathurst', ll. 69–70.

18 Jonathan Swift, *Prose Works*, ed. Herbert Davis (Oxford: Basil Blackwell, 1940) 3.6

19 Nicholson, *Writing and the Rise of Finance*, p. 7.

20 Ibid., p. 18.

21 Watts, *Literature and Money*, p. 119.

22 Ian A. Bell, *Defoe's Fiction* (London and Sydney: Croom Helm, 1985) p. 187.

23 Daniel Defoe, *Roxana*, ed. Jane Jack (London, Oxford and New York: Oxford University Press, 1969) p. 169.

24 Daniel Defoe, *Moll Flanders*, ed. G. A. Starr (Oxford: Oxford University Press, 1971) p. 189.

25 John Locke, *Two Treatises of Government* (1690), ed. P. Lazlitt (Cambridge, repr. 1963) e.g. p. 286.

26 Beth Swan, *Fictions of Law: An Investigation of the Law in Eighteenth-Century English Fiction* (Frankfurt: Peter Lang, 1997) Chapter 2.

27 Watts, *Literature and Money*, p. 86.

28 Bernard Mandeville, *The Fable of the Bees*, ed. F. B. Kaye, 2 vols (Oxford: Clarendon Press, 1924) 'The Grumbling Hive', 1.18–20.

29 Langford, *A Polite and Commercial People*, pp. 3–4. On luxury see, e.g., J. Sekora, *Luxury: The Concept in Western Thought from Eden to Smollett* (Baltimore: Johns Hopkins University Press, 1977).

30 John Gay, *The Beggar's Opera* (1728) in *Eighteenth-Century Comedy*, ed. W. D.Taylor (London: Oxford University Press, 1929) Act 1.1.

31 Nicholson, *Writing and the Rise of Finance*, p. 134.

32 Ibid., p. 10.

33 Terry Castle, *Masquerade and Civilization: The Carnivalesque in Eighteenth-Century English Culture and Fiction* (London: Methuen, 1986) p. 57.

34 Ian Donaldson, ' "A Double Capacity": *The Beggar's Opera*', in *The World Turned Upside Down: Comedy from Johnson to Fielding* (Oxford: Clarendon Press, 1970).

35 Ibid.

36 Ibid.

37 Ibid.

38 Nicholson, *Writing and the Rise of Finance*, p. 128.

Chapter 4   Men and Women – Love and Marriage

1   Henry Fielding, *The History of Tom Jones* (1749) (London: Dent, 1962). References are to Fielding's volume and chapter numbers.
2   Daniel Defoe, *Moll Flanders*, ed. G. A. Starr (Oxford: Oxford University Press, 1971) p. 20.
3   Samuel Johnson, *Lives of the English Poets* (1779–81), 2 vols (London: Oxford University Press, 1952) 2.101.
4   James Thomson, *The Seasons*, ed. James Sambrook (Oxford: Clarendon Press, 1981) 'Spring', pp. 580–1.
5   In the influential *A Father's Legacy to his Daughters* (1774) John Gregory, having noted that love can improve a man, says that 'if the fascination continue long, it will totally depress his spirit, and extinguish every active, vigorous, and manly principle of his mind. You will find this subject beautifully and pathetically painted in Thomson's Spring.' See Vivien Jones, *Women in the Eighteenth Century: Constructions of Femininity* (London: Routledge, 1990) p. 51.
6   William Hogarth, *Engravings*, ed. with commentary by Sean Shegreen (New York: Dover, 1973) plates 51–6.
7   Alexander Pope, *The Poems of Alexander Pope,* ed. John Butt (Bungay: Methuen, 1968) 'The Rape of the Lock', 2.88.90.
8   Extracted in Jones, *Women in the Eighteenth Century*, p. 29.
9   Ibid., p. 59.
10   'Philogamus', *The Present State of Matrimony* (1739), in Jones, *Women in the Eighteenth Century*, p. 78.
11   Valerie Rumbold, *Women's Place in Pope's World* (Cambridge: Cambridge University Press, 1989) p. 67.
12   Gillian Beer discusses this narrative extremely interestingly in ' "Our Unnatural No-voice": the Heroic Epistle, Pope, and Women's Gothic' (1981), repr. in Leopold Damrosch (ed.), *Modern Essays on Eighteenth-Century Literature* (New York and Oxford: Oxford University Press, 1988) pp. 379–411.
13   Jones, *Women in the Eighteenth Century*, pp. 217–18.
14   Beth Swan, *Fictions of Law: An Investigation of the Law in Eighteenth-Century English Fiction* (Frankfurt: Peter Lang, 1997) p. 20.
15   Janet Todd, *The Sign of Angellica: Women, Writing and Fiction, 1660–1800* (London: Virago, 1989) p. 7.
16   Jones, *Women in the Eighteenth Century*, p. 19.
17   Tobias Smollett, *Roderick Random* (1748) (London: Dent,1927) p. 428.
18   I discuss the trajectory of Roderick's life in 'From Tennis-Ball to Fruit Tree: Smollett's Story of the Scottish Self' in *Writing Region and Nation*, ed. M. W. Thomas (Swansea: University of Wales Swansea, 1994) pp. 549–60.

Chapter 5   Writing by Women

1   Roger Lonsdale, *Eighteenth-Century Women Poets* (Oxford: Oxford University Press, 1989).

2 See the general thesis of Jane Spencer, *The Rise of the Woman Novelist, from
   Aphra Behn to Jane Austen* (Oxford: Basil Blackwell, 1986) and especially
   part 1.3.
3 Penelope Aubin, *The Life of Madam de Beaumount* . . . (1721) pp. v–vii.
4 See, for instance, Lonsdale, *Eighteenth-Century Women Poets,* number 39.
   All the extracts in this section are taken from Lonsdale and are identified
   by the number he assigns to them.
5 John Milton, *Complete Shorter Poems*, ed. John Carey (London: Longman,
   1971) p. 125.
6 Alexander Pope, *The Poems of Alexander Pope*, ed. John Butt (Bungay:
   Methuen, 1968) p. 265.
7 Elaine Showalter, 'Towards a Feminist Poetics', in Mary Jacobus (ed.),
   Women Writing and Writing about Women, conveniently repr. in Rick
   Rylance (ed.), *Debating Texts* (Buckingham: Open University Press, 1987)
   pp. 243–4.
8 Mary Delarivier Manley, *The Adventures of Rivella; or, The History of the
   Author of the Atalantis* . . . (London, 1714) p. 8.
9 Spencer, *The Rise of the Woman Novelist*, p. 54.
10 Mary Delarivier Manley, *The Secret History of Queen Zarah, and the
   Zarazians* ('Albigion', 1705) pp. 8–9.
11 The arguments of this highly important *Preface* are summarised in the
   Appendix to this chapter.
12 J. C. Major, *The Role of Personal Memoirs in English Biography and Novel*
   (Philadelphia: University of Pennsylvania, 1935) p. 109.
13 M. Manley, *The New Atalantis*, ed. Rosalind Ballaster (London: Penguin,
   1992) p. vi.
14 Earl of Shaftesbury, *Characteristicks of Men, Manners, Opinions, Times*,
   revised edn (1713) p. 199.
15 Spencer, *The Rise of the Woman Novelist*, pp. 54, 56.
16 Manley, *The New Atalantis* (1992), p. ix.

Chapter 6   The Harmony of Things

1 James Thomson, *The Seasons*, ed. James Sambrook (Oxford: Clarendon
   Press, 1981), 'Autumn', pp. 773–6.
2 See also Chapter 7: 'Science and Nature' below.
3 Alexander Pope, *The Poems of Alexander Pope*, ed. John Butt (Bungay:
   Methuen, 1968) 'Windsor-Forest' pp. 413–22.
4 That the political context of *Windsor-Forest* was the century of civil war
   rather than the peace-making moment is argued in my 'The Composition
   of Pope's *Windsor-Forest*', *Durham University Journal*, Dec. 1974, pp.
   56–67.
5 Pope, *Poems*, ed. Butt, p. 273.
6 Pope, *Poems*, ed. Butt, p. 461.
7 See Dava Sobel, *Longitude* (London: Fourth Estate, 1996) Chapter 2.
8 Quoted by James Sambrook, *The Eighteenth Century: The Intellectual and*

Cultural Context of English Literature, 1700–1789 (London and New York: Longman, 1986) pp. 27–8, from Tillotson's popular sermon 'The Wisdom of God in the Creation of the World'.

9   *The Spectator*, ed. Donald F. Bond, 5 vols (Oxford: Clarendon Press, 1965) no. 465, 23 August 1712.
10 Jonathan Swift, *Gulliver's Travels* (1726), ed. Herbert Davis (Oxford: Basil Blackwell, 1965) Book 1.4.48
11 Howard Erskine-Hill, 'Alexander Pope: the Political Poet in his Time', *Eighteenth-Century Studies*, 15 (1981–2), repr. in Leopold Damrosch (ed.), *Modern Essays on Eighteenth-Century Literature* (New York and Oxford: Oxford University Press,1988) p. 133.
12 *Spectator*, ed. Bond, no. 10, 12 March 1711.
13 David Nokes, *Raillery and Rage: A Study of Eighteenth-Century Satire* (Brighton: Harvester Press, 1987) p. 97.
14 Stephen Copley and David Fairer, '*An Essay on Man* and the Polite Reader', in David Fairer (ed.), *Pope: New Contexts* (Hemel Hempstead: Harvester Press, 1990) p. 210.
15 Claude Rawson, *Order from Confusion Sprung: Studies in Eighteenth-Century Literature from Swift to Cowper* (London: George Allen and Unwin, 1985) p. 232.
16 Pope, *Poems*, ed. Butt, 501.
17 John Webster, *Three Plays*, ed. D. C. Gunby (Harmondsworth: Penguin, 1972) p. 189.
18 Douglas H. White and Thomas P. Tierney, '*An Essay on Man* and the Tradition of Satires on Mankind', *Modern Philology* 85 (1987) pp. 27–41.
19 Rawson, *Order from Confusion Sprung*, pp. 224, 228.
20 Ruth Perry, 'Anality and Ethics in Pope's Late Satires', repr. in Brean Hammond (ed.), *Pope* (London and New York: Longman, 1996) pp. 171, 176.
21 Rawson, *Order from Confusion Sprung*, p. 227.
22 Ibid., p. 227.
23 Pope, *Poems*, ed. Butt, p. 501.
24 Ibid., 570.
25 John Barrell and Harriet Guest, 'On the Use of Contradiction: Economics and Morality in the Eighteenth-Century Long Poem' (1987), repr. in Hammond (ed.), p. 121.
26 Maynard Mack traces the allusions Pope makes in this reworking of the Old Testament story of Balaam to Horace, *Odes* 3.16 (see *The Garden and the City: Retirement and Politics in the Later Poetry of Pope, 1731–1743* (Toronto: University of Toronto Press, 1969) pp. 86–9).
27 Sambrook, *The Eighteenth Century*, p. 43.

Chapter 7   Science and Nature

1   *The Spectator*, ed. Donald F. Bond, 5 vols (Oxford: Clarendon Press, 1965) 4.529–30.

2 Roy Porter, 'The Terraqueous Globe', in G. S. Rousseau and Roy Porter (eds), *Ferment of Knowledge: Studies in the Historiography of Eighteenth-Century Science* (Cambridge: Cambridge University Press, 1980) p. 291.

3 Marjorie Hope Nicolson, *Newton Demands the Muse: Newton's Opticks and the Eighteenth-Century Poets* (Princeton: Princeton University Press, 1948) p. 8.

4 Maynard Mack, 'Pope's Books: a Bibliographical Survey with a Finding List', in Maximillian Novak (ed.), *English Literature in the Age of Disguise* (Berkeley and Los Angeles: University of California Press, 1977).

5 Quoted by Colin Nicolson, *Writing and the Rise of Finance: Capital Satires of the Early Eighteenth Century* (Cambridge: Cambridge University Press, 1994) p. 16.

6 Sir William Denham, *Astro-Theology* (1715) p. 40.

7 Robert Knox, *An Historical Relation of the Island Ceylon . . .* (London, 1681) 'Preface'.

8 D. S. L. Cardwell, 'Science, Technology and Industry', in Rousseau and Porter (eds), *Ferment of Knowledge*, p. 454.

9 Draft preamble to the Royal Society statutes, cited by Peter Mathias, 'Who Unbound Prometheus? Science and Technological Change, 1600–1800' in A. E. Musson (ed.), *Science, Technology and Economic Growth in the Eighteenth Century* (London: Methuen, 1972) pp. 76–87.

10 Bernard Mandeville, *The Fable of the Bees*, ed. F. B. Kaye, 2 vols (Oxford: Clarendon Press, 1924) 2.144–5.

11 'Who Unbound Prometheus?', p. 78.

12 James Thomson, 'A Poem Sacred to the Memory of Sir Isaac Newton', in *Liberty, The Castle of Indolence and Other Poems*, ed. James Sambrook (Oxford: Clarendon Press, 1986) p. 9, ll. 76–81.

13 Elizabeth Rowe, *Miscellaneous Works in Prose and Verse* (1739), 1.86–92. Quoted by William Powell Jones, *The Rhetoric of Science: A Study of Scientific Ideas and Imagery in Eighteenth-Century English Poetry* (London: Routledge and Kegan Paul, 1966) p. 50.

14 Edward Young, *Night Thoughts*, ed. Stephen Cornford (Cambridge: Cambridge University Press, 1989) Night 1.285–87.

15 Young, *Night Thoughts*, ed. Cornford, p. 13.

16 *Spectator*, ed. Bond, no.10, 12 March 1711.

17 See *Spectator*, ed. Bond, 1.xxvii; 3.535 n.1.

18 *Spectator*, ed. Bond, 1.xxxix.

19 Jonathan Swift, *Gulliver's Travels* (1726), ed. Herbert Davis (Oxford: Basil Blackwell, 1959) 2.1.87.

20 James Sambrook, *The Eighteenth Century: The Intellectual and Cultural Context of English Literature, 1700–1789* (London and New York: Longman, 1986) p. 11.

21 For the outlines of this activity see *Gulliver's Travels*, ed. Davis, p. xiii.

22 'Spring' 853–60. The text is the 1746 text of *The Seasons*, edited by James Sambrook (Oxford: Clarendon Press, 1981).

23 After Bernard Fontenelle, *Entretiens sur la pluralité des mondes* (1689).

Chapter 8 Country and City, the Choice of Life

1 Samuel Johnson, *The History of Rasselas, Prince of Abyssinia*, ed. J. P. Hardy (London: Oxford University Press, 1968) Chapter 12.
2 George Farquhar, *The Beaux Stratagem*, ed. A. Norman Jeffares (Edinburgh: Oliver and Boyd, 1972) Act 1.1.
3 Alexander Pope, *The Poems of Alexander Pope*, ed. John Butt (Bungay: Methuen, 1968) p. 243.
4 A. R. Humphreys, *The Augustan World: Society, Thought and Letters in Eighteenth-Century England* (London: Methuen, 1954; repr. New York: Harper, 1963) p. 24.
5 Henry Fielding, *The History of Tom Jones*, ed. A. R. Humphreys, 2 vols (London and New York: Dent, 1962) 1.8–9.
6 James Thomson, *The Seasons*, ed. James Sambrook (Oxford: Clarendon Press, 1981) 'Spring' ll. 768–9.
7 These 'Sons of Riot', like Johnson's 'Lords of the street . . . Flush'd . . . with folly, youth and wine' (*London* 231–2) are clearly types of Milton's 'sons / Of Belial, flown with insolence and wine' (*Paradise Lost* 1.501–2) and as such manifestations of hellish horrors.
8 David Nokes, *Raillery and Rage: A Study of Eighteenth-Century Satire* (Brighton: Harvester Press, 1987) p. 41.
9 J. Paul Hunter, see *Before Novels: The Cultural Contexts of Eighteenth-Century English Fiction* (New York and London: Norton, 1990) Chapter 6, esp. pp. 141–56, quotation on p. 142.
10 The paradox of a developing sensibility that inheres only in an ever-diminishing circle of sympathetic minds is explored in John Mullan, *Sentiment and Sociability: The Language of Feeling in the Eighteenth Century* (Oxford: Clarendon Press, 1988).
11 Virginia C. Kenny, *The Country-House Ethos in English Literature, 1688–1750: Themes of Personal Retreat and National Expansion* (Brighton: Harvester Press, 1984) p. 210.
12 Maynard Mack, *The Garden and the City: Retirement and Politics in the Later Poetry of Pope, 1731–1743* (Toronto: University of Toronto Press, 1969) p. 3.
13 Ibid., 7.
14 W. B. Carnochan, *Confinement and Flight: An Essay on English Literature of the Eighteenth Century* (Berkeley, Los Angeles and London: University of California Press, 1977) pp. 173–8.
15 Ibid., 175.
16 Pope, *Poems*, ed. Butt, p. 707.
17 Mack, *The Garden and the City*, p. 66.
18 Mack reproduces this section of Roque's map.
19 'The Flight from History in Mid-Century Poetry' (1982), in Leopold Damrosch (ed.), *Modern Essays on Eighteenth-Century Literature* (New York and Oxford: Oxford University Press, 1988) pp. 422, 424.
20 James Boswell, *Life of Johnson*, ed. G. Birkbeck Hill, rev. L. F. Powell (Oxford, 1934) 1.127.
21 Samuel Johnson, *Poems*, ed. E. L. McAdam, with George Milne (New Haven and London: Yale University Press, 1964) 'London' 20, 19.

22 John Hardy, 'Johnson's "London": the Country versus the City', in *Studies in the Eighteenth Century*, ed. R. F. Brissenden (Canberra: Australian National University Press, 1968) p. 252.

23 Donald Greene, 'Introduction' to Paul Alkon and Robert Folkenflik, *Samuel Johnson: Pictures and Words* (Los Angeles: William Clark Andrews Memorial Library, 1984) p. iv.

24 Pat Rogers, *Samuel Johnson* (Oxford: Oxford University Press, 1993) p. 98. Cf. Fielding's comment that there would be 'no office so dull' as that of the travel writer who has nothing but 'the difference of hills, valleys, rivers' to write about, in *A Journey from this World to the Next and The Journal of a Voyage to Lisbon* ed. I. A. Bell and Andrew Varney (Oxford: Oxford University Press, 1997) p. 123.

25 Rogers, *Samuel Johnson*, p. 102.

26 Boswell, *Life of Johnson*, ed. Hill and Powell, 4.99.

27 'Samuel Johnson and Art', in Alkon and Folkenflik, *Samuel Johnson: Pictures and Words*, p. 83.

28 Johnson, *The History of Rasselas, Prince of Abyssinia*, ed. Hardy, p. 35.

29 Rogers, *Samuel Johnson*, p. 99.

30 John Wain, *Samuel Johnson* (London: Macmillan) p. 86.

Suggestions for Further Reading

Full references for works quoted in the text are given the first time they occur in each chapter.

Detailed lists of suggested reading for the principal authors discussed should be sought in, for instance, modern editions of particular works and studies of individual writers.

The following list comprises some works which help to broaden the base of understanding for readers pursuing early eighteenth-century topics. Some titles do indicate an author or work as a chief focus (for example, Rawson's *Gulliver and the Gentle Reader*) but they are included here because they have a wider resonance. In some cases brief annotation indicates where they are particularly helpful.

Castle, Terry, *Masquerade and Civilisation: The Carnivalesque in Eighteenth-Century English Culture and Fiction* (London: Methuen, 1986). Through the social phenomenon of masquerade opens many interesting lights on literary culture in the period.

Chambers, Douglas, *The Reinvention of the World: English Writing, 1650–1750* (London and New York: Arnold, 1996). Good on bearing of new geographies on the literary imagination.

Damrosch, Leopold, Jr, (ed.), *Modern Essays in Eighteenth-Century Literature* (New York and Oxford: Oxford University Press, 1988). Compendium of good modern essays on both major and minor figures.

Donaldson, Ian, *The World Upside-Down: Comedy from Jonson to Fielding* (Oxford: Clarendon Press, 1970).

Erskine-Hill, Howard, *The Augustan Idea in English Literature* (London: Edward Arnold, 1983).

Erskine-Hill, Howard, *The Social Milieu of Alexander Pope* (New Haven: Yale University Press, 1975).

Gill, Pat, *Interpreting Ladies: Women, Wit, and Morality in the Restoration Comedy of Manners* (Athens and London: University of Georgia Press, 1994). Part of the background to the representation of women in eighteenth-century writing.

Hill, Bridget, *Eighteenth-Century Women: An Anthology* (London: Allen and Unwin, 1984). Like Vivien Jones, below, many interesting and revealing texts.

Hogarth, William, *Graphic Works,* ed. Ronald Paulson, 2nd edn, 2 vols (New Haven: Yale University Press, 1970).

Humphreys, A. R. *The Augustan World: Society, Thought and Letters in Eighteenth-Century England* (London: Methuen, 1954).

Hunter, J. Paul, *Before Novels: The Cultural Contexts of Eighteenth-Century English Fiction* (New York and London: Norton, 1990). Very good on the new readers and their desires and expectations.

Jones, Vivien, *Women in the Eighteenth Century: Constructions of Femininity* (London: Routledge, 1990). Many excellently revealing extracts.

Jones, William Powell, *The Rhetoric of Science: A Study of Scientific Ideas and Imagery in Eighteenth-Century English Poetry* (London: Routledge and Kegan Paul, 1966).

Kenny, Virginia C., *The Country-House Ethos in English Literature 1688–1750: Themes of Personal Retreat and National Expansion* (Brighton: Harvester, 1984). Opens up themes of broad cultural resonance.

Langford, Paul, *A Polite and Commercial People: England 1727–1783* (London and New York: Guild Publishing with Oxford University Press, 1989). General history of the period highly responsive to cultural issues.

Lonsdale, Roger (ed.), *New Oxford Book of Eighteenth-Century Verse* (Oxford: Oxford University Press, 1984). Outstanding anthology.

Lonsdale, Roger (ed.), *Eighteenth Century Women Poets* (Oxford: Oxford University Press, 1990). Indispensable anthology containing, like his *New Oxford Book*, much material hard to find elsewhere.

Mack, Maynard, *The Garden and the City: Retirement and Politics in the Later Poetry of Pope, 1731–1743* (Toronto: University of Toronto Press, 1969).

McKeon, Michael, *The Origins of the English Novel 1600–1740* (Baltimore and London: Johns Hopkins University Press, 1987). Intellectually impressive revision in ideological terms of established accounts like Ian Watt's *The Rise of the Novel*.

Mullen, John, *Sentiment and Sociability: The Language of Feeling in the Eighteenth Century* (Oxford: Clarendon Press, 1988). Treats mainly later texts, but explains tendencies becoming apparent in first half of eighteenth century.

Nicholson, Colin, *Writing and the Rise of Finance: Capital Satires of the Early Eighteenth Century* (Cambridge: Cambridge University Press, 1994). On the financial revolution see also Cedric Watts, below.

Nicholson, Marjorie Hope, *Newton Demands the Muse: Newton's Opticks and the Eighteenth-Century Poets* (Princeton: Princeton University Press, 1946).

Nokes, David, *Raillery and Rage: A Study of Eighteenth-Century Satire* (Brighton: Harvester Press, 1987).

Novak, Maximillian (ed.), *English Literature in the Age of Disguise* (Berkeley and Los Angeles: University of California Press, 1977).

Nussbaum, Felicity A., *The Brink of All We Hate: English Satires on Women, 1660–1750* (Lexington: Kentucky University Press, 1984).

Porter, Roy, *English Society in the Eighteenth Century* (Harmondsworth: Penguin, 1982). Broad survey getting well beneath the skin of eighteenth-century culture.

Rawson, Claude, *Gulliver and the Gentle Reader: Studies in Swift and Our Time* (London: Routledge and Kegan Paul, 1973).

Rawson, Claude, *Order from Confusion Sprung: Studies in Eighteenth-Century Literature from Swift to Cowper* (London: George Allen and Unwin, 1985).

Rogers, Pat, *Hacks and Dunces: Pope, Swift and Grub Street* (London: Methuen, 1972; rev. edn 1980). Literary culture and subculture.

Rousseau, G. S. and Roy Porter (eds), *The Ferment of Knowledge: Studies in the Historiography of Eighteenth-Century Science* (Cambridge: Cambridge University Press, 1980). Essays with important implications about how the (scientific) past is read.

Rumbold, Valerie, *Women's Place in Pope's World* (Cambridge: Cambridge University Press, 1989).

Sambrook, James, *The Eighteenth Century: The Intellectual and Cultural Context of English Literature 1700–1789* (London and New York: Longman, 1986). Excellent guide to patterns of thought through the eighteenth century.

Sitter, John, *Literary Loneliness in Mid-Eighteenth Century England* (Ithaca: Cornell University Press, 1982).

Sobel, Dava, *Longitude* (London: Fourth Estate, 1996). Narrative of the quest for an accurate chronometer, but of broader interest as well.

Spencer, Jane, *The Rise of the Woman Novelist: From Aphra Behn to Jane Austen* (Oxford: Basil Blackwell, 1986). On women writers and the representation of women see also Janet Todd, below.

Swan, Beth, *Fictions of Law: An Investigation of the Law in Eighteenth-Century English Fiction* (Frankfurt: Peter Lang, 1997). Particularly important about position of women in relation to the law. Discusses many novels by women.

Todd, Janet, *The Sign of Angellica: Women, Writing and Fiction, 1660–1800* (London: Virago, 1989).

Todd, Janet, *A Dictionary of British and American Women Writers, 1650–1800* (London: Methuen, 1984).

Watt, Ian, *The Rise of the Novel: Studies in Defoe, Richardson and Fielding* (London: Chatto and Windus, 1957).

Watts, Cedric, *Literature and Money: Financial Myth and Literary Truth* (London and New York: Harvester Wheatsheaf, 1990). Places literature in the context of the financial revolution.

Index

Addison, Joseph, 7, 48, 149, 178, 187, 191, 207; *The Spectator*, 34, 35, 65–6, 67, 103, 150, 152–4, 171, 181–7
Alkon, Paul, 230
Anana, 1, 2, 3, 32; *see also* pineapple,
Ancients, 5
Anne, Queen, 97, 132, 136, 138, 172
Arbuthnot, John, 84, 172, 191; *The History of John Bull*, 80–1
Aubin, Penelope, novelist, 119–20, 226
Augustan Humanism/ists, 154, 168
Austen, Jane, 117; *Northanger Abbey*, 1, 4

Bacon, Francis, 10, 12, 25, 30, 173, 176, 196, 221
Backscheider, Paula R., 221
Bakhtin, Mikhail, 222
Ballaster, Rosalind, 119, 133, 138, 226
Bank of England, the, 6, 65, 69
Barrell, John, 166, 227
Battestin, M., 36, 52, 222, 223
Beer, Gillian, 55, 223, 225
Bell, Ian A., 20, 70, 222, 224, 230
Berkeley, Bishop, 4
Berlin, Isaiah, 28, 222
Bible, the, 32, 149
Blenheim Palace, 63
Blewett, David, 14, 21
Blount, Martha, Pope's friend, 118
Bolingbroke, Henry St John, Viscount, statesman, friend of Pope, 31, 149, 155, 161, 162, 210
Bond, Donald F., 224, 227, 228
Boswell, James, 212, 229, 230
Boyle, Robert, scientist, 173, 177

Bradshaigh, Lady, correspondent of Richardson, 118
Burke, Edmund, 66
Burlington, Richard Boyle, Earl of, patron, friend of Pope, 168–9
Burney, Fanny, 45, 117, 118
Butt, John, 22–7, 229

Cardwell, D. S. L., 175, 228
Carnivalesque, the, 24
Carnochan, W. B., 209, 229
Castle, Terry, 24, 83–4, 222, 224, 231
Centlivre, Susannah, dramatist, 117, 125
Chambers, Douglas, 8, 20, 65, 221–3, 231
Charles II, King, 7, 132
Charles Morton's Academy, Defoe educated at, 11
Cheyne, George, and natural religion, 177
Chudleigh, Lady Mary, poet, 127
Civic humanism, 5
Civil War, the, 36
clocks/clockwork, 97, 147, 148, 158, 166, 167, 176, 188
Collier, Jeremy, attacks the stage, 37, 222
comet(s), 149, 176, 190
Concordia Discors, 5
Congreve, William, *The Way of the World*, 33, 36–48, 52, 54, 198, 212
Copley, Stephen, 154, 227
Cornford, Stephen, 180–1, 228
Cruso, Timothy, Defoe's schoolmate, 11

Dampier, Captain William, 189
Damrosch, Leopold Jr, 225, 227 229, 231

Davis Herbert, 221, 228
Davys, Mary, author, 118
Defoe, Daniel, vii, viii, 32, 35, 66, 89, 175, 221, 224; *Captain Singleton*, 18, 221; *The Consolidator*, 13; *Moll Flanders*, vii, 11, 49, 70, 73–4, 88–9; *Robinson Crusoe*, ix, 1, 2, 4–6, 10, 11–23, 25, 29, 31, 131; *Roxana*, 11, 62, 65, 70–7, 80, 81, 224
Deism/ists, 150, 151, 152
Denham, William, and physico-theology,173, 177, 228
Descartes, René, 176
Donaldson, Ian, 84–5, 224, 231
Dryden, John, 36, 123, 151, 153
Dyer, John, poet, 66, 224

Egerton, Sarah, poet, 127–8
Erskine-Hill, Howard, 151, 227, 231

Fairer, David, 154, 227
Farqhar, George, 198; *The Beaux Stratagem*, 198–200, 207, 229; *The Recruiting Officer*, 198
Fermor, Arabella, 'Belinda', 103
Fielding, Henry, 60, 117, 132, 200, 207, 222, 225, 229, 230; *Amelia*, 35, 60; *Joseph Andrews*, 35; *Tom Jones*, 34, 35, 52, 60, 87–8, 91, 112–16, 152, 203, 207, 208
Fielding, Sarah, 117, 207
financial revolution, the, 62–86, 198; *see also* money
Finch, Anne, Countess of Winchelsea, poet, 123–5
Folkenflik, Robert, 214, 230
Fontenelle, Bernard, 'pluralité des mondes', 194, 228
France, 1, 66, 81, 175, 183

Garth, Dr Samuel, author and physician, 178
Gay, John, 84, 191, 223, 224; *The Beggar's Opera*, 62, 65, 68, 80–6
Gill, Pat, 44–5, 55, 58, 222, 223, 231

Gray, Thomas, poet, 60, 218
Greene, Donald, 214, 230
Gregory, John, anti-women, 225
Guest, Harriet, 166, 227

Hammond, Brean, 227
Hardy, John, 212, 230
Harley, Robert, Earl of Oxford, prime minister, 4, 31, 132
Hayes, Mary, author, 118
Haywood, Eliza, author, 117
High Church, 5
Hill, Bridget, 231
History of the Proceedings of the Mandarins . . ., 4, 5
Hobbes, Thomas, 85, 178
Hogarth, William, 166, 204, 231; *An Emblematical Print . . .*, 64–5, 67, 80; *Marriage à la Mode*, 95–7, 101
Holkham Hall, seat of Sir Thomas Coke, 63–4
Holland (the Dutch), 8, 31, 81
Hooke, Robert, secretary of the Royal Society, 174
Horace/Horatian, 120, 123, 154, 167, 199, 208
Hume, David, 173
Humphreys, A. R., 202, 229, 231
Hunter, J. Paul, 12, 18, 207, 221, 229, 232

Inchbald, Elizabeth, author, 117
Ireland, 28, 31, 190, 213

Jacobites/ism, 5, 125, 151, 152
Jennings, Sarah (Churchill), Duchess of Marlborough, 132, 136, 138
Johnson, Esther (Swift's 'Stella'), 118
Johnson, Dr Samuel, 197, 198, 207, 225, 229, 230; *The Idler*, 214; *Journey to the Western Islands*, 214; 'Life of Milton', 90, 218; *London*, 212–14, 220; *The Rambler*, 218; *Rasselas*, 197, 215–20, 229; *The Vanity of Human Wishes*, 214–15, 220
Jones, Vivien, 99–100, 225, 232

Jones, William Powell, 186–7, 190, 228, 232
Jonson, Ben, 207
Juan Fernandez (island), 4

Kenny, Virginia, 207–8, 229, 232
King, William, author, 178
Knox, Captain Robert, travel author, 173–4, 228

Langford, Paul, 67, 79–80, 224, 232
Leguat, Francis, travel author, 13, 221
Lennox, Charlotte, novelist, 118
Linnaeus, 2
literacy, 7, 174, 198
Locke, John, 74–5, 85, 146, 149, 150, 151, 173, 224
London/city of London, 64, 65, 71, 153, 200, 201–2, 204, 212, 213, 219, 220
longitude/Longitude Board, 7, 30, 148, 189, 226
Lonsdale, Roger, 119, 121–31, 225, 226, 232
Louis XIV, king of France, 31, 66, 81, 183
Low Church, 5

Mack, Maynard, 172–3, 209, 210, 227, 228, 229, 232
Major, J. C., 133, 226
Mandeville, Bernard, vii, 77, 175, 224, 228; *The Grumbling Hive/Fable of the Bees*, 77–9, 80
Manley, Mary Delarivier, vii, 117, 131–44; *Atalantis*, 117, 119, 131–3, 135, 137, 139, 226; *Queen Zarah*, 132, 136, 137, 140–4, 226; *Rivella*, 131, 133–7, 139, 226
Marlborough, John Churchill, Duke of, 31, 63, 131, 132, 135, 136
marriage, 39, 44–6, 48, 49, 75–6, 81, 87–116
Marvell, Andrew, 60, 66, 202, 207
mathematics, 30, 172, 175, 176, 188, 190

Mathias, Peter, 175, 228
McKeon, Michael, 5, 9, 10, 22, 221, 222, 232
Misson, F. H., author, 221
Milton, John, 59, 121, 150; *Comus*, 45; *Paradise Lost*, 79, 89–91, 95, 97, 171, 194, 229; *Paradise Regain'd*, 90; *Samson Agonistes*, 90
Moderns, 5
money, 16–18, 20, 31, 37, 48, 49, 62–86, 157–8, 166–7, 199; *see also* financial revolution
Moreton, Arabella, poet, 129–30
Mullan, John, 229, 232

Natural Religion, 150, 151, 152, 177
navigation, 7, 175, 188, 189
Newton, Isaac, 7, 146, 149, 172, 173, 176–9, 181, 182, 190–2
Nicholson, Colin, 67, 68, 81, 83, 85, 223, 224, 228, 232
Nicolson, Marjorie Hope, 172, 182, 228, 232
Nokes, David, 23, 28, 36, 65, 153, 206–7, 211, 222, 223, 227, 229, 232
Novak, Maximillian, 228, 232
Nussbaum, Felicity, 232

Odysseus, 9, 10
Ovid, 103

paper-money, 67–71
Pemberton, Henry, populariser of Newton, 173
Perry, Ruth, 158, 227
Petis de la Croix, Francis, fils, travel author, 13, 221
Phillips, Katherine, poet, 119
physico-theology, 173, 177, 178
pineapple(s), vii, 1–4, 20, 32; *see also* Anana
Piozzi, Hester Thrale, friend of Johnson, 118
pirates/piracy, 8
political economists, 5
Pope, Alexander, vii, viii, 35, 40, 63–4, 66, 68, 84, 123, 149, 151,

152, 172, 173, 191, 198, 205, 207, 209, 211, 217, 218; *The Dunciad*, 25, 117, 154, 155, 158, 179, 209; *Epistle to Arbuthnot*, 163, 209; *Essay on Criticism*, 34, 148, 153, 172; *An Essay on Man*, 145, 147, 148, 154–62, 163–4, 178–80, 192; *Imitations of Horace*, 211; minor verse, 147, 200–1, 207, 210; *Moral Essays*, 17, 62–3, 67–8, 78, 148–9, 154, 157–9, 162–70, 208, 209; 'On Solitude', 124, 208–10; *The Rape of the Lock*, viii, ix, 12, 13, 50, 87, 91, 97–103, 117; *Windsor-Forest*, vii, 66, 146–7, 156–7, 159, 208, 216

Porter, Roy, 172, 183, 228, 232, 233
Portugal/Portuguese, 8, 31
Prior, Matthew, poet, 178
privateer(s), 8

Radcliffe, Mrs Anne, novelist, 117
Rawson, Claude, 23, 24, 154, 157, 159, 222, 227, 232
Rediker, Marcus, 6
Reeve, Clara, novelist, 118
religion, 5, 6, 32, 145–70
restoration, restoration culture, theatre, etc., 6, 35–8, 48, 50–1, 58, 90, 198, 199, 212
Richardson, Samuel, 35, 70, 89, 223; *Clarissa*, viii, 33, 35, 36, 38, 48–61, 82, 91, 105, 129, 208; *Pamela*, 55, 133, 208; *Sir Charles Grandison*, 52, 208
Rights, Bill of (1689), 183
Rochester, John Wilmot, Earl of, poet, 50, 89
Rogers, Pat, 214, 216, 230, 232
romance(s), 119, 133, 136, 140–2, 184
Roque, John, cartographer, 211, 229
Rousseau, G. S., 228, 233
Rowe, Elizabeth, poet, 126, 179, 228
Royal Society, the, 7, 9, 174–7, 190; *Philosophical Transactions*, 175, 178, 191
Rumbold, Valerie, 103, 225, 233

Sambrook, James, 63, 66, 168, 221, 223, 224, 227–9, 233
science, 5, 7, 91, 171–96
Scotland, 106, 213, 214
Scriblerus Club, the, 84, 190, 191
Sekora, J., 224
Selkirk, Alexander, 4
Settlement (1689) The (Act of), 6, 151
Shaftesbury, Earl of, 85, 134, 149, 151–2, 226
Sheridan, Frances, novelist, 118
Sheridan, Richard, dramatist, 33–4
Showalter, Elaine, 125, 226
Sitter, John, 211, 233
Sobel, Dava, 226, 233
Smollett, Tobias, viii, 35; *Roderick Random*, 87, 91, 106–13, 225
South Sea Bubble Company, 7, 64, 119
Spain, 8, 80
Spanish Succession, War of the, 31, 81
Spectator, The, see Addison, Joseph
Spencer, Jane, 132, 137, 226, 233
Sprat, Thomas, and Royal Society, 9
Starr, G. A., 221, 223, 224
Steele, Sir Richard, 65, 181
Sterne, Laurence, *Tristram Shandy*, 25, 35
Swan, Beth, 75, 104–5
Swift, Jonathan, viii, 68, 71, 172, 178, 221, 222, 224; *The Examiner*, 68, 139; *Gulliver's Travels*, vii, ix, 1, 2, 5, 6, 10, 12, 13, 23–32, 81, 151, 171, 186–92, 208; *A Tale of a Tub*, 151, 192; verse, 88, 130, 131, 192

Thomas, Elizabeth, poet, 128–9
Thomas, M. W., 225
Thomson, James, vii, viii, 1, 66, 97, 105, 149, 171, 172, 211, 221, 225, 226, 228; *The Seasons*, vii, 171, 180, 192–6, 203, 206, 207; 'Spring', 91–5, 200, 203–4, 208, 225; 'Summer', 1–4, 204, 221; 'Autumn', 145–6, 159,

238 *Index*

Thomson, James – *cont.*
204–6; 'Winter', 50, 206; *A
Poem . . . to . . . Newton*, 176, 228
Tierney, Thomas P., 157, 227
Tillotson, John, Archbishop, 149–50
Todd, Janet, 105, 225, 233
Tory(ies), 4, 5, 31, 131, 132, 137,
139, 152, 212
Traugott, John, 24, 222
Twickenham, Pope's villa at, 64, 156,
172, 198, 208, 210, 211, 212

Utrecht, Peace of (1713), 31, 139

W., Miss, poet, 130, 131
Wain, John, 219, 230
Wales, 120, 212–14
Walpole, Sir Robert, prime minister,
50, 69, 80, 81, 152, 210, 212,
220
Watt, Ian, 4, 221, 233
Watts, Cedric, 62, 69, 77, 223, 224,
233
Webster, John, dramatist, 156, 227

Wesley, John and Charles, 126
Whalley, Peter, author, 4, 221
Whig(s), 5, 31, 63, 131, 132, 152,
183, 210
White, Douglas H., 157, 227
Wilkes, Wetenhall, anti-women,
98–9
William III, King, 6, 69, 138
Williams, Raymond, 62, 223
Wollstonecraft, Mary, author, 117
women, legal status of, 104–5, 118,
166
Wordsworth, William, 197, 212
Wortley Montagu, Lady Mary, as
poet, 7, 117, 121–2
Wren, Sir Christopher, 174
Wright, Mehetabel, poet, 126
Wycherley, William, 58

Yarico and Inkle, story of, 55, 103–4
Young, Arthur, agriculturalist, 62–4,
223
Young, Edward, poet, 179–80, 218,
228